GUIDE 1994

This symbol is based on information provided by the tourist attraction and is awarded to those attractions which have fulfilled the following two criteria:
1. The approach to at least one public entrance is on firm terrain by ramped or level access.
2. Sufficient public areas are accessible (ramped or level route, wide doorways) to make a visit worthwhile for wheelchair users.

This symbol indicates members of the East Anglia Tourist Board. 1000 of East Anglia's hotels, guesthouses, B&Bs, restaurants, tearooms and tourist attractions are members of the East Anglia Tourist Board. Like us they care about visitors to East Anglia and they work with us to provide the highest standards of courtesy and cleanliness and service. Look out for the membership sticker, it means you're welcome.

The Guide contains complete details of all eligible attractions which have signed the Code of Practice and which we are confident to promote, throughout the counties of Bedfordshire, Cambridgeshire, Essex, Norfolk and Suffolk. Information about Hertfordshire attractions is restricted to members of the East Anglia Tourist Board only. Hertfordshire Tourist Information Centres (listed on pages 116-117) will be able to give further information about attractions in their immediate area.

Published by East Anglia Tourist Board,
Toppesfield Hall, Hadleigh, Suffolk IP7 5DN
Telephone: (0473) 822922 Fax: (0473) 823063
Editor: Alison Smith
Advertising: Michael Penn
Production Manager: Elizabeth Woolnough
Editorial Assistant: Grahame MacDonald

East Anglia for the Children

By Caroline Putus

Where to take the children? It's a perennial problem whether you're on holiday, or just looking for something to do one weekend afternoon. East Anglia has lots of attractions that will keep the kids amused. This is just a personal selection, tried and tested by one energetic four year old and assorted friends aged up to seventy. Some of the best we've visited recently include **Sacrewell Farm and Country Centre** near Peterborough, with a lovely nature trail and where children are, almost uniquely these days, encouraged to use, handle and examine the exhibits and the **Dinosaur Natural History Park** at Weston Longville, where realistic dinosaurs stalk the wooded parkland, and there's a maze, adventure playground, interpretative centre, clean loos and baby-changing room, and a good shop stocked with blood-curdling dinosaur souvenirs!

Bedfordshire has some good children's attractions, including the evergreen **Woburn Safari Park**. There's the **Shuttleworth Collection** with its world renowned vintage aircraft, flying displays and close up views of maintainance and restoration projects. Take a ride on **Leighton Buzzard Railway's** three miles of track, and older children will enjoy a visit to **Stockwood Craft Museum and Gardens** at Farley Hill, Luton. The museum traces the history of rural trades and crafts, while the gardens show the history of gardening since medieval times. There's a marvellous collection of horse drawn vehicles too, including replicas used in the making of "Ben Hur" and "Out of Africa".

Ripley's Believe It or Not is Great Yarmouth's newest attraction and is fascinating for adults and older children. Making clever use of models, video, holograms, and the genuine thing, it is a collection of the weird, wonderful, and just plain unbelievable. There's a section on ghastly foods, where the menu includes real caterpillars and soup made of cremated human bones; there's a real shrunken head, a handbag made of chewing gum wrappers, and handpainted crisps. There's a cinema showing film of stomach-churning feats like the man who could pull his girlfriend along on a trolley - with his eyelids! - or the man (why were they all men?) who blew up balloons through his eyes. There's a real live talking leprechaun, and a tantalisingly disappearing naked lady. An unusual attraction, right opposite the beach, so that young members of the family could play in the sand, while the older ones prepare to be amazed, amused, and disgusted!

Go back in time at Kentwell Hall

Feeding the elephants, Woburn Safari Park

The **Kingdom of the Sea** has two sites in East Anglia: one at Hunstanton, which we visited, and one at Great Yarmouth. I thought this a very impressive attraction, and one that will appeal to all ages. A series of well-interpreted underwater scenes explains marine life off the British coast. Fish native to our waters can clearly be seen in a natural environment. Our party, which ranged in age from 3 to 70, were all captivated. As well as lobsters, crabs, eels, dogfish, rays, plaice and all the other fish, at Hunstanton you can see seals recovering from injury or illness at the Seal Hospital. There were three there when we visited; sleek, fat torpedoes whizzing through the water with such consumate grace that one of them didn't even bother to open its eyes! The children liked the Touch Pools best. Here, starfish, mussels, sea anemones, and crabs patiently allowed eager fingers to pluck them out of the water and discover their secrets. Have you ever seen a starfish's legs? The Kingdom of the Sea has a good quality and clean fast-food restaurant, nice clean loos, a baby-changing room, and a really good gift shop stocked with a wide range of good-quality and affordable "fishy" gifts. All in all, we thought it one of the best attractions we've visited.

Kentwell Hall, a mellow, moated red brick mansion is a fascinating place to visit at any time. The annual Historical Re-Creation is something really special. We visited during the summer of 1593, when Thomas Clopton was the owner of the house, and the news was of plague and Popery, witches and wage claims(4d per day for labourers and 26/8d per year for a good servant). Once we had passed through the "time tunnel", we left the 20th century behind and entered a world of barefoot servants, scholarly gentlemen, unruly schoolchildren, and all the bustle of a typical day at this great house in 1593. In the hot smokey kitchen, we watched the cooks preparing peacock, peach pies and stuffed mushrooms in pastry cases, while outside a kitchen boy rested in a sunny corner, back against warm red brick. We met fine ladies sewing, reading or just strolling, watched the gentlemen play the newfangled "game out of France, bill-i-ard", and our 20th century children thrilled deliciously to the schoolmaster who roared, "in the schoolroom, I am KING!" We chatted to ladies sharing a deep, nasturtium scented bath tub, practised archery, and learned about weaving and the very new art of knitting. We joked with cottagers working in the bailiff's garden and, well, I can't go into details about the parts a sprig of tansy is supposed to reach! Conversations are, fascinatingly, carried on in the language of the time, and although I detected occasional 16th century impatience

with 20th century questions perhaps this was understandable at the end of a long season. Crowded though it was with visitors bringing with them all the paraphenalia of the 20th century, this was a magical melting away of 500 years: a visit to remember. Be warned: this is a day visit with lots of walking and no availability of 20th century snacks like burgers or icecreams. It's expensive to get in (see page 21 for further details), but it really is worth every penny. We bought a little turned wooden cup and ball toy, tossed and caught with great aplomb by the 16th century children at Kentwell. Us 20th century kids haven't got the hang of it.

Built for Henry II in 1165, **Orford Castle** is perhaps not the most obvious place for a children's day out, but ours love it. The massive keep, all that remains, looms over marvellously steep earthworks: perfect for picnics and lots of rushing about and roly-poly. Inside, children really get a feel for what 12th century life must have been like. Narrow dark corridors, steep stairways, guard rooms and tiny bedchambers, and - most intersting of all - 12th century loos with botty-freezing drops into the moat. Climb to the top of the keep, and there is a stupendous view over pretty red brick Orford, marshes, river and the sea.

Orford Castle

Fresh strawberries, Tourism Section, Essex County Council

Regional Food

By Ruth Watson, owner of Fox & Goose at Fressingfield

Red herrings might not have been seen for years, and Suffolk cheese has always been regarded as a joke - Stilton was sold in Cambridge-shire, not made there - but East Anglians need feel no shame. Countless other glorious food stuffs are grown, caught, reared or produced in this fertile region.

With a long coast line that starts near Kings Lynn, bulges lavishly around Norfolk and Suffolk and finishes at Southend on Sea in Essex, fish and shellfish have always been a notable part of the East Anglian diet. Quotas may have brought anguish to the east coast fishing industry, but North Sea herring are still cured in Lowestoft to provide kippers, buckling and bloaters, and family-owned boats such as the Pinneys' in Orford, bring small catches of beautiful turbot, skate, cod and sole home each day.

As for shellfish, molluscs and the like, shifting sands might suspend the cockle harvest in Hunstanton from time to time, and Bonamia might have wrought devastating damage on the native oyster, but Cromer is still famous for its crabs, Leigh on Sea for its brown shrimps, Southwold to Felixstowe for divine, juicy lobsters, and Portuguese and Pacific oysters have taken quite happily to the beds left vacant in Colchester, Brancaster and Butley by their ill-fated brethren. Their flavour may not be quite as fine, but they do have one important advantage for the gastronome - they are available all year round - so no more having to remember where the R's occur in the calendar.

From the north Norfolk beaches too, comes a bright green, fern-like plant called samphire. Gathered in the late summer months, and tasting faintly of asparagus, it is best eaten lightly steamed with butter, and fittingly it makes a marvellous accompaniment to fish dishes.

Since the 17th century, Suffolk and Norfolk have been famous for rearing turkeys, geese and ducks. Huge droves of turkeys used to be driven via Colchester to London, from as far away as the Fens to the north or Ipswich to the east. Buttons of Redgrave continue to rear legions of Aylesbury ducks, and no one can be ignorant of the "bootiful" company which sells turkey in every conceivable guise. But for a really old-fashioned turkey, with an almost gamey flavour, try a bronze turkey reared and hung for a goodly time by Mr Munton of Boxted near Colchester.

Consumption of goose has certainly diminished over the years, but Norfolk Geese of Pulham Market amongst others, continue to pro-duce fine birds. For an occasional treat, the goose's unhealthy fattiness should be overlooked and the wonderful richness of its meat relished to the full.

Suffolk, and Norfolk particularly, have also long been synonymous with game shooting, and despite the deleterious effect that modern agricultural methods have had on much wild life, there is still no shortage of pheasant and partridge in the autumn and winter months. Butchers have to be licensed to sell game, but most small towns boast at least one dealer, and at R T Harvey of Norwich it can be difficult to see inside the shop for the serried rows of feathered and furry bodies in the window.

Venison, perhaps more readily associated with Scotland than Suf-folk, is now farmed widely, and one of the best producers of this healthy-for-humans meat, is the Denham Estate near Bury St Ed-munds. The flavour of farmed deer may be a little less intense than wild deer, but a much tenderer texture seems to be a fair exchange.

After the Agricultural Revolution, with its links to Norfolk in the persons of Coke of Holkham and "Turnip" Townshend of Raynham, and to Suffolk by Arthur Young of Bradfield Combust, production of cereals, peas, beans, carrots, parsnips and cabbages grew tenfold. These basic foodstuffs still grow in great abundance, along with sugar beet and oil seed rape. But thankfully for those who prefer the finer things in life, delicious vegetables and fruits are also grown in East Anglia.

Specialities

Still truly seasonal and very special because of its relatively short growing season from May to June, asparagus must count as one of the glories of the eastern counties. Asparagus, like sweetcorn, should ideally be eaten within an hour of cutting. So come the spring, pitch camp near Colin Goddard of Redgrave, or N Baldry and Son, near Aldeburgh, and with melted butter dripping down your chin, indulge in some of the most beautifully fresh asparagus you are ever likely to come across.

Apples, pears, damsons and plums, all flourish in this dryish, windy region. Eliza Acton, one of England's most famous 19th century cookery writers and a native of Ipswich, suggested in 1845 that Norfolk biffins should be used in her recipe for Black Caps. It is doubtful if any of Norfolk's once most famous apple survive now - perhaps in a far corner of some derelict orchard - but newer varieties, grafted on smaller and more easily tended stock, as well as carefully cherished older varieties are still widely grown.

From apples, unsurprisingly, come apple juice and cider, and while Aspalls of Debenham and Copella near Stoke by Nayland are nationally famous for their excellent products, even more appealing are the three unblended juices that James White of Brandeston presses - the slightly acidic Bramley, nuttily sweetish Cox's and sumptuously rich Russet should been sought out by any discerning palate.

A fitting accompaniment, Hintlesham Hall wine cellar

In 1724, at Hengrave Hall near Bury St Edmunds, Sir William Gage planted a plum tree imported from France which had lost its label. The green fruits subsequently borne became known as greengages, and from the 18th century onwards, with the proliferation of corn and wheat growing, these fruits would have been among the gooseberries, currants, damsons and plums which were turned into the pastry dominated desserts of dumplings, puddings, pies, tarts and cakes.

It should be apparent to even the most cynical gastronome, that East Anglia is not just the cereal and sugar bowl of England, but the fruit, fish, meat and vegetable bowl too. Good foodstuffs of infinite variety have always been produced here. But the particular marvel has been the burgeoning of countless small enterprises which are either marketing native produce in new and enticing forms, or just as excitingly, going back to old methods and recipes, to produce traditional foods seemingly vanished forever. Buy a 1lb of sweet-cured bacon from JR Creasey in Peasenhall, and know that real food is alive and well, at least in East Anglia.

Further details of local produce can be found on page 101. For a listing of some of the best eating places in East Anglia to sample delicious local food, turn to pages 102-109.

Mending fishing nets at Aldeburgh beach

Feasts in the East
Your festival guide.......

By Gerry O'Keeffe, Eastern Arts Board

Snape Maltings

Opera Circus, at the 1993 King's Lynn festival

A is for **ALDEBURGH**, of national renown
With the Maltings at Snape and the old seaside town.
Mr Britten so loved it he made it his base
On account of its soothing and rhythmical pace.
Now tourists enjoy its great music and charm
As they walk on the beach, in the cool and the warm.

B is for **BURY**, with a fine set of places
Of historical beauty and contemporary graces.
The theatre is Georgian, and the pillars are Greek.
And there's markets as well on most days of the week.
The cathedral fills up when the orchestras play
And the hostelries there stay open all day.

C is for **CHELMSFORD**, with not one but two
Arts festivals - one old and one new.
Cathedral events favour classical voices -
The Spectacular offers pop stadium choices.
Within this great spectrum is something for you;
Be it something renowned or totally new.

D is for Diss, with no feast of its own
But **WINGFIELD** is near and it's easy to phone.
This medieval college houses sculpture and art
And arranges bright workshops in which to take part.
But the music events are the best of the best -
As the churches and centres nearby will attest.

E is for Essex, so misunderstood -
A county of wheat fields and great barns made of wood
Indeed, **CRESSING TEMPLE** is six centuries old
So sit down by its lake and let history unfold.
They play purest music amid wattle and beam
And if you get peckish, there's strawberries and cream.

F is for **FELIXSTOWE**, an old Roman Port -
Nowadays it's more used to the Folk Music sort.
They come to hear people with hands over ears
Amid all the laughter and good local beers.
This British tradition looks certain to last,
On account of its love of both present and past.

G is for **GORLESTON**, Great Yarmouth's kin
Where St Andrew's festival's packing them in.
Some acts hark from Yorkshire or from Himalayas
- You see it depends on available players.
But come November, concerts, talks and plays
While away those wistful Autumn days.

H is for **HUNSTANTON**, on the North Norfolk coast,
Where they know how to play at the holiday host.
There's a showcase for talent and music galore
And afterwards time for a stroll on the shore.
The theatre there has a warm friendly glow -
And a warm seaside welcome as folk come and go.

I is for **IPSWICH**, and close to that town
A number of festivals are scattered around.
There's **RAMSEY** and **HADLEIGH** and **CLACTON** makes three
And just up the road is the **HAVERHILL** spree.
At **WOOLPIT** the arts make a marvellous sight
Before heading back into town late at night.

J is for Jollies, for that's what you're on
And J is for jazz in sunny **CLACTON**.
At festival **BRENTWOOD** they go for be-bop
And reckon they bring you the pick of the crop.
New jazz, funk and rock are in **FAKENHAM** too
And singing and playing designed just for you.

K is for **KINGS LYNN**, a musical feast
With people arriving on Network SouthEast,
To savour the style of this historic town
Where the tempo is up and the prices are down.
They play in fine buildings just next to the sea
While rare birds wheel round in the skies and the lea.

L is for **LUTON**, and it's Carnival time
Bank Holiday Spring in music and mime.
Charities trade and the big bands parade
As everyone joins in this masquerade.
Whatever you think, Carnival is free -
Free to be just what you want it to be.

M is for Midsummer, as **BROXBOURNE** can tell
With the festival weaving its own special spell.
From Rye House in Hoddeston to grand Temple Bar,
Exhibitions and shows bring the young from afar.
Barbecues and fetes gives arrivals a meal
While the talented artists give added appeal.

N is for **NORFOLK**, and **NORWICH** as well
For the N and N festival has tickets to sell
In town and in county and further afield
To ensure this season has maximum yield.
International in flavour and full of delight,
In October there's something to do every night.

O is for "**OUR WORLD**" Nineteen Ninety Four
A lively fun festival held mainly outdoors.
In Chapelfield Gardens in Norwich you'll find
Multi cultural acts set to broaden the mind.
Performers have travelled from far distant lands
To join in the fun with more local based bands.

P is for **PETERBOROUGH**, whose cathedral site
Is the focus for music that's selected just right -
But art too and poets are featured each year
Together with concerts at which you can hear
Great music picked out from the classical card
Played 'neath the wonderful arching facade.

Q is for queues which so often appear
For festivals here growing bigger each year.
So drop in and visit your good T.I.C.
(That's Tourist Information Centre to you and me)
For they'll be delighted to show you the way
To make local festivals part of your stay.

R is for **RICKMANSWORTH**, fun on the water,
Whose canal celebration spells good fun and laughter.
Steam narrow boats gather at old Batchworth Lock
And the Union Canal soon becomes chock-a-block.
Meanwhile back on land there are concerts galore
To celebrate 200 years and more.

S is for **SWAFFHAM**, the Peddlar's town
Who dreamed of a fortune hid in the ground.
And nearby is **WATTON**, with its own celebration
Which the locals join in with much joyful elation.
These mid Norfolk towns, with their markets and fairs
Will help you forget all your troubles and cares.

T is for **THAXTED**, an old Essex spot
Whose cobbles and spire have not changed a lot
Since horses and carriages made way for cars
But now **THAXTED** Festival welcomes the stars -
Who travel from Europe, making music not war
Reminding the listener of what it's all for.

U is for unfortunates, like those people who
Come to East England, unsure what to do.
Who never once think of attending events
In churches, in parks or in candy striped tents.
Our festivals want them, yes want every one
- To come by themselves or for family fun.

V is my vote of thanks to the readers who
Made it to this point where I'm trying to
Interest them in festivals and all other arts
Which give such choice to visitors and people from these parts.
Arts events should bring you in and never leave you out
- So go enjoy the arts this year, find what it's all about.

W is for **WANGFORD**, quite close to Southwold town,
Whose music and good eating will never let you down.
A lovely location of churches and choirs
With a Summer Ball of which nobody tires.
Tranquil and friendly and sometimes baroque -
A very good place to turn back the clock.

X, **Y** and **Zed**,
I think enough's been said...............

See page 84 for details of the Festival phoneline

Festival of Street Entertainers 1993, Southend-on-Sea

Conserving the Countryside

With an introduction by the Countryside Commission

The words on the leaflet sounded inviting. They spoke of a willow-fringed River Stour winding its way to Flatford Mill through a timeless English scene of pastoral meadows, flowering hedgerows and misty trees. Small wonder that this tranquil part of Dedham Vale, 90 square kilometres of East Anglia's finest rural landscape, was designated an *Area of Outstanding Natural Beauty* by the Countryside Commission some 21 years ago.

But the land made famous by John Constable's many paintings did not just happen by chance. Like most of England's beauty spots, it has been shaped by agricultural policies and farming methods over generations; influenced considerably by the work of local authorities, voluntary bodies and statutory undertakings whose ambition has been to conserve and enhance the area's scenic landscape as a legacy for future generations.

Ironically, at a time when people were awakening to the value of their environment, new technology and new demands were taking their toll. Field amalgamation - the polite term for saying that hedgerows are being ripped up to make bigger, more manageable fields - was forging ahead; familiar features such as coppiced woodland and grasslands were disappearing at an alarming rate, and ponds were being filled in. At the same time, the much-loved wayside Elm trees were succumbing to Dutch Elm disease, leaving lifeless skeletal remains, or ugly hedgerow gaps where they had been removed in a vain attempt to stop the spread of the plague.

But the pendulum has swung the other way. Where life-sustaining hedgerows were ripped out, miles of new ones have now appeared. And where coppices had been cleared, new woodland planting has paved the way for a mosaic of greenery. Even the dead elm trees have been replaced by more robust species, and new ponds have been created as wildlife havens for a myriad of creatures.

Working with local authorities and voluntary bodies such as the County Wildlife Trusts, the Countryside Commission undertakes conservation and visitor management projects. Acting as a catalyst, it has been estimated that £2.5 million Commission funding of countryside management projects in 1989/90 generated a further £10 million - and that is not including the benefits, in financial terms, of the huge amount of volunteer work.

East Anglia may never again be the same as when Constable knew it. But, for those entrusted with caring for our local countryside, it will not be for the want of trying!

Projects under way

Some exciting projects are under way to protect sensitive or vulnerable areas. Two sites have recently been granted national nature reserve status which means extra funding from the European Commmunity. These are **Redgrave and Lopham Fen**, owned by the Suffolk Wildlife Trust, and **Wicken Fen**, owned by The National Trust.

Redgrave and Lopham Fen, at the source of the River Waveney on the Norfolk/Suffolk border is one of the best examples of a lowland valley-head fen. Over the last 35 years abstraction for public water supply has been a problem and the drying out of the fen led to serious concern for its resident wetland wildlife. Since the site was surveyed by David Bellamy in 1958, many species of plants have disappeared. The new status will go a long way towards redressing the problem as European Community funding will enable the bore hole to be moved which is presently causing the fen to dry out. The Suffolk Wildlife Trust, National Rivers Authority, Suffolk Water Company and English Nature are partners in the project. Recognition of the importance of this site also means continued funding from English Nature for the annual management of the fen for such things as the cutting of sedge beds and grazing of the surrounding area. European Community funding will also be used to help restore the fen by paying for scrub removal, digging, better grazing and more mowing.

Wicken Fen, south of Ely in Cambridgeshire is the only readily accessible remnant of the once extensive fens of East Anglia's Great Level. It is a rare example of traditional land use based upon ancient drainage systems effective until the 19th century. Parts of it have been owned and managed by the National Trust since 1899.

For hundreds of years the fen was used by local people who gathered peat for fuel, sedge and reeds for thatch, and hay for their animals. Harvesting these products created a mosaic of different habitats and they now harbour the exciting range of flora and fauna (especially invertebrates) for which Wicken is famous.

The Fen is now the focus for three projects within English Nature's Species Recovery Programme. They are Fen Violet, Fen Ragwort and the Swallowtail Butterfly. The reintroduction of the Swallowtail, which became extinct in 1951, is now possible because of an increased number of the Milk Parsley plant, on which the butterfly lays its eggs. This is linked to the success of a waterproofing exercise carried out in 1989-90 which prevented further seepage of water from Wicken Fen to the surrounding, low level area. Large Swallowtail larvae were released onto the best Milk Parsley plants in a phased programme in July and August last year.

An area of countryside recently aquired by the National Trust deserves special mention. It is at **Orford Ness** on the Suffolk Coast and was purchased from the Ministry of Defence with aid of a £2.3 million grant by the Countryside Commission, the largest ever given. Much debris has to be

Dedham Vale project, school children on tree maintenance

cleared and the Trust will then pursue a policy of minimum intervention, allowing nature to take over. Visitors will have access from 1995. The Ness is one of the few areas in Britain where sea pea is increasing. Avocets and short-eared owls are among nesting birds.

Another coastal project is taking place at the RSPB's well known reserve at **Minsmere**. At first sight digging up the reedbed seems a strange way to help bitterns but this is what the RSPB is doing! What's more, the digging is also going to help avocets.

Research has shown that bitterns need really wet reedbeds so that their favourite prey - eels, fish and frogs - can move easily through the reeds and into the bills of waiting birds. However, a build up of leaf litter is causing a gradual drying out, and drastic action is planned to redress this.

Whilst the reedbeds are suffering from a surplus of vegetation, the avocet's habitat - an area of shallow water and open mud, man-made from former dry reedbed - is suffering from a deficit.

So the Trust plans to dig some of the dried-out areas to form new shallow water and mud habitat for the avocets and at the same time let the areas of what was avocet-habitat revert to reedbeds. The plan is to rotate the habitats over a 15-20 year period, thus maintaining the best conditions for both bitterns and avocets!

Finally, back to where we began, at the **Dedham Vale** and the **Stour Valley**. Work here is under way to recreate valued landscapes which have been lost over the years. Hedgerows are being carefully managed for the benefit of wildlife and for their scenic beauty, with sensitive farming preserving the special nature of the surrounding countryside.

The project also ensures the upkeep of footpaths to encourage visitors to sample the areas where Constable sat to do his paintings, and to explore the countryside around the honeypot villages of Dedham and Flatford.

More adventurous has been the work carried out on the **Stour Valley Path**, a 60 mile route to link with the Suffolk Coast Path. In the first 3 months alone, 4 bridges, 20 sites and some 60 waymark posts have all been erected and local ramblers have offered to oversee sections of the path to ensure that it remains trouble free.

Details of how to visit the places mentioned above, plus many more nature reserves in the region can be found on pages 63-65.

Boating on the
River Great Ouse

Ely cathedral rising majestically from the fens

By Alison Smith

The Norfolk Broads often spring to mind as one of the major waterways of the region, a popular holiday destination for many thousands of visitors. The Broads however only form part of an extensive network of rivers, canals and sea cuts. My journey starts at Hilgay, a village on the edge of the fens in Norfolk where I board a small cabin cruiser borrowed for the week. The River Wissey which passes through the village is quite narrow and we wend our way slowly downstream, enjoying the gentle chugging of the engine creating a wave of small ripples behind us.

After a short ride is the confluence with the River Great Ouse. Heading downstream would take us to Denver Sluice from where the river becomes tidal on its journey to the Wash, we head upstream towards Ely. There is plenty of room on the river with not much passing traffic. Over the floodbanks lie the fens, a rich agricultural area with its characteristic dark peaty soil. The flat fenland makes the sky appear endless. Soon Ely Cathedral comes into view rising majestically from the heart of this small city. Ely is a useful stopping point to replenish water, fuel and stock up on food supplies if you are self-catering. Motor cruisers are adequately equipped for cooking although waterside pubs and inns can be very tempting. From a mooring by the quayside, it is an enjoyable stroll up the hill to explore the city and the beautiful cathedral.

Several miles after leaving Ely, the river branches. To the left it becomes the Cam and to the right, the Old West River which takes us to Earith and the River Great Ouse once more. This stretch of river is particularly pretty and a delightful place to moor for a peaceful evening. Sleeping on board is a little strange at first as your bed rocks gently and water laps the sides of the boat, but soon the rhythm and the sounds of nightfall lull you to sleep. If the weather is on your side you may be lucky enough to waken to a misty morning and watch the sun slowly disperse the mist as the river comes to life. Coots and moorhens are the most common water birds, seen scuttling amongst the reeds. Grebes are there one minute and the next have disappeared

15th century bridge spanning the river at St Ives

Houghton Mill, belongs to the National Trust

glimpse of the New Bedford River which provides a very direct route to Denver Sluice. As it is tidal the journey would need to be carefully timed to avoid being stuck on a mud bank until the next high tide.

Back on the Great Ouse, the river meanders through Holywell and on to St Ives. An impressive 15th century multi arched stone bridge spans the river at St Ives and above the central pier stands a chapel built originally for passing travellers. A good place to moor is just before the bridge, from there it is a short walk to visit this attractive market town. The ride to St Neots passes through some picturesque riverside villages. The church of Hemingford Grey has an unusual stump for a tower, the original spire was blown into the river by a hurricane in the 18th century. Its neighbouring village is Hemingford Abbots. A little further along is Houghton where you can visit Houghton Mill. This 17th century timbered building belongs to the National Trust and is the only surviving watermill on the Great Ouse. Heading further upstream is Huntingdon, separated from Godmanchester by attractive water meadows. This is Oliver Cromwell country, he was born and educated in Huntingdon and trained his troops for the civil war in this area. After navigating a deep lock we are now at St Neots, another of old Huntingdonshire's busy market towns.

underwater in search of food. A solitary heron stands very still on the river's edge gazing intently for a fish to move and then like a flash it retrieves its prize. A pair of swans is always a graceful sight, if their cygnets are newly hatched a youngster may be seen hitching a ride on a parent's back.

Leaving the night's mooring behind, the Hermitage is the first lock to encounter, one of the few manned ones. Mastering the mechanics of a lock is all part of the fun and there are plenty more ahead. Caution is needed motoring in and when moored, the lock gates should be closed behind you. Using a lock handle, the paddles on the upstream gates need to be slowly wound open causing water to rush in and fill the lock. Once the turbulence has subsided the gates can be pushed open and you are now at a higher level. Many of the locks have gates at one end and a guillotine at the other; the guillotine works by lowering or raising it to control your passage. Passing Earith catch a

I am now on the last part of the journey to Bedford, passing through Eaton Socon and Great Barford. The latter village was once the upper limit of the river to motor boats but this stretch of river has now been cleaned up so you can reach Bedford. The ancient county town of Bedford is well known as the home of John Bunyan, who was imprisoned in the County Gaol for his beliefs. The Embankment is very attractive with its flower displays and suspension bridge. The town has a compact shopping centre, some historic buildings and good recreation facilities.

It has taken four days gentle motoring to reach my destination, stopping off at leisure en route. It has been a lovely relaxing holiday and the journey could easily have taken longer but now the return trip beckons. A longer journey could include some of the tributaries of the Great Ouse, such as the Cam to Cambridge, New River to Wicken Fen or maybe the River Lark to Prickwillow.

Attractive waterfront at Bedford

Further Information: Details of Boat Hire in the region are given on pages 84-85.

"The Inland Waterways Guide" is a useful annual handbook covering the British Isles, costing £2.50. It includes where to cruise, buy or book your holiday boat and find waterside facilities. Tel: (0372) 741411.

Houses with Stories to Tell

By June Shepherd

A story at Holkham Hall about the symmetry of the building has it that if all the doors linking the State Rooms were closed in one straight line, there would then be a clear view through the resulting row of perfectly aligned keyholes! Who knows whether the theory has ever been put to the test? Such stories are part of the fusion of legend, rumour and belief that grows around every historic house.

Take ghost stories. Surely the saddest and most chilling is the one connected with Blickling Hall in Norfolk. Here lived the young Anne Boleyn, who married Henry VIII, and was ultimately beheaded on his orders. It is said that on the anniversary of her execution in 1536, a coach is seen driving up to this Jacobean mansion. Not only is the coach drawn by headless horses and driven by a headless coachman, but Anne herself sits in the coach, head on lap! Not a spectral sight for the faint-hearted.

All these tales, be they fiction, fact or a blend of both, add insight to our visits to historic homes, for any house is more than just a pile of building materials. The people who build a house, live in it and call it home, imprint their personalities on its character and atmosphere, as do others who follow them. It is impossible to see individual touches such as recent needlework at Woburn Abbey or fresh flowers and family photographs at Euston Hall, and not wonder about the people who live here.

Because many of our historic houses were built by influential families of the day, they form a direct link with our national past and a vanished society. Those open to the public then, offer to visitors a rich field of thought, as well as hours of enjoyment - even if this is tinged with a certain relief that, back at home, we don't have miles of corridors to heat and all that silver and marble to clean! One member of staff at Luton Hoo told me that it takes him six hours to clean one of the beautiful crystal chandeliers in the dining room.

A personal selection from the many historic houses of different architectural styles open to the public in this region is drawn mostly from those still lived in as family homes, in some cases by descendants of the families who built them. Holkham Hall in Norfolk is still inhabited by descendants of Thomas Coke, the first Earl of Leicester (ancestor of the famous agricultural pioneer 'Coke of Norfolk'), who built this vast Palladian mansion in the 18th century.

Holkham Hall's austerely classical exterior houses a luxurious interior, where the famous marble hall rises the full height of the building, and impressive pictures, furnishings, statues, rare manuscripts and books are housed in rooms with magnificent gilded ceilings and hung with silk and rich tapestries. All this is enhanced by the softening touch of fresh flowers.

The present inhabitant, who lives here with his wife and family, is not the 6th Earl of Leicester, who lives abroad, but his son Edward, Viscount Coke. Surprisingly Lord Coke was not born to a title. This is because the 5th Earl had daughters, but no son, and the title, which descends only through the male line, therefore passed to the Earl's cousin, Edward Coke's father. Visiting this graceful place, set amidst formal gardens and a landscaped deer park, it is easy to appreciate why the building took 30 years to complete. I like the Old Kitchen here, where apparently, 'eighteen large turkeys' were roasted on a vast spit one long-ago Christmas.

Still in Norfolk, moated Oxburgh Hall near Swaffham, has been the home of the Bedingfield family since it was built in the 15th century, and is still the family's home, although now owned by the National Trust. Once described as 'the most exciting medieval house in

Marble Hall, Holkham Hall

Norfolk', Oxburgh is built of red brick, and has an impressively tall gatehouse whose towers rise 80 feet. Inside the hall, you can see needlework hangings worked by Mary Queen of Scots during her captivity, some of the few in existence worked by her. If you find the interior somewhat dimly lit at Oxburgh, there is a good reason. Sunlight, which can so easily damage ancient wallcoverings and textiles, has to be carefully controlled here by blinds, in order to preserve the materials.

Over the border in Suffolk, Euston Hall is the home of the Duke of Grafton. Built in the 1660s by Lord Arlington, father-in-law of the first Duke, the hall is of great interest to art lovers, for its stars are paintings. The glowing art collection includes magnificent portraits by Van Dyck, Reynolds and Stubbs. It is a miracle that all these pictures survived a fire earlier this century when two wings of the original hall were destroyed. This is a real family home - visitors are quite likely to see the present Duke's favourite tweed caps lying on a table in the entrance hall.

Our overseas visitors enjoy Ickworth, an extraordinary house built in the Palladian style, begun by the wayward 4th Earl of Bristol, who was also Bishop of Derry. Wanting to house his proud collection of paintings and sculptures, the unfortunate man lost most of these before the house was completed, as he was clapped in prison in Rome by Napoleon, and his treasures confiscated. The oval rotunda has two curved corridors leading to the opulent state rooms. Among the fine collection here is a stunning array of Georgian silver, which I would hate to clean, but enjoy looking at.

But not all historic houses are stately homes. Still in Suffolk, Wingfield Old College is no longer a college (it was established in 1362 by the will of John de Wingfield partly as a pre-university boarding school), but is the private home of Ian Chance, and the home also of an all-year round arts and music festival. A combined love of architecture, history and the arts prompted Ian to buy and restore this medieval timber-framed building with an 18th century facade, and use it as both dwelling and venue for the successful Wingfield Arts and Music Festival, which he started in 1981. This unusual building, with its beautiful great hall, cloister, church and topiary garden, is well worth a visit.

That sharing a private home with the public can add a rewarding dimension to the satisfaction of living in an historic building, is something which Alan and Gwenneth Casey know all about. They bought The Priory in Lavenham as a derelict building in 1979, and 'rescued' it. You will find an interesting photographic display on this restoration in the Merchant's Room. In 1983, the Caseys opened their home to the public in the real meaning of the term, for all the rooms you see here are the family's everyday living quarters, rather than rarely used state rooms. Outside, their courtyard, lawns and herb garden are also open for visitors to wander around at their leisure.

At The Priory, the phrase 'painstaking restoration' is apt: the building's entire timber frame has been exposed, as well as a Jacobean staircase, Elizabethan wall paintings and a fine inglenook fireplace in the original 13th century hall at the heart of the place. This intimate building has a rich history, having been owned by Benedictine monks and the Earls of Oxford, and lived in by rich cloth merchants, the Rectors of Lavenham, and more recently, by farmworkers. Today, its unique, restful atmosphere is enhanced by the unusual stained glass and paintings of Hungarian artist Ervin Bossanyi, who was a family friend of the Caseys.

In Cambridgeshire stands one of England's most important Elizabethan houses: Burghley House, built in 1587 by Elizabeth I's Lord Treasurer, William Cecil, and occupied by his descendants ever since. A stunningly beautiful building surrounded by a landscaped park, its exterior is an intricacy of towers, turrets, chimneys and windows. Inside is a fine art collection, unusual silver fireplaces, and amazing ceilings painted by Verrio, who spent 11 years working here! All are tended by helpful guides and staff. Visitors enter via the kitchen, one of the earliest rooms in the house, where unusual sights include a collection of turtle skulls. See if you can spot here the brass bootwarmer.

Splendid plaster work ceilings, interesting family portraits, fine wood carvings - and quite superb beds - can be seen at Burghley House. The Heaven Room, Verrio's masterpiece is breathtaking, the colours as fresh today as when they were painted. One notable inhabitant of Burghley was the 6th Marquess of Exeter who, as Lord Burghley, was a famous Olympic gold medallist during the nineteen-twenties. It was he who, on inheriting the house in 1956, decided to open it to the public. His daughter, Lady Victoria Leatham, now lives

The Priory, Lavenham

with her husband and family at Burghley House, looking after it on behalf of the family charitable trust. Amazingly, though, she never saw her grandfather, the Fifth Marquess, and never visited Burghley House during his lifetime, as he refused to receive Lady Victoria and her mother because of her father's divorce from his first wife.

Well-known as the presenter of the television series on stately homes, 'Heirs and Graces', Lady Victoria has described Burghley as 'a magical place for a child to grow up'. Because neither her uncle, the 7th Marquess, nor her cousin, the present Marquess, chose to live at Burghley, she has been since 1982 the custodian of the great house she first saw when she was nine years old, when her father inherited the title.

One member of the remarkable Cecil family became Lord Salisbury, who lived at Hatfield House in Hertfordshire, where his descendants still live. The present house is Jacobean, but its design follows the Elizabethan 'E' plan, being two wings linked by a central block. This is a delightful place, where tours are well guided. Some fine portraits include the famous Rainbow portrait of Elizabeth I, who was sitting beneath an oak tree in the grounds here when she heard of her accession. In the gardens, look out for mulberry trees, whose cultivation was encouraged by James I.

Inheriting an historic home can pose problems, as Nicholas and Sheila Charrington found when they took over the running of Layer Marney Tower in Essex from Nicholas's parents in 1990. This handsome building is set amidst a hundred and ten acres of land, insufficient for a commercial arable farm. So the enterprising young couple have established a Deer and Rare Breed Farm Park on their land, and opened it to the public. Visitors can see unusual animals including Red Poll cattle, Soay lambs and Norfolk Horn Sheep, and also look around the atmospheric Tudor Gatehouse, said to be the tallest in the country.

It is well worth travelling miles to see, at Luton Hoo in Bedfordshire, an incomparable art collection - tapestries, porcelain, paintings, rare Italian Renaissance bronzes. It was Sir Harold and Lady Zia Wernher who first opened this house to the public in 1950, displaying for a sad reason - as a memorial to their only son, Alex, killed in the 2nd world war - the priceless collections inherited from both parents.

It may seem odd to find a flavour of old Russia here in an English setting. The exquisite jewelled pieces by Fabergé, many touching personal mementoes of the last Imperial family, and robes worn at the Tsar's court, were acquired through Lady Zia, who was a Russian Countess. Consider the heavily embroidered red court dress, a 'uniform' worn by the Tsarina's maids of honour, of whom there were 100 at state occasions, each holding the train of the dress in front, and reflect that it took them an hour to walk past in procession! This is one more of the many fascinating stories that our historic houses have to tell.

Fabergé jewelled flowers, Luton Hoo

Please mention East Anglia Guide when replying to advertisements

HISTORIC HOUSES

BEDFORDSHIRE

Luton Hoo, Luton: Historic House built in 1767, exhibiting paintings, tapestries, porcelain, jewellery by Carl Fabergé and mementoes of the Russian Imperial family. *1 Apr-16 Oct, Fri, Sat, Sun and Bank Holiday Mon. Park and Gardens, 1200-1700, House 1330-1700 (last adm); Bank Holiday Mon opens 1030; Pre-booked parties only, Tue, Wed, Thu. House and gardens £5.00/£2.00/£4.50. Gardens only £2.50/£1.00/£2.25. Tel: (0582) 22955.*

Woburn Abbey, Woburn: One of the finest showplaces in England, Woburn Abbey has been the home of the Dukes of Bedford for more than 300 years. Set in a 3,000 acre deer park, it was built in the mid 18th century and extensively altered by Henry Holland, the Prince Regent's architect. The Abbey contains an important and extensive art collection, including paintings by Canaletto, Rembrandt, Holbein, Velasquez and many others. Restaurant and picnic areas. *1 Jan-26 Mar, Sat, Sun, 1100-1600 (last adm); 27 Mar-30 Oct, daily, 1100-1700 (last adm). £6.50/£3.00/£5.50 (inc private apartments); £6.00/£3.00/£5.00 (exc private apartments). Tel: (0525) 290666.* &

CAMBRIDGESHIRE

Anglesey Abbey, Lode: 13th century abbey, later Tudor house, paintings, furniture. Outstanding 100 acre garden. Fairhaven collection of paintings and furniture. Watermill. *26 Mar-16*

Anglesey Abbey, near Cambridge

Oct, Wed-Sun, Bank Hols, 1300-1700 Garden open 26 Mar-10 Jul, Wed-Sun plus Bank Holidays, 1100-1730, 11 Jul-6 Sep, daily, 1000-1730, 7 Sep-16 Oct, Wed-Sun, 1100-1730. £4.75/£2.35. Tel: (0223) 811200. &

Burghley House, Stamford: The largest and grandest house of the first Elizabethan age. House was built in 1585. Features paintings, tapestries, silver fireplaces, porcelain, furniture. *1 Apr-2 Oct, daily, 1100-1700. House closed 3 Sep. £4.80/£2.50/£4.50 (93). Tel: (0780) 52451.*

Elton Hall, Elton: Historic House and Gardens open to the public. Fine collection of paintings by Gainsborough, Reynolds, Alma Tadema, Constable and Millais. Furniture, books. Henry VIII's prayer book. Restored rose garden. New knot sunken gardens and recently planted arboretum. No guided tours on Bank Holidays. *All Bank Holidays, Sun, Mon, 1400-1700; Jul, Wed, Sun, 1400- 1700; Aug, Wed, Thu, Sun, 1400-1700. £3.80/£1.90. Tel: (0832) 280468.*

Hinchingbrooke House, Brampton Road, Huntingdon: Large country house - origins in 12th century Nunnery, home of the Cromwell family and Earls of Sandwich. *1 May-31 Aug, Sun, 1400-1700. £2.00/£1.00/£1.00. Tel: (0480) 51121.* &

Kimbolton Castle, Kimbolton: Tudor house remodelled by Vanbrugh. Pelligrini mural paintings, Adam gatehouse, fine parklands. *3,4 Apr, 29,30 May, 17,24,31 Jul, 7,14,21,28 Aug, 1400-1800. 60p/20p/20p. Tel: (0480) 860505.*

Peckover House, North Brink, Wisbech: Merchant's house on North Brink of River Nene, c. 1722. Fine plaster and wood rococo interior, notable and rare Victorian garden with unusual trees. *House open 26 Mar-30 Oct, Sun, Wed, Bank Holiday Mon, 1400- 1730, Garden Sat-Wed, 1400-1730. House and Garden £2.40/£1.20. Garden only £1.00/50p. Tel: (0945) 583463.*

Wimpole Hall, Arrington: 18th century house in landscaped park. Folly and Chinese

Ingatestone Hall, Essex

17

ENJOY 300 YEARS OF HISTORY IN A DAY

Holkham Hall is one of Britain's most majestic Stately homes, situated in a 3,000 acre deer park on the beautiful north Norfolk coast. This classic 18th Century Palladian style mansion is part of a great agricultural estate, and is a living treasure house of artistic and architectural history.

Attractions include: Holkham Hall, Bygones Museum, Pottery, Garden Centre, Gift Shop, Art Gallery, Tea Rooms, Deer Park, Lake and Beach.

OPENING TIMES & ADMISSION CHARGES

Daily (except Fridays & Saturdays) from 29th May to 29th September, 1.30 p.m.-5.00 p.m. Also Easter, May, Spring & Summer Bank Holiday Sundays & Mondays, 11.30 a.m.-5.00 p.m. Last admission 4.40 p.m.

Hall & Park:
Adults £3.00 Children £1.50
Bygones & Park:
Adults £3.00 Children £1.50
All inclusive:
Adult £5.00 Children £2.50
10% reduction on pre-paid parties of 20 or more

**Holkham Hall, Wells-next-the-Sea, Norfolk, NR23 1AB.
Tel. (0328) 710227**

Please mention East Anglia Guide when replying to advertisements

bridge. Plunge bath and yellow drawing room in house, work of John Soane. Home Farm - Rare breeds centre. Museum, children's corner, adventure playground. *Hall open 27 Mar-30 Oct, Tue, Wed, Thu, Sat, Sun, 1300-1700 Farm open Sat,Sun all year; 1300-1700; 27 Mar-30 Oct 1030-1700. House £4.50/£2.25, Farm £3.50/£1.75, joint £6.00/£3.00. Tel: (0223) 207257.* ♿

ESSEX

⚜ **Audley End House and Park**, Saffron Walden: Palatial Jacobean house remodelled in 18th-19th century. Magnificent Great Hall, 17th century plaster ceilings. Rooms/furniture by Robert Adam. Park by "Capability" Brown. *1 Apr-30 Sep, Wed-Sun, Grounds 1200-1800, House 1300-1700, Closed Christmas. Tel: (0799) 522842. £4.90/£2.40/£3.70 (93).* ♿

Gosfield Hall, Gosfield: Tudor house built around courtyard with later alterations. Old well and pump house. 100 foot Elizabethan gallery with oak panelling. *1 May-30 Sep, Wed & Thu, grounds 1400-1700, tours of house, 1430 & 1515. Grounds free, tours of house £1.50/50p. Tel: (0787) 472914.*

⚜ **Ingatestone Hall,** Ingatestone: Tudor House and gardens, the home of the Petre family since 1540. Family portrait collection, furniture and other heirlooms on display. *2 Apr-12 Jul, Fri-Sun; 13 Jul-1 Sep, Wed-Sun; 2-25 Sep, Fri- Sun; 1300-1800; Open 4 Apr. £3.00/£1.00/£2.50. Tel: (0277) 353010.*

⚜ **Layer Marney Tower**, Layer Marney: Tallest Tudor Gatehouse in the country built by Henry 1st Lord Marney, Lord Privy Seal to Henry 8th. Flamboyant Italianate style with fine terracotta work. Formal gardens and deer in surrounding fields. Rare Breed Farm Park allowing a chance to meet the animals. *1 Apr-2 Oct, Sun-Fri, 1400-1800, Bank Holidays 1100-1800. £3.00/£1.50/£3.00. Tel: (0206) 330202.* ♿

⚜ **Paycockes**, West Street, Coggeshall: Half-timbered merchants house built c. 1500. Richly carved interior. Special display of local crafts. *27 Mar-9 Oct, Tue, Thu, Sun, Bank Holiday Mon, 1400-1730. £1.40/70p. Tel: (0376) 61305.*

Knebworth House, set in a 250 acre park

HERTFORDSHIRE

⚜ **Hatfield House**, Hatfield Park, Hatfield: Twenty-one miles north of London, easy to reach by road and rail. There are two exhibitions, the National Collection of Model Soldiers and a William IV kitchen built in 1833. *25 Mar-9 Oct; Park daily, 1030-2000; Gardens Mon-Sat 1100-1800; House Tue-Sat, guided tours 1200-1600, Sun no guided tours 1330-1700, Bank Holidays no guided tours 1100-1700; Closed 1 Apr. £4.70/£3.10/£3.90. Tel: (0707) 262823.* ♿

⚜ **Knebworth House**, Gardens and Park, Knebworth: Home of the Lytton family since 1490, refashioned in the 19th century by Bulwer-Lytton. There is a fine collection of manuscripts, portraits and furniture. Jacobean Banquet Hall with Minstrels Gallery. British Raj Exhibition. Formal gardens with Jekyll Herb Garden, large adventure playground with "Fort Knebworth". Set in 250 acre country park which is the setting for many special events throughout the summer. Gift shop, licensed cafeteria in restored 400 year old Tithe Barn. *26 Mar-17 Apr, Tue-Sun; 23 Apr-22 May, Sat, Sun and Bank Holidays; 28 May-4 Sep, Tue-Sun; 10 Sep-2 Oct, Sat, Sun. Park open Mon, House open Bank Holiday Mon; Park 1100-1730, House and Gardens, 1200-1700 (last adm 1630). House, Gardens and Park £4.00/£3.50/£3.50 (93); Park only £2.50/£2.50/£2.50 (93). Tel: (0438) 812661.*

NORFOLK

⚜ **Beeston Hall and Grounds**, Beeston St Lawrence: Smaller historic house close to Norfolk Broads, built in 1786 by the Preston Family who still live there. In Gothic style but with classical interiors, it is faced with squared knapped flints unusual for a country house. Portraits and furniture associated with Preston family since 1640. Objects from Russia. *10 Apr-18 Sep, Fri, Sun, Bank Holidays, Aug Wed only, 1400-1730. House and Grounds £2.50/£1.00, Grounds only 60p/free. Tel: (0692) 630771.* ♿

⚜ **Blickling Hall**, Blickling: Jacobean red brick mansion. Garden, orangery, parkland and lake. Fine tapestries and furniture. Picnic area, shop and restaurant. Plant centre. *Open Apr-Oct, 1300-1700, Tue, Wed, Fri, Sat, Sun; Garden and shop open from 1200, Restaurant open from 1100, Plant Centre open 1000-1700, Parkland open daily, dawn-dusk. £4.50/£2.25. Tel: (0263) 733084.* ♿

Oxburgh Hall, Norfolk

HISTORIC HOUSES

Dragon Hall, 115-123 King Street, Norwich: Dragon Hall is a magnificent medieval merchants hall, described as, 'The secular equivalent of East Anglia's great medieval churches'. With a wealth of beautiful features including an outstanding crown-post roof, intricately carved and painted dragon and screens passage, the hall is a monument to medieval craftsmanship. Built for the sale and display of cloth, a staple of the local economy for five centuries, Dragon Hall is also a unique legacy of 15th century mercantile trade. *2 Apr-31 Oct, Mon-Sat, 1000-1600; 1 Nov-31 Mar, Mon-Fri, 1000-1600; closed 1,4 Apr, 24 Dec-2 Jan. £1.00/free/50p. Tel: (0603) 663922.* &

Felbrigg Hall, Felbrigg: 17th century country house with original 18th century furniture and pictures. Walled garden, orangery, parkland and lake. Walks, picnic area, shop. *Open 26 Mar-30 Oct, Mon,Wed,Thur,Sat,Sun, Gardens 1100-1700, Hall 1300-1700; park and woodland walks open all year. Hall and gardens £4.60/£2.20, gardens only £1.80/80p. Tel: (0263) 837444.* &

Holkham Hall, Wells-next-the-Sea: Classic 18th century Palladian style mansion is part of a great agricultural estate, and is a living treasure house of artistic and architectural history. One of Britain's most magestic Stately homes, situated in a 3,000 acre deer park on the beautiful north Norfolk coast. Attractions include: Bygones Museum, pottery, garden centre, gift shop, art gallery, tea rooms, deer park, lake and beach. Bygones Museum includes working pump room; traction engines; vintage cars; Victorian kitchen and tack room; brewery tapping room; steam days. *29 May-30 Sep, Sun-Thu, 1330-1700; also Easter, May, Spring and Summer Bank Holiday, Sun & Mon, 1130-1700; last adm 1640. £3.00/£1.50. Tel: (0328) 710733.*

Houghton Hall, Houghton: Built for Sir Robert Walpole, the first Prime Minister of England, in the early 18th century. Much of the original furnishings by William Kent in the State Rooms. Collection of approx 20,000 model soldiers and other militaria. Stables with heavy horses and ponies. Picnic area and cafeteria, gift shop, children's playground. *3 Apr-25 Sep, Thu, Sun and Bank Holiday Mon. Tel for times. £4.00/£2.00/£3.50 (93). Tel: (0485) 528569.* &

Oxburgh Hall, Oxborough, King's Lynn: 15th century moated red brick fortified manor house. Magnificent 80ft gatehouse. Mary Queen of Scots needlework. Catholic priests hole. Garden. Woodland walks. Catholic chapel. *26 Mar-30 Oct, Sat-Wed; Hall, 1300-1700; Garden, 1200-1730; 4 Apr, 1100-1700. £3.80/£1.40. Tel: (0366) 328258.* &

Sandringham, home of HM The Queen

Sandringham: The country retreat of H.M. The Queen. Set in 60 acres of beautiful grounds and lakes, Sandringham is complemented by a museum of Royal vehicles and memorabilia. House and grounds are surrounded by 600 acres of country park with visitor centre and shop. *1 Apr-2 Oct, House and Museum, Mon-Sat, 1100-1645, Sun, 1200-1645; Grounds, Mon-Sat, 1030-1700, Sun 1130-1700; House closed 19 Jul-4 Aug; Grounds and Museum closed 23 Jul-3 Aug; House and Grounds closed whenever HM The Queen or any member of The Royal Family in residence. House, grounds and Museum £3.50/£2.00/£2.50. Grounds and Museum £2.50/£1.50/£2.00. Tel: (0553) 772675.* &

SUFFOLK

Christchurch Mansion, Christchurch Park, Ipswich: Fine Tudor Mansion built between 1548 and 1550. Good collection of furniture, panelling and ceramics, clocks and paintings from 16th-19th century. *All year, Tue-Sat, and Bank Hol Mon, 1000-1700, Sun, 1430-1630. Tel: (0473) 253246.*

Euston Hall, Euston, Thetford: Euston Hall was built in the 1660s by the father-in-law of the first Duke of Grafton, Lord Arlington. Fine collection of portraits of Charles II, his family and court, hang in the house and includes works by Van Dyck, Lely and Stubbs. The Pleasure Grounds were designed by John Evelyn and the Park and Temple by William Kent. The 17th century church of St Genevieve has a beautiful panelled interior, and contains monuments to members of the FitzRoy family. *2 Jun-29 Sep, Thu, 1430-1700; 26 Jun, 4 Sep, 1430-1700. £2.50/50p/£1.50. Tel: (0842) 766366.*

Haughley Park, Haughley: Jacobean manor house with lovely gardens and woods set in parkland. *May-Sep, Tue, 1500-1730; Closed Easter,Christmas. £2.00/£1.00. Tel: (0359) 240205.* &

Interior of Dragon Hall, Norwich

⚜ **Ickworth House**, Park and Gardens, Ickworth: Ickworth is one of England's most extraordinary houses, a Rotunda begun in 1795, the inspiration of the Earl of Bristol and Bishop of Derry, housing a major collection of pictures, including works by Titian, Gainsborough and Velasquez and Georgian Silver. The house is set in a 'Capability' Brown Park and surrounded by an Italian Garden. Range of waymarked woodland walks, deer enclosure with hide and adventure playground. *House open 26 Mar-30 Oct, Tue,Wed,Fri,Sat,Sun and Bank Hols 1330-1730; Park open all year, daily, 0700-1900 Closed 1 Apr, open 2,3,4 Apr, 1330-1730. House, Park and Gardens £4.30/£2.00. Park and Gardens £1.50/50p. Tel: (0284) 735270.* ⅄

⚜ **Kentwell Hall**, Long Melford: Mellow red brick Tudor Manor surrounded by moat. Family home interestingly restored. Tudor costume display. 15th century Moat House, Tudor Rose brick paved maze. Unique Re-Creations of Tudor life over Bank Holidays, other selected weekends and during 19 Jun-17 Jul when Kentwell Hall re-creates a given year in the Tudor period with up to 250 people in costume taking part each day. *20 Mar-18 Jun, Sun; 1-8 Apr, 30 Apr-2 May, 28 May-3 Jun, daily; 19 Jun-17 Jul, Sat, Sun & 15 Jul for main Historical Re-Creation; 20 Jul-25 Sep, daily; Oct, Sun. 1200-1700; Bank Holidays and Re-Creations 1100-1800. Full ticket £4.00/£2.50/£3.50. Moat House, Gardens and Farm only £2.40/£1.60/£2.00. Increased charges for Re-Creation days. Tel: (0787) 310207.*

⚜ **Little Hall**, Market Place, Lavenham: 15th century hall house with crown post roof. Contains Gayer-Anderson collection of furniture, pictures, sculpture and ceramics. Small walled garden. *1 Apr-31 Oct, Wed, Thu, Sat, Sun, Good Fri, Bank Holiday Mon 1430-1730; Closed Christmas. £1.00/50p. Tel: (0787) 247179.*

⚜ **Melford Hall**, Long Melford: Turreted brick Tudor Mansion with 18th century and Regency

Somerleyton Hall, near Lowestoft

interiors. Collection of Chinese porcelain. Gardens. *Apr, Sat,Sun and Bank Holiday Mon, 1400-1730; 1 May-30 Sep, Wed, Thu, Sat, Sun; 1400-1730; Oct, Sat,Sun, 1400-1730. £2.70/£1.35. Tel: (0787) 880286.* ⅄

⚜ **Otley Hall**, Hall Lane, Otley: 15th century moated medieval hall. Rich in architecture and family history, set in ten acres of garden, including canal, mount, nuttery, herbaceous and rose garden. *1-4 Apr, 29,30 May, 29,30 Aug, 1400-1800. £4.00/£2.50. Tel: (0473) 890264.* ⅄

⚜ **The Priory**, Water Street, Lavenham: Through the ages the home of Benedictine monks, medieval wool merchants, an Elizabethan rector. Timber-framed. Herb garden, with culinary, medicinal and dyers herbs. Kitchen garden, orchard and pond. Superb medieval building in the heart of Lavenham, yet backing onto rolling countryside. *12 Mar-30 Oct, daily, 1030-1730; Closed Christmas. £2.50/£1.00/£2.50. Tel: (0787) 247003.*

⚜ **Somerleyton Hall and Gardens**, Somerleyton Hall, Somerleyton: The home of Lord and Lady Somerleyton. Rebuilt in Anglo-Italian style in 1846. Magnificent state rooms, furnishings and paintings. Fine gardens; maze, garden trail and miniature railway. Shop and refreshment room for light luncheons and teas. *3 Apr-25 Sep, Sun, Thu, Bank Holidays; Jul and Aug also Tue, Wed; 1400-1700, Gardens open from 1230. £3.50/£1.60/£3.50. Tel: (0502) 730224.* ⅄

⚜ **Wingfield College**, Wingfield: Founded in 1362 on the 13th century site of the Manor House by Sir John de Wingfield. Magnificent medieval great hall. Mixed period interiors with 18th century neo-classical facade. Walled gardens and topiary. Homemade teas, celebrated arts and music season based at Wingfield College. Regular exhibitions Adjacent church with tombs of college founder and benefactor the Dukes of Suffolk. *2 Apr-25 Sep, Sat, Sun, Bank Holidays, 1400-1800; Closed 25,26 Dec. £2.20/£1.00/£2.00. Tel: (0379) 384505.*

The Priory, Lavenham

Prices appear in the order Adults/Children/Senior Citizens. Where prices are not available at the time of going to press, the 1993 (93) price is given. If no price is given, admission is free. See Touring Maps on pages 119-124 for locations of places to visit.

GARDENS AND VINEYARDS

BEDFORDSHIRE

Stockwood Craft Museum and Gardens, Stockwood Park, Farley Hill, Luton: Museum set in period gardens and Hamilton Finlay sculpture garden. Craft demonstrations at weekends. *1 Apr-31 Oct, Tue-Sat, 1000-1700, Sun, and Bank Hol Mon, 1000-1800; 1 Nov-31 Mar, Sat-Sun, 1000-1600; Closed 25,26 Dec, 1 Jan. Tel: (0582) 38714.* &

🌐 **The Swiss Garden**, Biggleswade Road, Old Warden: Main features include original buildings, numerous trees and plants, some rare, and adjacent lakeside picnic site. *Jan-Mar, Sun and New Year's Day, 1100-1600; Apr-Oct, Mon, Wed-Sat, 1330-1800, Sun and Bank Holidays 1000-1800. £2.00/75p/£1.00 (less 25% Jan-Feb). Tel: (0234) 228330.* &

Wrest Park House and Gardens, Wrest Park, Silsoe: 150 years of English Gardens, laid out in the early 18th century. Includes a Painted Pavilion, Chinese Bridge, lake, classical temple and Louis XV style French Mansion. *Apr-Sep, Sat, Sun and Bank holidays, 1000-1800. £1.70/85p/£1.30. Tel: (0525) 860152.* &

CAMBRIDGESHIRE

🌐 **Chilford Hundred Vineyard**, Chilford Hall, Balsham Road, Linton: Winery housed in interesting old buildings. Collection of sculptures on view, vineyard, cafe, shop *1 May-30 Sep,* *1000-1730. Tours 1100-1600. £3.50/free/£3.50. Tel: (0223) 892641.* &

Docwra's Manor Garden, 2 Meldreth Road, Shepreth: Walled gardens round 18th century red brick house and wrought iron gates. Barns, 20th century folly and unusual plants. Plants for sale. *All year, Mon, Wed, Fri, 1000-1700; first Sun of Apr-Oct, 1400-1700; Bank Holiday Mon, 1000-1700. £1.50. Tel: (0763) 261473.* &

University of Cambridge Botanic Garden, Cory Lodge, Bateman Street, Cambridge: Arboretum, rockgarden, scented garden, winter garden, glasshouses. *Nov-Jan, daily, 1000-1600; Feb-Apr, daily, 1000-1700; May-Sep, daily, 1000-1800; Oct, daily, 1000-1700; Closed 25,26 Dec. Nov-Feb, Mon-Fri, free. Other times £1.50/£1.00/£1.00. Tel: (0223) 336265.* &

ESSEX

B B C Essex Garden, Ongar Road, Abridge: Garden; Decorative with shrub beds, seedsowing, flower border, vegetable plot, two greenhouses, summer house and dahlia area. Weekends are worked in summer by Jack Kimms (vegetable and dahlias) with Shelia Love working remainder. *Open all year, daily, 0900-1730, Closed Christmas. Tel: (0708) 688581.* &

Bridge End Gardens, Bridge End, Saffron Walden: A Victorian garden of great interest, featuring garden ornaments, rose garden, Dutch

Docwra's Manor Garden

garden and pavilions. Hedge maze - only open by appointment. Some fine trees. *All year, daily, any time. Tel: (0799) 526637.* &

Felsted Vineyard, The Vineyards, Crix Green, Felsted: Wine and cider making, vineyard work. Wine and vines may be bought. *All year, Sat, 1000-1900, Sun, 1200-1500; 1 Apr-30 Sep, Tue-Fri, 1000-1900; Bank Holiday Mon, 1000-1900; 1 Apr, 1200-1500; closed 25 Dec. 75p. Tel: (0245) 361 504.*

The Fens, Old Mill Road, Langham: Undulating 2 acre cottage garden with pond. Woodland and ditch with a wide variety of interesting plants. Nursery stocking unusual hardy plants. *1 Mar-31 Aug, Thu-Sat; also 3 Apr, 24 Apr, 22 May, 10 Jul. £1.00/50p. Tel: (0206) 272 259.* &

🌐 **New Hall Vineyards**, Chelmsford Road, Purleigh: Guided tours, May-Sep. Vineyards and cellars where wine can be tasted. Vineyard trail through vines. Press house, and slide shows, fermentation, bottling and wine tasting. *All year, Mon-Fri 1000-1700, Sat, Sun, 1000-1330. £3.50/50p/£3.50. Tel: (0621) 828343.* &

Mark Hall Gardens, Muskham Road, Off First Avenue, Harlow: Three walled gardens developed as an ornaamental fruit garden, a 17th century style garden with parterre, and a large walled garden demonstrates a number of gardening styles and techniques. Gardens form part of Mark Hall Cycle Museum. *All year, Sun-Fri, 1000-1700. Admission prices on application. Tel: (0279) 439680.*

RHS Garden, Hyde Hall

Priory Vineyards, Priory Place, Little Dunmow: 10 acre vineyard with winemaking. Off licence. Medieval farmhouse dating from 13th century, originally part of Augustinian Priory. Vineyard is on site of Priory buildings and fishponds. The original Flitch Trials took place in the farmhouse which is shown in the 18th century engraving. *31 Mar-31 Oct, Sun, 1200-1500, Tue-Sat, 1100-1700. £1.50. Tel: (0371) 820577.* &

⚜ **RHS Garden** - Hyde Hall, Rettendon, Chelmsford: All year round garden of 8 acres set in a hill with fine views. Woodland garden, spring bulbs, extensive rose garden, ornamental ponds with lilies and fish, flowering shrubs and trees, herbaceous borders, glasshouses and national collections of malus and viburnum. *27 Mar-23 Oct, Wed, Thu, Sat, Sun, Bank Holidays, 1100-1800. £2.50/50p/£2.50. Tel: (0245) 400256.* &

Saling Hall Garden, Great Saling: 17th century house not open. 12 acre garden with old walls, water, small park and young collection of rare trees. *May-Jul, Wed, 1400-1700, 26 Jun, Sun, 1400-1800. £1.50/free/£1.50. Tel: (0371) 850243.* &

Spains Hall Gardens, Finchingfield: Beautiful grounds including flower and kitchen gardens and large Cedar of Lebanon tree planted 17th century. *Gardens only May-Aug, Sun, Bank Hol Mon, 1400-1700. £1.00/50p/£1.00. Tel: (0371) 810266.*

Congham Hall Herb Garden

HERTFORDSHIRE

⚜ **The Gardens of the Rose**, The Royal National Rose Society, Chiswell Green, St Albans. The Royal National Rose Society's Garden, 20 acres of showground. 30,000 roses of all types with 1,700 different varieties. Especially interesting are trial grounds where new varieties submitted by leading hybridists worldwide undergo a 3 year trial. *11 Jun-16 Oct, Mon-Sat, 0900-1700, Sun and Aug Bank Holiday, 1000-1800. £4.00/free/£4.00. Tel: (0727) 850461.* &

Gardens of the Rose, St Albans

NORFOLK

Alby Gardens, Cromer Road, Erpingham: 4 acres of garden with observation hive, bee garden and ponds, beside craft centre. Primroses - April; Wild Orchids - late May; Iris - June; Roses and lilies - July are specialities *1 Apr-30 Sep, Tue-Sun, 1000-1700, closed Mon except Bank Holiday; closed 25 Dec. £1.00/free/£1.00. Tel: (0263) 761226.* &

⚜ **Bressingham Steam Museum & Gardens**, Bressingham: Steam museum with gardens, 2 acre plant centre and display area. (Adrian Blooms Garden is open once a month through the year please ring to confirm exact dates). *1 Apr-31 Oct, daily, 1000-1730; telephone for details of opening times at Easter and Christmas. £3.50/£2.50/£2.50. Tel: (037 988) 386.* &

Congham Hall Herb Garden, Lynn Road, Grimston: Over 250 herbs in formal beds with wild flowers and potager garden. Over 150 herbs for sale in pots. *1 Apr-30 Sep, daily except Sat, 1400-1600. Tel: (0485) 600250.*

⚜ **Fairhaven Garden Trust**, 2 The Woodlands, Wymers Lane, School Road, South Walsham: 170 acres of natural woodland and water gardens including private inner broad and separate bird sanctuary for bird watchers. Peace and tranquility away from crowds. Primulas, azaleas, rhododendrons, giant lilies, 900 year old oak, rare shrubs. *Easter Week 1 Apr-10 Apr; Primrose weekend 16,17, Apr; 24 Apr, 1,2, May; 4 May-25 Sep, Wed-Sun and Bank Holidays; Candelabra Primula Weekend 21,22 May; Autumn Colours Week, daily, 23-30 Oct; Weekday times 1100-1800, Sat, 1400-1800;. £2.00/£1.00/£1.50. Tel: (0603) 270449.* &

⚜ **Fritton Lake Countryworld,** Fritton: 250 acres of woodland and water which features boating, fishing, 9 hole golf, putting, childrens adventure playground, wildfowl collection, mature gardens, cafe with home baking, gift shop, basket making demonstrations. Main attractions are the large undercover falconry centre with flying displays twice daily (not Fridays) whatever the weather; The heavy horse stables with Shires and Suffolks. Free cart rides. *1 Apr-25 Sep, 1000-1730, last admission 1615. £3.00/£2.00/£2.00. Tel: (0493) 488208.* &

Gooderstone Water Gardens, Crow Hall Farm, Gooderstone: 7 1/2 acres; grass paths beside waterways. Ten bridges over streams. Shrubs, trees and flowers. A small nature walk crossing river Gadder from the garden - also small aviary. *1 Apr-31 Oct, daily, 1000-1730. £1.00/30p/£1.00. Tel: (0366) 328645.*

Hoveton Hall Gardens, Hoveton Hall, Wroxham: Approx 10 acres gardens featuring principally daffodils, azaleas, rhododendrons and hydrangeas in a woodland setting. Large walled herbaceous garden. Victorian kitchen garden. Woodland and lakeside walks. *3 Apr-18 Sep, Wed, Fri, Sun, Bank Holidays (also Thu during May), 1400-1730. £2.00/50p. Tel: (0603) 782798.* &

Please mention East Anglia Guide when replying to advertisements

Helmingham Hall Gardens

◎ **Mannington Gardens**, Mannington Hall, Norwich: Gardens with lake, moat and woodland. Outstanding rose collection. Heritage rose exhibition. Saxon church and Victorian follies. Country walks and trails. Refreshments. Manor house by prior arangement for specialist groups. *Apr-Oct, Sun, 1200-1700; May-Aug, also Wed-Fri, 1100-1700. £2.50/free/£2.00. Tel: (026 387) 4175.*

Natural Surroundings, Bayfield Estate, Bayfield: A wild flower centre set in 8 acres of the Glaven Valley. Demonstration gardens, nature trail, bird hide, information room and a well stocked shop and sales area, ideal for the wildlife and organic gardener. Learn how to create your own wildlife area or just enjoy the hundreds of wild flowers. *3 Jan-31 Mar, Wed-Sun, 1000-1730; 1 Apr-31 Oct, daily, 1000-1730; 1 Nov-24 Dec, Wed-Sun, 1000-1730. £1.50/free/£1.00. Tel: (0263) 711091.* ♿

◎ **Norfolk Lavender Ltd**, Caley Mill, Heacham: Caley Mill is the home of the National Collection of Lavenders. See many varieties of lavender and a large miscellany of herbs. Hear about the harvest and the ancient process of lavender distillation. The Gift Shop stocks the full range of Norfolk Lavender's products. The Herb Shop has many varieties of lavender and herb plants, together with unusual gifts for gardeners. Cottage Tea Room. *All year, daily, 1000-1700; Closed 23 Dec-5 Jan. Guided tours £1.00/50p. Tel: (0485) 70384.* ♿

◎ **Rainthorpe Hall and Gardens**, Tasburgh: Large gardens of Elizabethan manor house. Fine trees of botanical interest, includes a collection of bamboos. Conservation lake. Plant sales and display gardens. *House by appointment only; Gardens, 1 Apr-Mid Oct, Wed, Sat, Sun & Bank Hol Mons, 1000-1700. Tel: (0508) 470618.* ♿

Raveningham Gardens, Raveningham: Extensive gardens surrounding an elegant Georgian house provide the setting for many rare, variegated and unusual plants and shrubs. Large nurseries, sculptures, parkland and church. *Mid Mar-mid Sep, Sun, Bank Holidays, 1400-1700, Wed, 1300-1600. £2.00/free/£1.00. Tel: (050 846) 222.* ♿

Pulham Vineyards Ltd, Mill Lane, Pulham Market: Vineyard, winemaking, bottling and tasting. *Jun-Sep, Tue-Sat, 1000-1730, Sun, 1000-1530, by appt only. £2.50/free/£2.00. Tel: (0379) 676672.*

SUFFOLK

Akenfield, 1 Park Lane, Charsfield: 1/2 acre council house garden full of flowers and vegetables. Homemade wine on view. As seen on BBC Gardeners World. New fish pool. *1 Apr-25 Sep, daily, 1030-dusk. £1.00/free/75p. Tel: (047 337) 402.*

◎ **Blakenham Woodland Garden**, Little Blakenham, Blakenham, Ipswich: 5 acre woodland garden with many rare trees and shrubs. Especially lovely in the spring with daffodils, bluebells, camellias, magnolias and cornus followed by roses in the early summer. No dogs please. *1 Mar-30 Jun, Sun-Fri, 1300-1700. £1.00/£1.00/£1.00. Tel: (0473) 830344.*

Boyton Vineyard, Hill Farm, Boyton End, Stoke by Clare: Vineyard and gardens of listed period farmhouse. Tours of vineyard followed by talk and wine tasting. *1 Apr-31 Oct, daily, 1030-1800. £1.50/free/free. Tel: (0440) 61893.*

◎ **Bruisyard Vineyard and Herb Centre**, Church Road, Bruisyard: 10 acre vineyard, winery, herb and water gardens, wooded picnic area and childrens' play area. Crafts and souvenirs. Producers of the award winning Bruisyard St Peter English wine. Restaurant. *2 Jan-24 Dec, daily, 1030-1700. Tours £2.50/£1.00/£2.30. Tel: (072 875) 281.* ♿

Gifford's Hall, Hartest, Bury St Edmunds: 12 acres of vines and a winery offering free tastings. *1 Apr-30 Sep, daily, 1200-1800. £2.75/free/£2.25. Tel: (0284) 830464.*

◎ **Helmingham Hall Gardens**, Estate Office, Helmingham: Moated and walled garden with many rare roses. Also highland cattle and safari rides in park to view red/fallow deer. *1 May-11 Sep, Sun, 1400-1800. £2.50/£1.50/£2.30. Tel: (0473) 890363.* ♿

Letheringham Watermill Gardens, Letheringham Mill, Woodbridge: Watermill (with newly restored wheel) in nearly 5 acres of gardens, river walk and watermeadows. Home made teas. Plants for sale. Well stocked aviary of exotic pheasants. Gallery. *27 Mar-end May and 3 Jul-end Aug, Sun and Bank Holiday Mon, 1400-1730. £1.50/free/£1.00. Tel: (0728) 746349.* ♿

◎ **The Priory**, Water Street, Lavenham: Superb timber framed medieval building in the heart of Lavenham, backing onto rolling countryside. Herb garden with culinary, medicinal and dyers herbs. Kitchen garden, orchard and pond. *12 Mar-30 Oct, daily, 1030-1730; Closed Christmas. £2.50/£1.00/£2.50. Tel: (0787) 247003.*

◎ **Shawsgate Vineyard**, Badingham Road, Framlingham: 17 acre vineyard with modern winery making award winning English wines. Guided tours, vineyard walk, wine tastings, picnic area, children's play area. Shop open all year for wine sales. *1 Mar-31 Oct, daily, 1030-1700. £3.00/free/£2.50. Tel: (0728) 724060.*

◎ **Somerleyton Hall and Gardens**, Somerleyton: The home of Lord and Lady Somerleyton. Rebuilt in Anglo-Italian style in 1846. Fine gardens, maze, garden trail and miniature railway. Shop and refreshment room for light lunches and teas. *3 Apr-25 Sep, Sun, Thu, Bank Holidays; Jul and Aug also Tue, Wed, 1400-1700, Gardens open from 1230. £3.50/£1.60/£3.50. Tel: (0502) 730224.* ♿

Wyken Hall Gardens and Wyken Vineyards, Stanton, Bury St Edmunds: Seven acres of vines and four acres of garden. An Elizabethan Manor House and 16th century barn. Spectacular woodland walk through ancient woodland. *1 May-1 Oct, Thu, Sun, 1000-1800; Mid Nov-Christmas, Sat, Sun, 1000-1800. £1.50/free/£1.00 Tel: (0359) 50240.*

Norfolk Lavender Ltd, Heacham

Prices are in the order Adults/Children/Senior Citizens. Where prices are not available at the time of going to press, the 1993 (93) price is given. If no price is given, admission is free. See Touring Maps on pages 119-124 for locations of places to visit.

NURSERIES AND GARDEN CENTRES

Stonham Barns, Pettaugh Road, (A1120), Stonham Aspal, Stowmarket, (just off A140). A delightful garden and leisure centre in the middle of the Suffolk countryside. Privately owned, many attractions have evolved over the years. The garden centre has all manner of plants, trees, tools, equipment and sundries, and also specialises in Cymbidium Orchids. Look out for the open days during the spring. Our Restaurant serves home made lunches, cakes, teas and coffees, and welcomes coach parties, parties and functions by appointment. A large selection of locally grown fruit and vegetables are on sale in the Farm shop, as well as gifts and crafts - ideal for presents to take home, countrywear and home furnishings. This is the home of Stonham Hedgerow - a hand made range of jams, marmalades and chutneys, featured recently on Anglia TV. Apart from all this, there are a number of other rural enterprises, including a pine shop, bygones, floristry, fish centre, golf driving range, picture framing and bonsai shop. *Open all year, Apr-Oct, daily, 0930-1730; Oct-Apr, daily, 1000-1700. Coaches and groups welcome by appointment. Talks and demonstrations on orchids, fruit growing or ribbon craft organised on request, linked in with refreshments. Tel: (0449) 711755 Fax: (0449) 711174.*

Fisk's Clematis Nursery, Westleton, nr Saxmundham, Suffolk IP17 3AJ (midway between Aldeburgh and Southwold on the B1125): Call and see many varieties of clematis in flower, on walls, pergola and in greenhouses, or send 75p for our colour catalogue. *Open Mon-Fri,0900-1700 Sat and Sun in summer 1000-1300, 1400-1700, Tel: Westleton (072873) 263*

Norfolk Lavender Ltd.,Caley Mill, Heacham, (on A149) Norfolk. Caley Mill is the home of the National Collection of Lavenders. See many varieties of lavender and a large miscellany of herbs. Hear about the harvest, and the ancient process of lavender distillation. The Countryside Gift Shop stocks the full range of Norfolk Lavender's famous products, together with a wide choice of other gifts to suit all pockets. The Herb Shop has many varieties of lavender and herb plants, together with unusual gifts for gardeners. The Cottage Tea Room specialises in cream teas, home made cakes and light lunches. Admission to car park and grounds free. *Open daily 1000-1700 (closed for Christmas holiday). Tea Room opening – Please see Afternoon Teas Section. Tel: (0485) 70384*

Peter Beales Roses, Attleborough. A large and world famous collection of roses featuring over 1100 rare, unusual and beautiful varieties. The National Collection of Rosa Species is held here with 250 unique varieties. Browse through 2 ½ acres of rose gardens or make a selection from thousands of container roses available in the summer months, or order for winter delivery. Experts are always on hand for advice or help in the selection of new varieties. *Open Mon-Fri, 0900-1700, Sat,0900-1630, Sun, 1000-1600. Catalogue available on request. Peter Beales Roses, London Road, Attleborough, Norfolk. Tel (0953) 454707.*

Taverham Garden Centre, Fir Covert Road, Taverham, Norwich (Situated 7 miles from Norwich on the A1067 Norwich/Fakenham road). Taverham Garden Centre is set in 15 acres of beautiful contryside in the pretty Wensum Valley to the west of the city of Norwich. The Garden Centre offers a riot of colour all year round, with acres of greenhouses packed with beautiful flowers and pot plants, all grown to the highest standards in the on-site propagating unit. For gardeners, there is an unrivalled choice of plants, shrubs and trees and an extensive range of bulbs and seeds, as well as attractive garden furniture and ornaments, terra-cotta pots and planters, paving slabs, pools and conservatories. Plus dried and silk flowers, books petfood, coffee bar, craft complex. Facilities for the disabled; coach parties welcome. Car parking for 1000 cars. *Open Mon-Sat, 0900-1730. Sun, 1000-1730. Tel: (0603) 860522*

Long Street Nursery Tropical Butterfly House.

Bruisyard Vineyard and Herb Centre. One of the largest ornamental herb gardens in East Anglia. We have a wide variety of culinary, medicinal and pot-pourri herbs for sale as well as a good range of vines. We also offer vineyard and winery tours, a secluded picnic area, childrens play area, restaurant, a shop selling herb seeds, wines, herbal teas, local produce and crafts. Admission to the car park and gardens is free. *Open daily from 2 Jan-24 Dec, 1030-1700, at Church Road, Bruisyard, Saxmundham, Suffolk IP17 2EF. Tel: Badingham (072875) 281.*

Frinton Road Nurseries Ltd, Kirby Cross, Frinton-on-Sea, Essex. On your way to the peaceful resort of Frinton-on-Sea call and inspect our wide range of top quality plants, shrubs and trees. Many of these are grown in our own nurseries, which you are invited to wander around at leisure. Our attractive shop and pot plant house stocks a wide range of sundries, tools and furniture and offers service from friendly and helpful staff. "The Applegarth", our new coffee shop is now open. *Open Mon-Sat, 0830-1730. Tel: (02556) 74838.*

Wootten's of Wenhaston: A beautifully laid out nursery with superbly grown herbaceous plants, many of them rare. An extraordinary range of plants thumping with health. Masses of salvias, a huge collection of of Barnhaven primulas, at least 10 different sorts of foxgloves and more than 40 irises. More than 80 kinds of old fashioned scented leaved pelargoniums. "To get there, I spent seven hours in the car driving through a monumental Cloud burst. It was worth it" Anna Pavord, The Independent. *Wootten's Plants, Blackheath, Wenhaston, Suffolk IP19 9HD. Tel: (050270) 258. Open daily 0930-1700. One and a half miles off the A12 south of Blythburgh.*

Notcutts Garden Centres: No visit to East Anglia is complete without a visit to Notcutts the nationally known and respected nursery and garden centres. Enjoy a stroll through the display grounds which include a children's playground, display borders and fine specimens of many interesting plants. Or browse through the pot plant centres, planterias or shops where attractive garden and house plants or garden tools and furniture are available. Whatever your interests, there will be plenty for you at: *Ipswich Road, Woodbridge, Suffolk, Tel: (0394) 383600. Also at Station Road, Ardleigh, Essex, Tel:(0206) 230271; Daniels Road (Ring Road), Norwich, Tel: (0603) 53155;Oundle Road, Orton Waterville, Peterborough, Tel: (0733) 234600.*

Long Street Nursery, Great Ellingham, (off the A11 Attleborough bypass) confidently claims to be Norfolk's fastest growing Garden Centre. A full range of garden goods and a particularly good selection of over 1500 different varieties of trees, shrubs and perennials attract gardening enthusiasts from all over East Anglia. An unusual added attraction is the beautifully landscaped TROPICAL BUTTERFLY GARDEN (See Animal Collections), where visitors walk among hundreds of free flying exotic butterflies. Coffee Shop, Tea Garden, Gift Shop, PYO Fruit in season, Picnic Area. *Open all year, Mon-Sat, 0900-1800, Sun, 1000-1800 and Bank Holidays. Winter closing 1700.*

Grow your own souvenir of East Anglia at Laurel Farm Herbs where you'll find a wide selection of top quality potted herb plants. They are attractive, fragrant, tasty, easy to grow and the ideal way to remember your holiday in East Anglia -

every time you take a cutting. Meet local herb specialist Chris Seagon who will be glad to take you round the 160 herb varieties in his gardens. *Open every day (except Tue) from 1000-1700 so come along and say hello. Laurel Farm Herbs, main A12 at Kelsale between Saxmundham and Yoxford. Tel (0728) 77223.*

Thorncroft Clematis is a small family run nursery specialising in growing clematis, they have a large sales area displaying around 200 varieties, as well as a display garden showing different ways to grow them. There is always someone available to give advice on selecting and planting. *Open from 1 Mar-31 Oct from 1000-1700 daily except Wed when it is closed all day.Directions are – On the B1135 exactly halfway between Wymondham and East Dereham, Norfolk. Tel: (0953) 850407.*

Mill Race Nursery, Aldham, Nr Colchester, just off the A604. Our nursery consists of 12 acres which border the peaceful River Colne. We have an excellent range of herbaceous plants, flowering and evergreen shrubs, ornamental and flowering trees, conifers, climbers as well as top and soft fruit, alpines, bedding plants and hanging baskets. Our dried flower shop specialises in the exotic and unusual. Garlands, swags and arrangements are made on the premises. *Open 7 days a week, light refreshments, riverside picnic garden, coach parties welcome. Tel: (0206) 242324.*

Tony Clements' African Violet Centre, Terrington St Clement, King's Lynn, Norfolk. Wide variety of gold medal winning African Violets on show. Cultural advice given. Good selection of African Violets and other seasonal plants for sale. Attractive and inexpensive gift shop and tearoom for light refreshments. Ample parking, coach parties welcomed. Talk and demonstration to parties, by appointment. *Open daily from 1 Mar-31 Oct, 1000-1700. Find us on the A17, near King's Lynn. Tel: (0553) 828374.*

Please mention East Anglia Guide when replying to advertisements

MILLS

BEDFORDSHIRE

⚙ **Bromham Mill**, Stagsden Road (Bridge End), Bromham: Restored watermill in working condition; static displays of machinery and interpretation of waterways and milling. Art gallery, craft sales, natural history room, picnic site. *Apr-Oct, Wed-Fri, 1030-1630; Sat, Sun and Bank Holidays, 1130-1800.* 60p/30p/30p. Tel: (0234) 228330.

⚙ **Stevington Windmill**, Stevington: Fully restored 18th century postmill. Keys available from the Royal George Public House in Silver Street for a returnable deposit of 50p. *All year, daily, 1000-1900 (or dusk).* 60p/30p/30p. Tel: (0234) 228330.

CAMBRIDGESHIRE

Bourn Windmill, Caxton Road, Bourn: Precivil War post-mill which may well be the oldest of its type in England. Thoroughly restored in 1980s for which a Civic Trust Commendation and a Europa Nostra Diploma were received. *4 Apr; 8,30 May; 26 Jun; 24 Jul; 29 Aug; 25 Sep; 1400-1700.* £1.00/25p.

Downfield Windmill, Fordham Road, Soham: Working windmill, dating back to 1726. Flour is produced for sale to visitors and local shops. *All year, Sun, Bank Holiday Mon, 1100-1700; closed 25 Dec-2 Jan.* 70p/35p. Tel: (0353) 720333.

Hinxton Watermill, Mill Lane, Hinxton: 17th century watermill restored to working order with working machinery grinding flour. *8 May, 5 Jun, 10 Jul, 7 Aug, 4 Sep , 1430-1730.* £1.00/25p.

⚙ **Houghton Mill**, Houghton: Large timber built water mill on island in River Ouse. Much of the 19th century mill machinery intact, and some restored to working order. *26 Mar-16 Oct, Sat, Sun and Bank Hol Mon, 1400-1730; 27 Jun-7 Sept also Mon-Wed, 1400-1730.* £1.80/90p, Sun £2.20/£1.10. Tel: (0480) 301494.

⚙ **Lode Watermill**, Lode: Watermill. See entry under Anglesey Abbey. Tel: (0223) 811200.

⚙ **Sacrewell Farm and Country Centre**, Sacrewell, Thornhaugh: 500 acre farm with working watermill. Farmhouse gardens, shrubberies, nature and general interest trails. Farm, rural and domestic bygones. Childrens play area. *All year, daily, 0900-2100.* £2.00/£1.00 (2-10 years 50p/£1.50. Tel: (0780) 782222. ♿

⚙ **Wicken Fen Nature Reserve**, Lode Lane, Wicken: Last remaining undrained portion of great Fen levels of East Anglia. Rich in plant, bird and invertebrate life. Working windpump. Fen cottage restored as it might have been in the 1930's. 3/4 mile board walk gives easy access to the heart of the Fen. *All year, daily, ex 25 Dec, dawn-dusk. Parties must pre-book.* £2.50/£1.25. Tel: (0353) 720274. ♿

The Windmill, Swaffham Prior, Cambridge: Tarred brick and clunch four storied tower mill built c1860 and worked commercially until 1946. Restored by present owner and producing traditional stoneground wholemeal flour with french burr stones powered by four double-shuttered patent sails. *Apr-Oct, first and third Sun in each month, 1400-1700; 4 Apr, 2,30 May, 29 Aug, 1400-1700;* £1.00/50p/50p. Tel: (0638) 741009.

ESSEX

⚙ **Aythorpe Roding Post Mill**, Aythorpe Roding: 18th century post mill restored to working order. *24 Apr, 8 and 29 May, 26 Jun, 31 Jul, 28 Aug, 25 Sep, 1400-1700. Donations welcome.* Tel: (0245) 492211.

⚙ **Bourne Mill**, Bourne Road, Colchester: 16th century fishing lodge converted into a mill. Machinery now in working order. *All Bank Holiday Sun & Mons; Jul & Aug, Sun and Tue; 1400-1730.* £1.30/65p. Tel: (0206) 572422.

John Webb's Windmill, Thaxted: Four floors of mill can be explored, main machinery is intact and on view. Rural museum on two lower floors. One pair of sails are now clothed so that when the mill has a volunteer available and the wind is favourable, they may turn in the wind. *1 May-30 Sep, Sat, Sun, Bank Holidays, 1400-1800; Easter 1-4 Apr, 1400-1800.* 50p/25p. Tel: (0371) 830366.

⚙ **Mountnessing Windmill**, Roman Road, Mountnessing: Early 19th century post mill restored to working order. *8 and 15 May, 19 Jun, 17 Jul, 21 Aug, 18 Sep, 16 Oct, 1400-1700. Donations welcome.* Tel: (0245) 492211.

Stansted Mountfitchet Windmill, Millfields, Stansted: Best preserved tower mill in Essex, built 1787. Most of original machinery remains including rare boulter and curved ladder to fit cap. *Apr-Oct, first Sun in every month, also Bank Hol Sun and Mon, every Sun in Aug, 1400-1800.* 50p/25p. Groups by appt, Tel: (0279) 813160.

NORFOLK

⚙ **Berney Arms and Mill**, Great Yarmouth: Most splendid and highest remaining Norfolk marsh mill in working order, 7 floors. Built late 19th century by millwrights Stolworthy. Situated on Halvergate Marsh. Access by boat (river trips from Great Yarmouth) or train, difficult walk across marshes. Site exhibition. *31 Mar-30 Sep, daily, 0900-1300, 1400-1700.* £1.10/60p/90p. Tel: (0493) 700605.

Billingford Windmill, Billingford: Fully restored cornmill with all internal machinery intact, in addition to wind driver machinery. *All year, Mon-Sat, 1100-1500, 1800-2300; Sun, 1200-1500, 1900-2230; key available from pub.* 70p/30p/30p. Tel: (0379) 740414. ♿

⚙ **Bircham Mill**, Great Bircham: Norfolk cornmill with working machinery. Small bakery museum. Tea rooms and ponies. *1 Apr-30 Sep, daily, 1000-1800; Tea rooms and Bakery closed Sat.* £2/£1.25/£1.75 (93). Tel: (048 523) 393. ♿

Stevington Mill, Bedfordshire

Saxtead Mill

Thurne Dyke Windpump, Thurne: Fully restored windpump. Exhibition of windpumps in Broadland. Tower very distinctive, painted white. *May-Sept, Sun and Bank Holiday Mon, 1500-1800. Donations welcome. Tel: (0692) 670764.*

Wicklewood Mill, Wicklewood: Mill contains much of the original machinery. Good views. Five storey tower. *May-Sep, 3rd Sun in every month, 1400-1700. 70p/30p.*

SUFFOLK

Buttrums Mill, Burkitt Road, Woodbridge: Six storey brick tower dating from 1836. Fully restored with 4 shuttered sails and working fantail for turning cap and sails to face the wind. Last worked in 1928, it retains intact milling machinery including 4 pairs of millstones. Ground floor contains a display of the history and workings of the mill. *1 May-25 Sep, Sat, Sun, Bank Holidays, 1400-1800. 50p/20p/50p. Tel: (0394) 382045.*

Herringfleet Marsh Mill, Herringfleet: Octagonal smock drainage mill clad in tarred weatherboards with a boat-shaped cap. 4 Common sails, spread with cloth when the mill works. Cap turns to face the wind by means of a winch. External scoopwheel. Dating from the 1830's, it is now the last of the old wooden pumping mills in Broadland. In working order. *8 May, 1300-1700 and other days which are advertised locally.*

Pakenham Water Mill, Grimestone End, Pakenham: Fine 18th century working Water Mill on Domesday site, complete with oil engine and other subsidary machinery. Mill recently restored by Suffolk Preservation Society. *1 Apr-30 Sep, Wed, Sat, Sun, Bank Holidays, 1400-1730. £1.25/60p/£1.00. Tel: (0787) 247179.*

Saxtead Mill, Saxtead Green: Elegent white windmill dating from 1776. Fine example of traditional Suffolk post mill. Climb stairs to 'buck' to see machinery all in working order. *1 Apr-30 Sep, Mon-Sat, 1000-1300, 1400-1800. £1.20/60p/90p. Tel: (0728) 685789.*

Thelnetham Windmill, Mill Road, Thelnetham: Early 19th century four floor towermill with conical cap, powered by four large "Patent" sails which drive two parts of French millstones. The mill is working whenever possible (wind permitting) on open days. Visitors may purchase stoneground flour and other grain products. *Jul-Sep, Sun, 1100-1700; Bank Holidays except 1 Apr, 25 Dec; Open 3,4 Apr 1100-1900; 1 Jan, 1100-1700. 60p/20p/60p. Tel: (0473) 742388.*

Thorpeness Windmill, Thorpeness: Working windmill housing displays on Suffolk coast and Thorpeness village as well as mill information. *1-4 Apr, 1400-1700; May, Jun, Sep, Sat and Sun, 1400-1700; Jul, Aug, daily, 1400-1700; Donations welcome. Tel: (0473) 265177.*

Woodbridge Tide Mill, Tide Mill Quay, Woodbridge: Standing on the picturesque Woodbridge quayside. The tide mill was built in 1793, and used until 1957. After full restoration it was opened to the public in 1973. The machinery works at varying times and for varying periods, depending on tides. *1-3 Apr, 1 May-30 Sep, daily, 1100-1700; Oct, Sat, Sun, 1100-1700. 80p/40p/80p. Tel: (0473) 626618.*

Boardman's Mill, How Hill Trust, Ludham: Unique open framed trestle windpump with turbine. No exhibits. *All year, daily, Tel: (068 262) 555.*

Clayrack Windpump, How Hill, Ludham: Remains of Ranworth Hollow Post, taken to How Hill and rebuilt. *All year, daily.*

Cley Mill, Cley next the Sea: Tower mill used as a flour mill until 1918, converted to guest house in 1983. Built early 1800's. Outstanding example of preserved mill with sails/machinery. *1 Apr-30 Sep, daily, 1400-1700. £1.50/75p/75p Tel: (0263) 740209.*

Dereham Windmill, Cherry Lane, Norwich Road, Dereham: Brick tower mill built in 1836. Restored 1984-87. Now complete with cap, fantail and sails. Some machinery intact. Permanent exhibition on windmills. *3 Apr-25 Sep; Sun, 1430-1630; Thu, Fri and Sat, 1200-1500.*

Gunton Park Sawmill, Gunton Park, Hanworth: Grade II water powered sawmill. Timber framed and weatherboarded. Saw frame inside fully restored. *24 Apr, 23 May, 26 Jun, 24 Jul, 26 Aug, 25 Sep, 1400-1700. £1.00/free/£1.00.*

Horsey Windmill, Nr B1159, Horsey: Windpump four storeys high and gallery with splendid views across the marshes. *26 Mar-30 Sep, daily, 1100-1700; Jul and Aug, 1100-1800. £1.00/50p.*

Letheringsett Watermill, Riverside Road, Letheringsett: Working mill (1802) restored to working order. Mills approx 2 tons of flour per week. Doomsday site. On working days fully demonstrated displays of mill working with staff on hand to help and explain workings of mill. *All year, Tue-Fri, 0900-1300, 1400-1700; Whitsun-Sep, also Sun 1400-1630; closed 1 Apr. Working demonstrations, £2.25/£1.50/£1.75. Viewing only, £1.25/£1.00. Tel: (0263) 713153.*

Little Cressingham Mill, Fairstead Lane, Little Cressingham: Combined wind and water mill in process of restoration. Pumphouse with water powered cylinder pump built by Joseph Bramah. Hydraulic rams. Picnic area. *10 Apr, 8 May, 12 Jun, 10 Jul, 14 Aug, 11 Sep, 9 Oct, Sun, 1400-1700. £1.00/25p (93).*

Saint Olaves Windpump, St Olaves: Tiny trestle windpump in working order. *All year, daily; key held by Mr Miller at Bridge Stores St Olaves.*

Snettisham Watermill, The Mill House, Snettisham: 18th century Watermill with original machinery restored to working order. See miller grind corn and explain history. Exhibition of local history. Shop. *14 Jul-15 Sep, Thu, Aug Bank Holiday Sun and Mon. 1000-1730. £1.50/75p/£1.00. Tel: (0485) 542180.*

Starston Windpump, Starston: Restored windpump. *All year, daily.*

Stow Mill, Paston: Tower Mill, built in 1827 with working fantail and sails. Restoration to full working order in progress. *All year, daily, 1000-dusk. 50p/30p. Tel: (0263) 720298.*

Stracey Arms Windpump, Stracey Arms, Acle: Exhibition of photos and history of wind-pumps in Broadland. Fully restored drainage pump. Access by 2 ladders to cap showing brakewheel and gears. Also shop selling souvenirs and snacks. *1 Apr-30 Sep, daily, 0800-2000. 70p/30p.*

Sutton Windmill and Broads Museum, Stalham. Tallest mill in the country, milling machinery complete. *1 Apr-30 Sep, daily, 1000-1730. £2.00/£1.00. Tel: (0692) 581195.*

Prices are in the order Adults/Children/Senior Citizens. Where prices are not available at the time of going to press, the 1993 (93) price is given. If no price is given, admission is free. See Touring Maps on pages 119-124 for locations of places to visit.

29

BEDFORDSHIRE

Leighton Buzzard Railway, Page's Park Station, Billington Road, Leighton Buzzard: A preserved narrow gauge railway operating rare steam and diesel engines on passenger trains through uniquely varied scenery around Leighton Buzzard. A large locomotive collection includes 9 steam engines and many preserved diesels. Wagons are restored and demonstrated in authentic industrial train displays and a variety of special events are held. This volunteer run railway is a true working museum. *20 Mar-16 Oct, Sun and Bank Hols, 1100-1630; 1 Jun-25 Aug, also Wed, 1100-1510; 4-25 Aug also Thu, 1100-1510; 3-24 Dec, Sat,Sun. £4.00/£1.00/£3.00. Tel: (0525) 373888.* &

The Mossman Collection, Stockwood Country Park, Farley Hill, Luton: Over 70 historic vehicles depicting the history of horse-drawn transport from Roman times up to the Second World War. There is a splendid, possibly unique, example of a Royal Mail Coach, state coaches and examples of omnibuses. *1 Apr-31 Oct, Tue-Sat, 1000-1700, Sun, 1000-1800; 1 Nov-31 Mar, Sat, Sun, 1000-1600; Open all Bank Holidays, except 25,26 Dec, 1 Jan. Tel: (0582) 38714.* &

◉ **Shuttleworth Collection,** Old Warden Aerodrome, Biggleswade: Unique historic collection of aircraft from 1909 Bleriot to 1942 Spitfire in flying condition and cars dating from 1898. Many other events held throughout the year including several Aeromodeller and motor rally events. *All year, 1000-1600, last admission 1500. Nov-Mar, closes 1500, last admission 1400. Closed Christmas. £4.00/£2.50/£2.50 Tel: (0767) 627288.* &

CAMBRIDGESHIRE

◉ **Imperial War Museum**, Duxford Airfield, Duxford: A former Battle of Britain fighter station, home to the largest collection of military and civil aircraft in Britain. Special exhibitions, ride simulator, adventure playground, shops, restaurant and picnic area. Pleasure flying during summer weekends. Education groups welcome. Special events during summer. Narrow gauge railway. *All year, Mar-Oct, 1000-1800; Oct-Mar, 1000-1600. £5.80/£2.90/£4.00 (93). Tel: (0223) 835000.* &

◉ **Nene Valley Railway**, Wansford Station, Stibbington: Regular steam trains operate over the line to Peterborough - a return trip of 15 miles. Many steam locomotives are kept on this line including both British and Continental types. The railway has featured in television series including Hannay, London's Burning, Christobel and for breathtaking stunts in the James Bond film "Octopussy". *Services: All year, Sun, May-end Aug, some other mid weekdays; Sep & Oct, Sat & Sun. Tel for details of train fares and train times. Site adm £1.00/50p. Tel: (0780) 782854.* &

Prickwillow Engine Museum, Main Street, Prickwillow: Mirrlees Bickerton and Day diesel engine. Five cylinder, blast injection, 250 bhp, working unit. Vicker-Petter 2 cylinder 2 stroke diesel, and others. *1 Apr-30 Sep, daily, 0900-1900. Donations welcome. Tel: (035 388) 230.*

Stretham Beam Engine, Old West River, Green End, Stretham: Stretham old engine was erected in 1831 as part of the continuing need to drain the fenland. It replaced 3 wind pumps and was in turn succeeded by first a diesel and later electric pumps. The massive scoop wheel was driven by a Steam Beam Engine, which is preserved intact. From the upper floor there are extensive views across to Ely and Cambridge and over fenland with its wildlife. *1 Apr-31 Oct, daily except Tue, 1130-1700. £1.50/£1.00/£1.00. Tel: (0353) 649516.*

Museum of Technology, Riverside, Cambridge: Preserved Victorian pumping station containing gas and steam engines, working printshop and other items from the industrial past. *All year, first Sun of every month, 1400-1700 plus special steamdays; 3,4 Apr, 1000-1700. £1.00/ 50p/50p. Steam days £2.50/£1.00/£1.00. Tel: (0223) 68650.*

ESSEX

Audley End Miniature Railway, Audley End: Steam and diesel locomotives in 10.5 gauge running through attractive woodland for 1/2 miles. Crosses the River Cam twice. *27 Mar-16 Oct, Sat, Sun and Bank Holiday Mon, 1400-1700; 1-10 Apr, whitsun week, school summer holiday and 10-17 Dec, daily, 1400-1700. £2.00/£1.00/£2.00. Tel: (0799) 41354.*

Castle Point Transport Museum, The Old Bus Garage, 105 Point Road, Canvey Island: 1930 bus garage housing collection of buses and coaches in restored condition. Some examples are unique. Some now being restored. *1 Apr-31 Oct, 2nd & last Sat of month, 1000-1700. Donations welcome. Tel: (0268) 684272.*

◉ **Colne Valley Railway**, Yeldham Road, Castle Hedingham: Complete reconstruction of Victorian Edwardian Rural Branch Line, Stations, signal boxes, vintage engines and carriage displays. Museum. *1 Mar-23 Dec, 1000-1700; closed 24 Dec-1 Jan. £2.00/£1.00/£2.00. Steam days £4.00/£2.00/£3.00. Tel: (0787) 61174.* &

◉ **East Anglian Railway Museum**, Chappel Station, Colchester: The most comprehensive collection of period railway architecture and engineering in East Anglia. Based upon a busy Victorian country junction station. Preserved locomotives, passenger and freight rolling stock, working signal boxes, heritage centre. Fine transport bookshop, giftshop, buffet. Steam train rides on approx 30 days/year, miniature railway. Childrens play area. *All year, daily, 0930-1700 or dusk if earlier, Closed 25 Dec. £2.00/£1.00/£1.00. Steam days £3.50/£2.00/ £2.00. Tel: (0206) 242524.* &

Vintage Aircraft at the Shuttleworth Collection

East Anglian Railway Museum, Chappel

Mangapps Railway Museum, Burnham-on-Crouch: Large collection of railway relics, restored station, locomotives, coaches and wagons. Working railway line (1/4m). Also farm bygones and animals. *All year, Sat, Sun, Bank Holidays; 28 Mar-8 Apr, daily 1300- 1800 (1130 opening 3,4 Apr); Open throughout school holidays daily; 19 Dec-1 Jan, daily. Closed 25,26 Dec. £3.00/£2.00/£2.50. Tel: (0621) 784898.* &

Mark Hall Cycle Museum, off First Avenue, Muskham Road, Harlow: A unique collection of over 60 cycles and accessories illustrating the history of the bicycle from 1818 to the 1980's. Housed in converted 19th century stable block of Mark Hall Estate. *All year, Sun-Thu, 1000-1700; Closed Bank Hols. £1.00/50p/50p. Tel: (0279) 439680.* &

National Motorboat Museum, Wät Tyler Country Park, Pitsea: Museum devoted to the history and evolution of the motorboat, racing hydroplanes, power boats and leisure boats. Racing trophies. *All year, 1 Apr-31 Oct, Thu-Mon, 1000-1700, 1 Nov-31 Mar, Thu-Mon, 1000-1600. Tel: (0268) 550088.*

⊛ **The Working Silk Museum** New Mills, South Street, Braintree: Show of textiles and mill shop. Looms and ancient textile machines restored and working. Working looms Mon-Fri, Sat pm on the hour with weaving demonstrations. Evening tours with demonstrations by appointment. *All year, daily, except Sun and Bank Holidays, 1000-1230, 1330-1700; Guided Tours, Sat, 1400,1500,1600. £2.75/£1.50/£1.50. Tel: (0376) 553393.* &

NORFOLK

Barton House Railway, Hartwell Road, The Avenue, Wroxham: 3.5" gauge miniature steam passenger railway. 7.25" gauge battery-electric railway. Full size M & GN accessories including signals and signal box. *Apr-Oct, third Sun of each month, 1430-1730. 30p/10p/30p. Tel: (0603) 782470.*

⊛ **Bressingham Steam Museum and Gardens,** Bressingham: Fire museum, locomotive sheds, stationary engine display, Royal coach, traction engines, gardens, 2 acre plant centre and display area. (Adrian Blooms Garden is open once a month through the year, please ring to confirm exact dates). *1 Apr-31 Oct, daily, 1000-1730;*

telephone for details of opening times at Easter and Christmas. £3.50/£2.50/£2.50. Tel: (037 988) 386. &

⊛ **Bure Valley Railway** Aylsham Station, Norwich Road, Aylsham: This new narrow-gauge steam railway runs on 9 miles of the old Great Eastern trackbed through some of Norfolk's most beautiful Broadland countryside. Trains can be joined at either end of the route and the stations are conveniently placed in each town. Parking available in both places. Connections are possible with both the National Trust's Blickling Hall and the Broads. *1 Apr-31 Oct. £6.00/£3.50/£5.00 (93). Tel: (0263) 733858 for days and times.* &

Caister Castle and Car Collection, West Caister: Castle built in 1432 with large collection of motor vehicles from 1893 to present. *Mid May-30 Sep, Sun-Fri. Tel: (057284) 251 for opening times and prices.* &

Charles Burrell Museum, Minstergate, Thetford: The Museum draws together an impressive collection of exhibits to tell the story of Charles Burrell & Son, a name once famous throughout the world. The large exhibits are housed on the ground floor, together with a series of recreated workshops with original tools and machinery. Up in the gallery a series of photographs, letters and documents tell the story of the company and of the Burrell Family. *2 Apr-30 Oct, Sat,Sun and Bank Hols, 1000-1700. £1.25/75p/75p. Tel: (0362) 695333.* &

City of Norwich Aviation Museum, Old Norwich Road, Horsham St Faith: Exhibition building with displays of aviation memorabilia, photographs, models, maps and pictures. RAF Horsham St Faith display, 8th USAAF display, 2nd Air Division display, 458th Bomb Group display, collection of aircraft including Vulcan Bomber from Falklands Task Force. Souvenir shop. *1 Jan-30 Mar and 1 Nov-31 Dec, Sun, 1000-1600; 31 Mar-31 Oct, Sun, 1000-1700; 30 Apr-31 Aug, also Tue and Thu, 0730-dusk and Wed, 1400-1700; Bank Holidays open 1000-1700; closed 25 and 26 Dec. £1.50/50p/£1.00. Vulcan cockpit 50p/25p. Tel: (0603) 861348.* &

County School Station, North Elmham: Restored country railway station. Exhibition on the railway, county school and Wensum Valley. Small length of track with working diesel train and brake-van. *All year, daily, 0900-1800. Tel: (0362) 695333.*

Fenland Aviation Museum, Bambers Gdn Centre, Old Lynn Road, West Walton: The Vampire T11 aircraft is one of the finest examples in the country and has just undergone a complete respray and airframe check. Members of the public are welcome to sit in the cockpit and study the aircraft at close quarters. *5 Mar-30 Oct, Sat, Sun, Bank Hol Mons, 0930-1700; other times and days by appointment. 50p/25p/25p. Tel: (0945) 585946.* &

Forncett Industrial - Steam Museum, Low Road, Forncett St Mary: Unusual collections of large industial steam engines including one that used to open Tower Bridge. Seven of the largest can be seen working on steam days. Museum

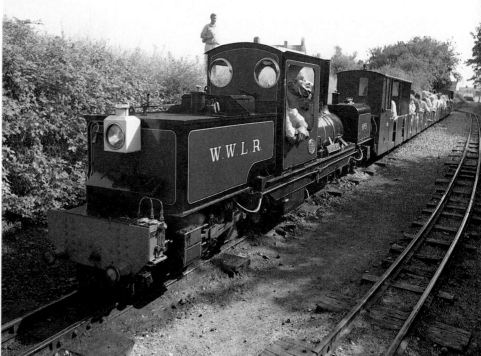
Wells Walsingham Railway

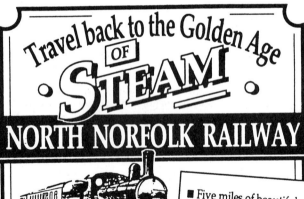
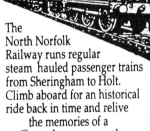

Please mention East Anglia Guide when replying to advertisements

won a 1989 Steam Heritage Award. *Public Steam Days, 1 May, 5 Jun, 3 Jul, 7 Aug, 4 Sep, 2 Oct, 6 Nov, 4 Dec, 1400-1800. £2.50/£1.25/£1.75. Tel: (050 841) 8277.* &

Lydia Eva Steam Drifter: see entry under Suffolk.

◉ **Muckleburgh Collection**, Weybourne Old Military Camp, Weybourne: The original NAAFI complex of this former military camp now houses a collection of tanks, armoured cars, lorries, artillery, bombs and missiles used by Allied armies during WWII and since. It incorporates the Suffolk & Norfolk Yeomanry Museum of uniforms, weapons, photographs and documents. There are items of artillery used in the Falkland Islands, also uniforms, weapons and other equipment recovered from Coalition and Iraqi armies in the Gulf War. Some post war aircraft on display and a maritime and RNLI exhibition. *20 Mar-30 Oct, daily, 1000-1700. £3.00/£1.60/£2.50 (93) Tel: (026 370) 210.* &

◉ **North Norfolk Railway**, Sheringham Station, Station Approach, Sheringham: The North Norfolk Railway operates steam trains along the 5 mile line from the seaside resort of Sheringham to the market town Holt. The journey affords beautiful views of the sea, pine forest and heathland. At Sheringham there is a museum of railway memorabilia, static exhibits, a station buffet and souvenir shop also a model railway and shop. Weybourne station gives access to Kelling Heath nature trail and is a typical rural station. Here is also our engine shed where historical locomotives and rolling stock are maintained and restored. A regular steam or vintage diesel hauled service. *Station open all year, daily, 0900-1800; trains operate Mar-Dec, varying times, phone for details; at Christmas Santa Specials/mince pie specials, steam service, phone for details. Station only 50p/25p. Sheringham to Holt return, £5.00/£3.00/£4.00. Tel: (0263) 822045.* &

Seething Airfield Control Tower, Station 146, Seething Aifield, Seething: A B24 Liberator base during World War II. Renovated USAAF control tower has model a/c room, diorama of Seething base, 448th Honour roll, display of WWII memorabilia, exhibition of "The 448th Bomb Group Collection". This includes diaries, photographs and personal stories from Americans based at Seething 1943-1945. *May-Oct, first Sun in every month, 1000-1700. Tel: (0508) 50787.* &

Strumpshaw Hall Steam Museum, Strumpshaw: Collection of steam vehicles including working beam engines, showman's road engine, portable and stationary steam engines, steam wagon and fairground organ. Railway running every day. *1,2,3,4 Apr, 1100-1600. 28,29,30 May, 0930-1100; 14 Jul-1 Oct, 1100-1600; £2.00/£1.00/£1.50. Tel: (0603) 712339.* &

◉ **Thursford Collection**, Thursford Green, Thursford: Musical evenings every Tue from end Jun to end Sep. Live musical show every opening - 9 mechanical organs and Wurlitzer show starring Robert Wolfe. *1 Apr-31 May, daily, 1300-1700; 1 Jun-31 Aug, daily, 1100- 1700; 1 Sep-31 Oct, daily, 1300-1700; Closed 25 Dec, 1 Jan. £4.20/£1.80/£3.80. Tel: (0328) 878477.* &

Wells Walsingham Railway, Stiffkey Road, Wells-next-the-Sea: Four miles of railway. The longest 10.25 inch railway in the world. New locomotive, Norfolk Hero now in service, largest of its kind ever built. *1 Apr-30 Sep, daily, 1000-1800; £3.50/£2.50 (93).* &

Enjoy a ride at Thursford

Wolferton Station Museum, Wolferton: The former royal retiring rooms built for King Edward VII and Queen Alexandra in 1898. Items and furniture from royal trains, Queen Victoria's travelling bed, railway relics and curios, Victorian/Edwardian fashions, jewellery, furniture, personal royal letters. A representation of a royal train carriage housed in an 1880's GER coach. *1 Apr-30 Sep, Mon-Fri, 1100-1730, Sat (craft shop and grounds only) 1030-1630, Sun, 1300-1700. £1.85/80p/£1.40. Tel: (0485) 540674.* &

SUFFOLK

Boat World, Sea Lake Road, Oulton Broad: Working exhibition of boat building craft skills. Visitors can view a variety of interesting craft under construction. Maritime book shop and tea rooms. *Whitsun-30 Sep, Mon-Fri, 1000-1600. £1.95/£1.50/£1.50. Tel: (0502) 500661.* &

◉ **East Anglia Transport Museum**, Chapel Road, Carlton Colville: Museum which is under constant development, where the emphasis is on movement. Working trams, trolley buses and narrow gauge railway. Also buses, cars, commercial vehicles and steam rollers. A period street is being developed complete with authentic street furniture. *3,4 Apr; May-Sep, Sun, Bank Hols, 1100-1700; Jun-Sep, also Sat 1400-1600; 18 Jul-4 Sep, daily, 1400-1600; £2.50/£1.50/£1.50 (93). Tel: (0986) 798398.* &

Ipswich Transport Museum, Old Trolleybus Depot, Cobham Road, Ipswich: A collection of over 70 historic commercial vehicles, housed in a former Ipswich Corporation Trolleybus Depot. The vehicles date from 1850-1983 and all have been built or used in the area. *3,4 Apr, 8 May, 19 Jun, 17 Jul, 21 Aug, 25 Sep, 16 Oct; 1100-1630. £1.50/75p/£1.00. Tel: (0473) 832260.* &

Long Shop Museum, Main Street, Leiston: The Long Shop dates back to 1853. Houses steam roller, steam tractor, CCS Potable, drills, threshing drum, living van and trolley bus. History of Leiston Town and its environs; story of the 2nd World War USAAF air base. History of Steam Exhibition. *1 Apr-31 Oct, Mon-Sat, 1000-1700, Sun 1100-1700. £1.50/75p/75p. Tel: (0728) 832189.* &

Lydia Eva Steam Drifter, Yacht Basin, Lowestoft Harbour, Lowestoft: One of the last steam drifters to be built and the last survivor of over 3000 drifters which came every autumn to Yarmouth and Lowestoft to fish for herring. Displays the hardships of life in an industry which dominated the two towns for a century. Lydia Eva was built in 1930 in King's Lynn and her engines and boiler were fitted in Great Yarmouth. *1 Apr-31 Jun at Great Yarmouth, daily, 1000-1630; 1 Jul-30 Sep at Lowestoft, daily, 1000-1630. Tel: (0502) 77602 (after 1630).*

Mid Suffolk Light Railway Society Museum, Brockford Station, Brockford: The setting up of a working museum dedicated to the Mid Suffolk Light Railway. Restoration of station and trackwork on part of original route of railway. Preservation of artefacts and memorabilia. *3 Apr-30 Sep, Sun, 1000-1700. 50p/free/50p. Open days £1.50/free/£1.50.*

Norfolk and Suffolk Aviation Museum, The Street, Flixton: 18 aircraft on display. Large indoor display of smaller items connected with the history of aviation. *Apr-Oct, Sun, Bank Holidays, 1000-1700, 19 Jul-15 Sep, Tue, Wed, Thu, 1000-1700; Jul & Aug, Wed & Thu, 1900-2100; Donations encouraged.* &

William Clowes Printing Museum, Newgate, Beccles: Development of printing from 1800. Large display of machinery, wood engravings, books. Guided factory tours by arrangement. *1 Jun-31 Aug, Mon-Fri, 1400-1600. Tel: (0502) 712884.*

Prices are in the order Adults/Senior Citizens. Where prices are not available at the time of going to press, the 1993 (93) price is given. If no price is given, admission is free. See Touring Maps on pages 119-124 for locations of places to visit.

33

MUSEUMS

Elstow Moot Hall

BEDFORDSHIRE

BEDFORD

⊛ **Bedford Museum,** Castle Lane: Bedford Museum is housed in a former brewery in a setting close to the River Great Ouse. The displays show aspects of community life in Bedford, re-created interiors of farmhouse and cottage, local rocks and fossils, birds and mammals from town and countryside, archaeology through the ages including important local archaeological finds and lacemaking. There is a full programme of temporary exhibitions, children's activities and special events. *All year, Tue-Sat, 1100-1700; Sun, 1400-1700; Closed 1 Apr and 25 Dec, telephone for details for remainder of Christmas. Tel: (0234) 353323.* ⅋

Bunyan Museum and Bunyan Meeting Free Church, Mill Street: Personal effects of John Bunyan (1628-1688) and copies of 60 of Bunyan's works including "The Pilgrim's Progress" in 169 languages, together with items relating to over 300 years of Church history. The Church contains bronze doors and stained glass windows depicting scenes from the "Pilgrim's Progress". *1 Apr-31 Oct, Tue-Sat, 1400-1600. 50p/30p/30p. Tel: (0234) 358075.* ⅋

⊛ **Cecil Higgins Art Gallery and Museum,** Castle Close: Award winning re-created Victorian Mansion, original home of Cecil Higgins. Rooms displayed to give 'lived-in' atmosphere including bedroom with furniture designed by William Burges (1827-1881). Adjoining gallery with outstanding collections of ceramics, glass and watercolours. *All year, Tue-Fri, 1230-1700, Sat, 1100-1700; Sun, 1400-1700, Bank Holidays, 1230-1700; Closed Mon; 1 Apr; 25,26 Dec; Tel: (0234) 211222.* ⅋

⊛ **ELSTOW Moot Hall,** Elstow Green, Church End: Medieval Market Hall containing exhibits of 17th century life. *2 Apr-30 Oct, Tue-Thu, Sat, Bank Holidays, 1400-1700, Sun, 1400-1730. 60p/30p/30p. Tel: (0234) 228330.*

LUTON

⊛ **Luton Museum and Art Gallery,** Wardown Park: Victorian mansion in 50 acres of parkland. Costume, lace, hat-making displays, Victorian street displays, natural history and the archaeology of South Bedfordshire. *All year, Mon-Sat, 1000-1700, Sun, 1300-1700. Closed 25,26 Dec and 1 Jan. Tel: (0582) 36941.* ⅋

⊛ **Stockwood Craft Museum and Gardens,** Stockwood Park, Farley Hill: Museum set in period gardens and Hamilton Finlay sculpture garden. Craft demonstrations at weekends. *1 Apr-31 Oct, Tue-Sat, 1000-1700, Sun, and Bank Hol Mon, 1000-1800; 1 Nov-31 Mar, Sat-Sun, 1000-1600; Closed 25,26 Dec, 1 Jan. Tel: (0582) 38714.* ⅋

CAMBRIDGESHIRE

BURWELL Museum Trust, Mill Close, Burwell: Rural village museum housed in re erected 18th century timber framed barn. Smithy and wheelwrights shop. *All year, Sun; Apr-Oct, also Bank Hols, 1400-1700.* ⅋

CAMBRIDGE

Cambridge and County Folk Museum, 2-3 Castle Street: The building was originally a 16th century farmhouse. From 17th century to 1934 it was an Inn. Houses wide variety of objects relating to everyday life of people in City and Country. Museum also has temporary exhibition programme and activity days. *2 Apr-30 Sep, Mon-Sat, 1030-1700, Sun, 1400-1700; 1 Oct-31 Mar, Tue-Sat, 1030-1700, Sun, 1400-1700; closed 1 Apr, 24 Dec-2 Jan. £1.00/50p/50p. Tel: (0223) 355159.* ⅋

Museum of Classical Archaeology, Sidgwick Avenue: Plaster casts of Greek and Roman sculptures. *All year, Mon-Fri, 0900-1700. Tel: (0223) 335153.*

Fitzwilliam Museum, Trumpington Street: The museum contains fascinating Egyptian, Greek, Roman and other antiquities, an internationally renowned collection of European paintings, an outstanding and varied display of ceramics, some fine furniture, clocks, watches, bronzes, medals, armour and fans. The original magnificent buildings dating from the mid-19th century and the

Painting by J van der Hoecke, Fitzwilliam Museum

Oliver Cromwell's House, Ely

additions built this century provide a splendid setting, resulting in one of the best museums of its type outside the major cities. *All year, Tue-Sat, 1000-1700, Sun, 1415-1700, Bank Holiday Mons 1000-1700; closed 24 Dec-1 Jan. Tel: (0223) 332900.* &

Kettle's Yard, Castle Street: Major collection of 20th century paintings and sculpture exhibited in a house of unique character. Temporary exhibitions gallery with changing contemporary art exhibitions, talks and discussions. *House open all year, Tue-Sun, 1400-1600; Gallery open from 1 Apr, Tue-Sat, 1230-1730, Sun, 1400-1730. Closed Christmas to New Year. Tel (0223) 352124.*

Sedgwick Museum, Dept of Earth Sciences, Downing Street: Large collection of vertebrate and invertebrate fossils from all over the world. Some mounted skeletons of dinosaur, reptiles and mammals. Also collection of rocks and building stones. *All year; Mon-Fri, 0900-1300, 1400-1700; Sat, 1000-1300; closed Easter weekend and Christmas/New Year. Tel: (0223) 333456.*

University Museum of Zoology, Downing Street: Material used in teaching and research in zoology including marine invetebrates, insects, fossils, recent fishes, amphibians, reptiles, birds and mammals. *All year, Mon-Fri, 1415-1645; closed Christmas and Easter week. Tel: (0223) 336650.*

Whipple Museum of the History of Science, Free School Lane: Extensive collection of scientific instruments. *All year, Mon-Fri, 1400-1600; May-Nov, also Sat, 1400-1600; Tel: (0223) 334540.*

ELY

Ely Museum, 28C High Street: Displays investigate the history of Ely and the surrounding area from the prehistoric period onwards. Particular exhibits include an archeology and Medieval history gallery, Fenland life (including audio-visual films), crafts. The Cambridgeshire Regiment, and the cycle of James Moore used on the day of the world's first bicycle race. *4 Jan-1 Apr, Tue-Fri, 1130-1530; Sat-Sun, 1130-1600; 2 Apr-11 Dec, Tue-Sun, 1030-1300, 1415-1700; £1.00/50p/50p. Tel: (0353) 666655.*

◉ **Oliver Cromwells's House,** 29 St Mary's Street: Family home of Oliver Cromwell. 17th century kitchen and parlour scenes, tourist information centre, souvenirs and craft shop. *1 Apr-30 Sep, daily, 1000-1800, 1 Oct-31 Mar, 1000-*

1715, Mon-Sat. Closed 25,26 Dec and 1 Jan. £1.80/£1.50. Tel: (0353) 662062.

Stained Glass Museum, The Cathedral: Examples of stained glass from 13th century to present day in specially lighted display boxes. Models of a modern workshop which explain the manufacture of a stained glass window. There are approximately 75 panels on display. *All year,*

Kettles Yard, Cambridge

Sun, 1200-1500; Sat and Bank Holidays, 1030-1630; 1 Mar-31 Oct, Mon-Fri, 1030-1600; Closed 1 Apr, 25 Dec. £1.50/70p/70p. Tel: (0353) 667735/6.

HUNTINGDON Cromwell Museum, Grammar School Walk: Housed in building where Oliver Cromwell and Samuel Pepys went to school. *1 Apr-31 Oct, Tue-Fri, 1100-1300, 1400-1700, Sat-Sun, 1100-1300, 1400-1600; 1 Nov-31 Mar, Tue-Fri, 1300-1600, Sat 1100-1300, 1400-1600, Sun, 1400-1600. Tel: (0480) 425830.*

MARCH & District Museum, High Street: General collection of artefacts relating to social history. Agricultural tools, many local photos and 19th century record material. Restored blacksmiths forge and Fen Cottage. *All year, Wed, 1000-1200, Sat, 1000-1200, 1400-1630. Tel: (0354) 55300.*

◉ **PETERBOROUGH Museum and Art Gallery,** Priestgate: Local history. Geology, Archaeology, natural history, folk life, world famous collection of Napoleonic POW work, costume period shop and many temporary exhibitions. *All year, Tue-Sat, 1000-1700. Closed Christmas. Tel: (0733) 343329.*

RAMSEY Rural Museum, The Wood Yard, Cemetery Road: Rebuilt farm buildings housing a collection of old farm implements of the fens and Victorian life in the home. Now including a chemist's shop and a cobblers. *1 Apr-30 Sep, Sun, Thu, 1400-1700. Closed Easter. Tel: (0487) 813823.* &

ST IVES Norris Museum, The Broadway: The Norris Museum is the museum of Huntingdonshire, with exhibits from every part of the county and every period of history. Oldest items on show are fossils and reconstructed models of animals that lived here in the time of the dinosaurs; more recent specimens include remains of the Woolly Mammoth, and archaeological remains from the Stone Age onwards. There are special displays on the Civil War, on French prisoner-of-war work from the prison camp at Norman Cross, and the local sport of ice-skating on the flooded Fens. The Museum is set in a picturesque riverside garden. *4 Jan-30 Apr, 1 Oct-31 Dec, Mon-Fri, 1000-1300, 1400-1600, Sat, 1000-1200; 1 May-30 Sep, Mon-Fri, 1000-1300, 1400-1700, Sat, 1000-1200, 1400-1700, Sun, 1400-1700; Closed 1 Apr, 24-28 Dec and 1-3 Jan. Tel: (0480) 465101.* &

THORNEY Heritage Centre, Station Road: Models, maps of development from monastic days, changes of Walloon, Fleming influence after Vermudens drainage. 19th century model housing by Duke of Bedford, recent village life. *1 Apr-31 Oct, Sat, Sun, 1400-1700; 1 Jun-30 Sep, Wed, Sat, Sun, 1400-1700. Tel: (0733) 270780.* &

WHITTLESEY Whittlesea Museum, Town Hall, Market Street: Archaeology, agriculture, hand tools, brickmaking, collection of local photographs. Sir Harry Smith exhibition, railways, costume display, temporary exhibitions. *All year; Fri & Sun 1430-1630; Sat, 1000-1200. 50p/20p/50p. Tel: (0733) 203608.*

WISBECH Wisbech & Fenland Museum, Museum Square: Museum founded in 1835. Premises purpose built in 1845. Collections cover: Applied Art, for example ceramics and Townshend collection, local geology, zoology archaeology, topography and history. Ethnography - mainly African. The building also houses two historic libraries, open by appointment, as well as local archives, including Parish Records and maps. Temporary Exhibition Gallery. New gallery on Thomas Clarkson, slavery and the slave trade. *All year, Jan-Mar, Tue-Sat, 1000-1600, Apr-Sep, Tue-Sat 1000-1700, Oct-Dec, Tue-Sat, 1000-1600. Closed Christmas. Tel: (0945) 583817.*

ESSEX

BILLERICAY Barleylands Farm Museum, Barleylands Road : Situated on a working farm. An extensive collection of vintage farm machinery, tractors and agricultural bygones illustrating rural life of the past, including a pair of Fowler steam engines with implements. Narrow gauge steam railway open summer Sun and Bank Holidays, weather permitting. Also working craft units. *All year, Wed-Sun, 1100-1700; closed 25,26 Dec. £2.00/£1.00/£1.00. Tel: (0268) 282090. Steam Railway 50p/50p/50p.*

BRAINTREE The Town Hall Centre, Market Square: Heritage centre shows the town's development from the Stone Age to the present and describes Braintree's international importance to wool, silk, engineering and early American history. The gallery houses changing exhibitions. Study room with local interest books and photographic collection. *All year, Mon-Sat, 1000-1700; Closed Bank Holidays. Tel: (0376) 552525.*

BRIGHTLINGSEA Museum, 1 Duke Street: Maritime and social history of the town. Also history of fishing, yachting, stowboating and oystering. *Apr-Oct, Mon and Thu 1400-1700, Sat 1000-1600. 50p/25p/25p.*

BURNHAM-ON-CROUCH Museum, Providence (off High Street): Small museum devoted to local history with maritime and agricultural features of Dengie Hundred. *Mid Mar-mid Dec, Wed, Sat, 1100-1600; Sun, Bank Holidays, Burnham Week and East Coast Boat Show, 1400-1630. 40p/10p/40p.*

CANVEY ISLAND Dutch Cottage Museum, Canvey Road: Early 17th century cottage belonging to one of Vermuydens Dutch workmen (responsible for drainage schemes in East Anglia). *30 May, 1030-1300, 1430-1700; 1 Jun-28 Sep, Wed, Sun, 1430- 1700. Tel: (0268) 794005.*

CHELMSFORD Chelmsford and Essex Museum, Oaklands Park, Moulsham Street: Permanent collections of fossils and rocks, archaeology, costume, decorative arts (Castle Hedingham Ware, English tinglaze pottery) glass, natural history. Also Essex Regiment Museum. New permanent display - The Story of Chelmsford, from the Ice Age to AD1600. Temporary exhibition programme. *All year, Mon-Sat 1000-1700, Sun 1400-1700; Closed 1 Apr, 25,26 Dec. Tel: (0245) 353066.*

COLCHESTER

Colchester Castle: Spectacular new displays of Colchester's early history including the destruction of Colchester at the hands of Boudica and the Iceni. Roman Colchester galleries feature many hands on exhibits of appeal to children and adults alike. Look out for the imaginative holiday events programme. *All year, Mon-Sat, 1000-1700, last adm 1630; Mar-Nov, also Sun 1400-1700; closed 24-27 Dec & 1 Jan. £2.00/£1.00/£1.00. Tel: (0206) 712931.*

Stained Glass Museum, Ely Cathedral

Hollytrees Museum, High Street: Collection of toys, costume and decorating arts from 18th to 20th century displays in a elegant Georgian Town House built in 1718. *All year, Tue-Sat, 1000-1200, 1300-1700; Closed 1 Apr, 24-28 Dec and 1 Jan. Tel: (0206) 712931.*

Natural History Museum, All Saints Church, High Street: Recently redisplayed to a high standard with "hands on" activities for children. *All year, Tue-Sat, 1000-1300, 1400-1700; closed 1 Apr, 24-28 Dec, 1 Jan. Tel: (0206) 712932.*

Social History Museum, Holy Trinity Church, Trinity Street: Town and country life in the Colchester area over the last two hundred years displayed in the medieval former Church of Holy Trinity with its Saxon tower. *Apr-Oct, Tue-Sat, 1000-1200, 1300-1700; closed 1 Apr. Tel: (0206) 712931.*

Tymperleys Clock Museum, Trinity Street: A fine collection of Colchester made clocks displayed in Tymperleys, a restored late fifteenth century timber framed house. *Apr-Oct, Tue-Sat, 1000-1300, 1400-1700; closed 1 Apr. Tel: (0206) 712931.*

DEDHAM

The Sir Alfred Munnings Art Museum, Castle House: Standing in attractive garden, two studios and other galleries contain many paintings, drawings, sketches and other works. *1 May-2 Oct, Sun, Wed, Bank Holidays, 1400-1700; also Thu, Sat in Aug. £2.00/25p/£1.00. Tel: (0206) 322127.*

Toy Museum, Dedham Centre, High Street: Small museum with collection of dolls, teddies, games, play house and pictures. *All year, Tue, Wed, Thu, Sat and Sun, 1030-1645 (closed lunchtimes). Open 1,4 Apr. Closed 25,26,27 Dec. 40p/20p/20p. Tel: (0206) 322666.*

EAST TILBURY Coalhouse Fort, Princess Margaret Road: Victorian Thames defence fortress. Thameside Aviation museum, military vehicles, artillery displays, rifle range and park. River Thames foreshore walk. *Open last Sun of every month and most bank holidays, 1200-1600. Guided tours £1.50/50p/£1.50. Tel:(0375) 844203*

FINCHINGFIELD Guildhall, Church Hill: 15th century Guildhall houses local museum of local artefacts including Roman remains.

Dedham Toy Museum

Exhibition Hall. *1 Apr-30 Sep, Sun and Bank Holidays, 1400-1730. Tel: (0371) 810456.*

GRAYS Thurrock Museum, Thameside Complex, Orsett Road,: An interesting display of artefacts, maps and models showing Thurrock's history from prehistoric to modern times. *All year, Mon-Sat, 0900-2000; Closed Sun and Bank Holidays. Tel: (0375) 382555.* &

GREAT BARDFIELD

Bardfield Cage, Bridge Street: 19th century village lock up. *1 Apr-30 Sep, Sat, Sun and Bank Holiday Monday, 1400-1730.*

Cottage Museum, Dunmow Road: 16th century Charity Cottage: A collection of mainly 19th and 20th century domestic and agriculture artefacts - some Rural Crafts mainly strawplaiting and corndollies. *1 Apr-30 Sep, Sat, Sun, Bank holidays, 1400-1730. Tel: (0371) 810689.*

HARLOW

Harlow Museum, Passmores House, Third Avenue: 5 Galleries covering archaeology, history, geology and natural history. Temporary exhibition gallery. *All year, Tue-Sat, 1000-1700, closed Sun, Mon and Bank Hols. £1.00/50p/50p. Tel: (0279) 454959.* &

Harlow Study and Visitors Centre, Netteswell Bury Farm: Study centre in a 13th century church. Visitors Centre in a medieval tithe barn with an exhibition on Harlow's new town story. *All year, Mon-Fri, 0930-1630; closed Christmas, Easter and New Year. Tel: (0279) 446745. £1.00/50p/£1.00.* &

HARWICH Maritime Museum, Low Lighthouse, The Green: Special displays relating to lifeboats. Royal Navy and commercial shipping. Fine views over unending shipping movements in harbour. *1 Apr-31 Oct, Sun only, 1000-1200, 1400-1700. 50p/free/50p. Tel: (0255) 503429.*

Colchester Castle

LINFORD Walton Hall Farm Museum, Walton Hall Road, Linford: Main collection housed in 17th century English Barn and other farm buildings. Collection includes farming bygones, tools, wagons, implements, harnesses, military, rare breed animals, shire horse, donkey, sheep, goats, fowl, pigeons, peacock, parrot, domestic bygones, motoring bygones. Representations of Victorian and Edwardian childs nursery with dolls, toys, collection of prams. Representations

Prittlewell Priory Museum, Southend-on-Sea

KELVEDON Feering & Kelvedon Local History Museum, Maldon Road: Artefacts from Roman settlement of Camonium. Manorial history, agricultural tools and bygones. *1 Mar-31 Oct, Mon 1400-1700, Sat, 0930-1230; 1 Nov-28 Feb, Sat 1000-1230; closed Bank Holidays, 1-4 Apr and 25 Dec. Tel: (0376) 570307.*

LEIGH-ON-SEA Heritage Centre, 13A High Street: Photographic exhibition, historical interpretive displays. *All year, daily, 1100-1500. Closed 24, 25,26 Dec. Tel: (0702) 470834.* &

of old time dairy, milk delivery pram, churns, bottles. Bird garden and picnic lawn. *1 Apr-24 Dec, Thu-Sun, 1000-1700 including Bank Holidays; £2.00/£1.00/£1.00. Tel: (0375) 671874.* &

MANNINGTREE and District Local History Museum, Manningtree Library, High Street: Local History museum with displays of old photographs, artefacts, books and local maps and plans. Some permanent displays with two major exhibitions of local interest each year (wartime,

schools). The museum provides a resource for local historical study by children and adults as well as any archive for research and a repository for the continuing acquisition of historical material. *All year, Fri, 1000-1200, 1400-1600, Sat, 1000-1200. Tel: (0206) 392747.* &

◉ **SAFFRON WALDEN Museum**, Museum Street: 150 year old museum of local history, decorative arts, ethnography, Great Hall gallery of archaelogy and early history. Ancient Egyptian room/tomb. New geology displays opened 1993. Norman castle ruins in grounds. *3,4 Apr 1430-1700; 5 Apr-31 Oct, Mon-Sat, 1000-1700, Sun 1430-1700; 1 Nov-31 Mar, Tue-Sat, 1100-1600, Sun 1430-1630; closed 24,25 Dec; Open 26 Dec, 1 Jan, 1430-1630. £1.00/free/50p. Tel: (0799) 510333.* &

SOUTHEND-ON-SEA

◉ **Central Museum and Planetarium**, Victoria Avenue: Edwardian building housing displays of archaeology, natural history, social and local history. Also houses only planetarium in south east of England outside London. *All year; Mon, 1300-1700; Tue-Sat, 1000-1700; Planetarium shows, Wed-Sat, 1000, 1100, 1200, 1400, 1500, 1600; closed Bank Holidays, Easter, Christmas and New Year. Planetarium £2.00/£1.10/£1.10. Tel: (0702) 330214.* & *(wheelchair access museum only)*

◉ **Prittlewell Priory**, Priory Park, Victoria Avenue: Remains of 12th century priory with later additions. Displays of natural history, medieval religious life and radios, gramophones and TV's. Set in Priory Park about 200 yards from the entrance. *All year, Tue-Sat, 1000-1300, 1400-1700; closed Easter, Christmas and New Year. Tel: (0702) 342878.* &

◉ **Southchurch Hall Museum**, Southchurch Hall Gardens, Southchurch Hall Close: Moated timber-framed 13 and 14th century manor house set in attractive gardens. *All year, Tue-Sat, 1000-1300, 1400-1700; closed Easter, Christmas and New Year. Tel: (0702) 467671.* &

SOUTHMINSTER Ewenny Farm Alternative Environment Centre, Southminster Road: Traditional windpump/wind generators, solar electric displays, organic garden, wildlife

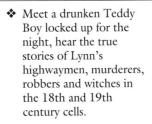

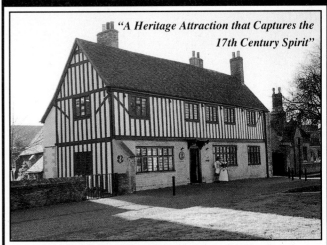
Please mention East Anglia Guide when replying to advertisements

garden, pond, tree nursery, herbs and visitors centre. *All year, daily, 1000-1800. Closed Christmas and New Year. £2.00/£1.50/£1.50, Tel: (0621) 773755.* ♿

STANSTED House on the Hill Toy Museum: Exciting, animated Toy Museum covering 7,000 sq. ft. featuring a huge collection of toys from Victorian times to the 1970's, offering a nostalgic trip back to childhood. *13 Mar-13 Nov, daily, 1000-1700; 14 Nov-31 Dec, weekends and school holidays, 1000-1700; closed 24-26 Dec. £2.80/£1.80/£2.30. Tel: (0279) 813237.*

WALTHAM ABBEY Epping Forest District Museum, 39-41 Sun Street: Tudor and Georgian Timber framed buildings; Tudor herb garden; Tudor panelled room. Temporary exhibitions, and general local history. *All year, Fri-Mon, 1400-1700, Tue, 1200-1700; closed 25, 26 Dec, 1 Jan. Tel: (0992) 716882.*

WALTON-ON-THE-NAZE Walton Heritage Centre, East Terrace: 100 years old former Lifeboat House, carefully restored. Exhibitions of local interest change annually eg. Maritime, Urban, seaside, development. *Mid Jul-mid Sep, daily, 1400-1700. 50p/family ticket £1.00. Tel: (0255) 672061.*

WEST MERSEA Mersea Island Museum, High Street: Local history, natural history, display of methods and tools used in marine, and wildlife. Fishing equipment, social history, fossils and mineral display. *1 May-2 Oct, Tue-Sun, 1400-1700. Open Easter. 50p/20p/25p. Tel: (0206) 385191.* ♿

WESTCLIFF-ON-SEA Beecroft Art Gallery, Station Road: A local topographical collection of watercolours, oils, and prints plus occasional displays of works from the permanent collection of 16th-20th century Contemporary art. Varied programme of temporary exhibitions, both local and regional. *All year, Tue-Sat, 0930-1700; Closed Bank Holidays, Easter and Christmas. Tel: (0702) 347418.* ♿

WITHAM Fossil Hall, Boars Tye Road, Silver End: 2000 replicas of fossils from museums of the world, archaeological items, minerals, fossils, and replicas for sale. Bookshop with 150,000 second-hand items in stock. *All year, Sat and Bank Holidays, 1000-1600; 75p/25p. Tel: (0376) 583502.*

Central Museum, Southend-on-Sea

HERTFORDSHIRE

ROYSTON and District Museum, Lower King Street: A local history museum containing many interesting items relating to Royston and the surrounding area. Also includes a fine collection of modern ceramics. A tapestry of the history of Royston has been recently started. *All year Wed, Thu, Sat, 1000-1700, 1 Apr-30 Sep, also Sun, 1430-1700. Tel: (0763) 242587.*

Royston Museum

NORFOLK

ALBY

Alby Lace Museum and Study Centre, Alby Craft Centre, Cromer Road: Wide variety of lace exhibits up to 300 years old, easily studied with magnifying glasses provided. Lacemaker's cottage shows conditions under which lace would have been made in late Victorian times. Wide variety of memorabilia and some modern lace on display. Bobbin lace demonstrated and sold, wide variety of equipment and books for sale. DMC Main agent for all embroidery supplies. *Jan- mid Mar, Sun, 1000-1300, 1400-1700; mid Mar-Dec, Tue-Fri, Sun, 1000-1300, 1400-1700; Open Bank Holidays, Closed 25 Dec. Tel: (0263) 768002.* ♿

Alby Bottle Museum Alby Craft Centre, Cromer Road:The Bottle Museum is part of a large craft complex complete with gallery, working craftsmen and gardens. No coaches July-Aug. *18 Mar-20 Dec, Tue-Sun, Bank Holiday Mons, 1000-1700. 30p/10p. Tel: (0263) 761327.*

BURGH ST MARGARET, Bygone Heritage Village: Re-creation of a 19th century village. Collection of steam road locomotives, fire appliances, cars and motorcycles. Steam driven sawmill, animals and crafts. *Easter to end Oct, daily 1000-1800. Tel to confirm opening and for prices. Tel: (0493) 369770.*

BURSTON Strike School: Scene of the longest strike in British History - 25 years. Building erected to house scholars of strike school. Interpretative exhibit of artefacts, documents and photographs. *All year, daily, 0700-dusk; closed 1 Apr, 25, 26 Dec, 1 Jan. Tel: (037 986) 8256.* ♿

COCKLEY CLEY Iceni Village and Museums: Reconstruction of an Iceni tribal village, medieval cottage/forge with museum, carriage, vintage engine and farm museums. Nature trail. Saxon church c630 AD. *1 Apr-31 Oct, daily, 1100-1730. £2.50/£1.00/£1.50. Tel: (0760) 721339.* ♿

COCKTHORPE Cockthorpe Hall Toy Museum, Cockthorpe Hall: Toys late 1800s to mid 60s. 7 rooms contained in 16th century Cockthorpe Hall. *Jan-Mar and Oct-Dec, Mon-Fri, 1200-1600, Sat,Sun, 1100-1600; 1 Apr-30 Sep, daily, 1000-1700; Closed 24,25,26 Dec. £2.00/£1.00. Tel: (0328) 830293.*

MUSEUMS

CROMER

Lifeboat Museum and Lifeboat, The Pier and Gangway: Museum houses the Oakley class lifeboat "H F Bailey" which served at Cromer from 1935 to 1947. This boat and crew saved 818 lives. The history of Cromer lifeboats is displayed in pictures, models, photographs. Henry Bloggs' medals are also on display. The present lifeboat "Ruby and Arthur Read II" is a new Tyne Class lifeboat and can be viewed at the Lifeboat house on the pier at the same times as the museum. *1 May-31 Oct, daily, 1000-1600; Easter week, 1000-1600. Tel: (0263) 512503.* &

Cromer Museum, East Cottages, Tucker Street: Late Victorian fisherman's cottage, displays on local history (fishing, bathing resort) geology, natural history and archaeology. *All year, Sun, 1400-1700, Mon, 1000-1300, 1400-1700, Tue-Sat 1000-1700; closed 1 Apr, 23-26 Dec, 1 Jan. £1.00/50p/60p. Tel: (0263) 513543.*

DEREHAM

Bishop Bonners Cottage Museum, St Withburga Lane: Building originally 3 cottages. Built 1502. Framed building. Walls of brick, flint, wattle and daub. Thatched roof, pargeting. Old pictures and artefacts. *3 May-1 Oct, Tue-Sat and Bank Holidays, 1430-1700. Closed Easter. Tel: (0362) 693107.*

Hobbies Museum of Fretwork and Craft Centre, 34-36 Swaffham Road: Museum of fretwork machines dating back 1900, magazines and hobbies weeklies from 1895 and samples of old fretwork designs. *1 Apr-30 Sep, Mon-Fri, 1000-1200, 1400-1600. Tel: (0362) 692985.* &

DICKLEBURGH 100th Bomb Group Memorial Museum, Common Road: Museum housed in original World War II control tower. Other buildings. History of the 100th Bomb Group plus 8th Air Force exhibits, with visitors centre. *All year, Sat, Sun, Bank Holidays, 1000-1630; 1 May-Sep, also Wed 1000-1700; Closed 25 Dec. Tel: (0379) 740708.*

DISS Museum, Market Place: Diss Museum portrays the past life of the market town of Diss and its local area, including the upper Waveney Valley. The 19th century is well represented, especially by Victorian photographs, work tools and women's clothing; *8 Jan-30 Apr and 1 Nov-24 Dec, Fri, Sat, 1100-1700; 1 May-31 Oct, Wed, Thu, Sun, 1500-1700, Fri, Sat, 1100-1700; Tel: (0379) 650618.*

Cromer Lifeboat Museum

DOWNHAM MARKET Bridge Farm - A Country Christmas, River Ouse Bank: Bridge Farm is a working arable farm with over a mile of frontage to the River Ouse. It is on the site of a medieval hermitage and there is the Hermitage Pilgrims Hall. The Chapel of the Nativity is unique. The main feature is a journey back to Dickens Christmas with Victorian Street scenes, ghosts and farm shop. A car and cart museum and country walk. *Oct-Dec, Wed, tour at 1500. £3.50/£2.00/£3.00. Tel: (0366) 383185.*

FAKENHAM Museum of Gas and Local History, Hempton Road: Complete small town gasworks with local history section; displays of working gas meters and ancillary exhibits. *1-10 Apr, Tue, Thu-Sun, 1000-1400; 28 May-18 Sep, Tue, Thu-Sun, 1000-1400; open Bank Holiday Mon (ex May day). £1.50/25p/£1.00(93). Tel: (0328) 863150.* &

GREAT YARMOUTH

Elizabethan House Museum, 4 South Quay: Merchant's house with late Georgian front and 16th century panelled rooms. Exhibits showing 19th century domestic life; Victorian toys; Lowestoft porcelain and glasses. *28 Mar-9 Apr,*

Sun, 1400-1700, Mon-Fri, 1000-1700; 29 May-1 Oct, Sun-Fri, 1000-1700. 80p/40p/50p. Tel: (0493) 855746.

Maritime Museum, Marine Parade: Maritime history of Norfolk, with herring fishery and Norfolk wherry, large collection of ship models. *28 Mar-9 Apr, Mon-Fri, 1000-1700, Sun, 1400-1700. 29 May-1 Oct, Sun-Fri, 1000-1700. 80p/40p/50p. Tel: (0493) 842267.*

Great Yarmouth Museums Exhibition Galleries, Central Library, Tolhouse Street: Local and travelling exhibitions. Permanent art collection on display. *29 May-10 Dec, Sun-Fri, 1000-1700; Oct-Dec, Mon-Sat, 1000-1700; dates subject to temporary exhibition programme, tel to confirm (0493) 855746.* &

North West Tower, North Quay: Medieval tower which was originally part of the town walls of Great Yarmouth. Exhibition about trading wherries, traditional craft used on the Broads. Broads Information Centre. *1 Apr-31 Oct, Mon-Sun, 0900-1700. Tel:(0493) 332095.*

Old Merchant's House, Row 111, South Quay: Typical 17th century town houses. One with splendid plaster ceilings contains local architectural and domestic fittings salvaged from other 'Row' houses. *1 Apr-1 Oct, daily, 1000-1300, 1400-1800. £1.20/60p/90p. Tel: (0493) 857900.*

Tolhouse Museum, Tolhouse Street: One of the oldest municipal buildings in England. Once the town's courthouse and gaol, prison cells can still be seen. Displays illustrating the long history of the town. *28 Mar-9 Apr, Sun, 1400-1700, Mon-Fri, 1000-1700; 29 May- 1 Oct, Sun-Fri, 1000-1700. Tel: (0493) 858900.*

GRESSENHALL Norfolk Rural Life Museum, Beech House: Former workhouse illustrating history of Norfolk over last 200 years. Union Farm is a working 1920s farm with traditional breeds of livestock. Crafts and exhibits, special events and activities, exhibitions. *27 Mar-30 Oct, Tue-Sat, 1000-1700, Sun, 1200-1730. £3.00/£1.00/£2.00 (93). Tel: (0362) 860563.* &

KING'S LYNN

Arts Centre and Guildhall of St. George, 27 King Street: Regional Arts Centre. Medieval Guildhall now houses theatre. Regular programme of daytime and evening events. Films, concerts, galleries and annual arts festival. *Jan-Mar and Oct-Dec, Mon-Fri, 1100-1600, Sat, 1100-1300, 1400-1600; 2 Apr-30 Sep, Mon-Fri, 1000-1700, Sat, 1000-1300 & 1400-1700, Sun, 1400-1700; 50p/25p/50p. Gallery closed Mon. Closed 1 Apr, Christmas and New Year. Tel:(0553) 774725.*

Lynn Museum, Old Market Street: Natural history, archaeology, local history; also temporary exhibitions. *Jan-30 Sep, Mon-Sat, 1000-1700. Tel for winter opening. 60p/30p/40p. Tel: (0553) 775001.* &

Tales of the Old Gaol House, The Old Gaol House, Saturday Market Place: Charts the history of Crime and Punishment over the last 3 centuries. Once through the Gaol House the tour takes you into the Undercroft of the Trinity Guildhall to view the King John Cup, Four Maces, Royal Charters and Mayoral Insignia. *2 Jan-31 Mar, Fri-Tue, 1000-1700 (last admission 1615); 1 Apr-31 Oct, daily, 1000-1700 (last admission 1615); 1 Nov- 31 Dec, Fri-Tue, 1000-1700 (last admission 1615); Phone to check Christmas opening times; Entrance through TIC. £2.00/£1.50/£1.50. Tel: (0553) 763044.* &

Elizabethan Cottage, Cockley Cley

King's Lynn Arts Centre and Guildhall of St George

Norwich Gallery, Norfolk Institute of Art and Design, St Georges Street: Regional venue for contemporary art with a national reputation for touring exhibitions. *All year, Mon-Sat, 1100-1700. Tel: (0603) 610561.* &

⊚ **Royal Norfolk Regimental Museum**, Shirehall, Market Avenue: Displays devoted to the history of the County Regiment from 1685. Includes the daily life of a soldier. Audio- visual displays and graphics compliment the collection. Linked to Castle Museum by prisoners tunnel and a reconstructed 1st World War communication trench. *All year, Mon-Sat, 1000-1700, Sun, 1400-1700. £1.00/50p/70p. Tel: (0603) 223649.*

⊚ **Sainsbury Centre for Visual Arts**, University of East Anglia: The Robert and Lisa Sainsbury Collection is wide-ranging, remarkable and of international importance. With the recent addition of Sir Norman Foster & Partners superb Crescent Wing seven hundred paintings, sculptures and ceramics are on permanent display with Picasso, Moore, Bacon and Giacometti shown alongside art from Africa, the Pacific and the Americas. The Centre also houses the Anderson Collection of Art Nouveau. Three special exhibitions a year. The Centre has a restaurant, buffet and coffee bar. *4 Jan-23 Dec, Tue-Sun, 1200-1700; £1.00/50p/50p. Tel: (0603) 56060.* &

⊚ **Saint Peter Hungate Church Museum**, Princes Street: 15th century church with fine hammerbeam roof and Norwich painted glass. Displays on art and craft in service of Christianity. Illuminated books, brasses, musical instruments. *All year, Mon-Sat, 1000-1700; Closed 1 Apr, 23-27 Dec, 1 Jan. Tel: (0603) 667231.* &

⊚ **Strangers' Hall Museum of Domestic Life**, Charing Cross: Late medieval town house with furnished rooms illustrating tastes and fashions 16th-19th century. Fine costume and textile collection. *All year, Mon-Sat, 1000-1700; closed 1 Apr, 23-26 Dec, 1 Jan. £1.00/50p/70p. Tel: (0603) 667229.*

⊚ **Town House Museum of Lynn Life**, 46 Queen Street: Discover the merchants, tradesmen and families who for nine hundred years have made Lynn such a prosperous place. The past comes to life in historic room displays, including costume, toys, a working Victorian kitchen and a 1950's living room. *1 May-30 Sep, Tue-Sat, 1000-1700, Sun, 1400-1700; 1 Oct-31 Apr, Tue-Sat, 1000-1600. £1.00/50p/60p. Tel: (0553) 773450.* &

True's Yard Heritage Centre, 3-5 North Street: Two fully restored fisherman's cottages with research facilities for tracing ancestry in King's Lynn, museum, gift shop and tea room. *All year, daily, 0930-1630, except Christmas Day. £1.80/£1.00/£1.50. Tel: (0553) 770479.* &

LITTLE DUNHAM Dunham Museum: Exhibition buildings showing collection of old working tools and machinery. Dairy, leathersmith, shoemakers. Stationary engines and bygones. *1 Apr-30 Sep, daily, 1000-1500. £1.00/25p. Tel: (0760) 23073.* &

⊚ **LITTLE WALSINGHAM Shirehall Museum**, Common Place: A Georgian country courthouse, local museum and tourist information centre. *31 Mar-30 Sep, Mon-Sat, 1000-1700, Sun, 1400-1700, closed Mon 1300-1400; 1-31 Oct, Sat, 1000-1700, Sun, 1400-1700; 60p/30p/40p. Tel: (0328) 820510.*

LUDHAM Toad Hole Cottage Museum, How Hill: 18th century building; 5 small rooms plus Broads information area. Cottage museum giving impression of home and working life of a family on the marshes, about 100 years ago. *1 Apr-31 Oct, daily; Apr, May, Oct, 1100-1700, Jun-Sep, 1000-1800. Tel: (069 262) 763.*

NORWICH

⊚ **Bridewell Museum of Norwich Trades & Industries**, Bridewell Alley: Display illustrating local industry during the past two hundred years. *All year, Mon-Sat, 1000-1700, closed 1 Apr, 23-27 Dec, 1 Jan. £1.00/50p/70p. Tel: (0603) 667228.*

⊚ **Castle Museum**, Castle Hill: Large Collection of art (including an important collection by Norwich School artists). Large collection of British Ceramic Teapots. Archaeology, natural history, temporary exhibitions. 12th century Castle Keep. Tours of battlements and dungeons. *All year, Mon-Sat, 1000-1700, Sun, 1400-1700. Closed 1 Apr, 23-27 Dec, 1 Jan. £1.80/70p/£1.40. Tel: (0603) 223624.* &

True's Yard, King's Lynn

Castle Museum, Norwich

SHERINGHAM Museum, Station Road: Local history museum includes social history and town life. *1 Apr-mid Dec, Tue-Sat, 1000-1600, Sun and Bank Holidays, 1400-1630. Tel: (0263) 822895.*

SWAFFHAM Museum, Town Hall, London Street: 18th century building, formerly brewers main house. Local history museum with significant temporary exhibitions. Displays on local heroes: Howard Carter and the discovery of Tutankhamun's Tomb, WE Johns, author of Biggles; Admiral Sir Kynvet Wilson VC. *1 Apr-31 Oct, Tue-Sat, 1100-1300, 1400-1600. 50p/free. Tel: (0760) 721230.*

THETFORD Ancient House Museum, White Hart Street: A museum of Thetford and Breckland life in a remarkable early Tudor House. Displays on local history, flint, archaeology and natural history. Herb garden in courtyard with Tudor plants. The building is noted for its fine carved oak ceilings. Museum is also the local Tourist Information Point with displays and leaflets. Occasional temporary exhibitions and special events. *All year, Mon-Sat, 1000-1700, Closed Mon, 1300-1400; 29 May-30 Sep, also Sun, 1400-1700; Closed 1 Apr. 60p/30p/40p. Tel: (0842) 752599.*

WELLS-NEXT-THE-SEA

⊛ **Bygones Collection**, Holkham Hall: One of Britain's most magestic Stately homes, situated in a 3,000 acre deer park on the beautiful north Norfolk coast. Attractions include: Bygones museum, pottery, garden centre, gift shop, art gallery, tea rooms, deer park, lake and beach. Bygones museum includes working pump room; traction engines; vintage cars; Victorian kitchen and tack room; brewery tapping room; steam days; History of Farming exhibition. *30 May-30 Sep, Sun-Thu, 1330-1700; also Easter, May, Spring and Summer Bank Holiday, Sun & Mon, 1130-1700; last adm 1640. £3.00/£1.50. Tel: (0328) 710733. &*

Wells Maritime Museum, Old Lifeboat Museum, The Quay: Museum houses the maritime history of Wells covering, fishing, port, wildfowling, coastguard, lifeboat and bait digging. *1 Apr-22 Jul, Tue-Fri, 1400-1700, Sat, Sun, 1000-1300; 23 Jul-7 Sep, Tue-Fri, 1000-1300, 1400-1700, 1800-2000; 8 Sep-mid Oct, Tue-Fri, 1400-1700, Sat, Sun, 1000-1300; Open Bank Holiday Mons. 50p/25p/50p.*

⊛ **WESTON LONGVILLE Dinosaur Natural History Park**, Weston Estate: Life size dinosaurs in natural woodland setting. Play area, wooded maze, Bygone museum, Information centre. Gift shop, picnic area and crazy golf. *Apr-Oct, daily, 1000-1800; Nov-Mar, Sun, 1400-1900. Tel: (0603) 870245. £3.50/£2.50/£2.50. &*

⊛ **WEYBOURNE Muckleburgh Collection**, Weybourne Old Military Camp: The original NAAFI complex of this former military camp now houses a collection of tanks, armoured cars, lorries, artillery, bombs and missiles used by Allied armies during and after WWII. It incorporates the Suffolk & Norfolk Yeomanry Museum of uniforms, weapons, photographs and documents. There are items of artillery used in the Falkland Islands, and uniforms, weapons and other equipment recovered from Coalition and Iraqi armies in the Gulf War. Some post war aircraft on display and a maritime and RNLI exhibition. *20 Mar-30 Oct, daily, 1000-1700. Tel: (026 370) 210. £3.00/£1.60/£2.50 (93). &*

WYMONDHAM Heritage Museum, 14A Middleton Street: The museum established in 1984 is housed in outbuildings of a Georgian House. Exhibits of local origin. Displays are generally changed annually or biannually. *2 Apr-28 May, Thu, Fri, 1400-1600, Sat, 1000-1600; 1 June-30 Sep, Mon-Fri, 1400-1600, Sat, 1000-1600; closed Bank Holidays. 50p/10p/25p. Tel: (0953) 604650.*

SUFFOLK

ALDEBURGH Moot Hall and Museum: 16th century listed ancient building with museum of items of local interest. *1 Apr-31 May, Sat, Sun, 1430-1700; 1-30 Jun, 1-30 Sep, daily 1430-1700; 1 Jul-31 Aug, daily, 1030-1230, 1430-1700. 35p/free/35p. Tel: (0728) 452871.*

⊛ **BRANDON Heritage Centre**, George Street: Details of the flint, fur and forestry industries in the Brandon area, together with a local interest section housed in former fire station premises. *2 Apr-22 Dec, Thu, Sat, 1030-1700, Sun, 1400-1700; 1 Nov-22 Dec, closes 1600. Open 4 Apr. 50p/40p/40p. Tel:(0842) 813707.*

BUNGAY Museum, Waveney District Council Office, Broad Street: 2 Small rooms upstairs. *All year, Mon-Fri, 0900-1300,1400-1600. 30p/free/20p. Tel: (0986) 892176.*

BURY ST EDMUNDS

Bury St Edmunds Art Gallery, Market Cross: Programme of changing exhibitions across the visual arts with a special emphasis on contemporary craftwork. Craft shop. *All year, Tue-Sat, 1030-1630. Closed 25 Dec-2 Jan & 1 Apr. 50p/30p/30p. Tel: (0284) 762081. &*

⊛ **Manor House**, Honey Hill: Collection of clocks and watches, fine and decorative arts, of national importance in magnificent 16th and 18th century buildings. *All year, daily, 1000-1700, Sun 1400-1700; Closed 1 Apr, 25,26 Dec. £2.50/£1.50/£1.50. Tel: (0284) 757072. &*

⊛ **Moyse's Hall Museum**, Cornhill: Norman domestic building containing local history, archaeology of West Suffolk. Relics of Maria Marten Red Barn Murder. Temporary exhibitions. *All year, daily, 1000-1700, Sun 1400-1700; Closed 1 Apr, 25,26 Dec. Tel: (0284) 763233. &*

Suffolk Regiment Museum, The Keep, Gibraltar Barracks: 1873 Victorian keep, Military, historical exhibits of the Suffolk and Cambridge Regiments. *All year, Mon-Fri, 1000-1200, 1400-1600; Closed Easter and Christmas. Tel: (0284) 752394.*

CAVENDISH Sue Ryder Foundation Museum, Sue Ryder Foundation Headquarters: Displays showing the reason for establishing the Sue Ryder Foundation and its work, past, present and future. *All year, daily, 1000-1730, closed 25 Dec. 80p/40p/40p. Tel: (0787) 280252.* &

COTTON Mechanical Music Museum Trust, Blacksmith Road: A large selection of mechanical musical items. Small music boxes, polyphones and organettes, larger street pianos and player organs and large fair organs, dance band and cafe organs plus a number of unusual items. Wurlitzer theatre pipe organ, housed in a purpose built building with interior roof adorned with hundreds of old records and horned gramaphones. *Jun-Sep, Sun, 1430-1730. £2.50/50p/£2.50. Tel: (0449) 613876.* &

DUNWICH Museum, St James's Street: History of Dunwich from Roman times chronicling its disappearance into the sea. Local wildlife. *1 Apr-30 Sep, daily, 1130-1630; Oct, daily, 1200-1600; 1 Nov -31 Mar, by appointment only. Tel: (072 873) 796.*

◎ **FELIXSTOWE Landguard Fort**: Items relevant to the history of the fort, an early 18th century monument. Hour long tours. *1 Jun-25 Sep, Wed, Sun,1430-1700. £1.20/60p. Tel: (0394) 286403.*

◎ **FLATFORD, Bridge Cottage**: 16th century building, tea garden and shop. Constable exhibition. *1 Apr-31 May, Oct, Wed-Sun and Bank holidays, 1100-1730, 1 Jun-30 Sep, daily, 1000-1730, Nov, Wed-Sun, 1100-1530. Tel: (0206) 298260.* &

FRAMLINGHAM Lanman Museum, Framlingham Castle: Rural exhibits relating to everyday life in Framlingham and surrounding area, including paintings and photographs. *1 Apr-30 Sep, daily, 1030-1300,1400-1630 except Sun. Mon morning.30p/10p/10p. Tel: (0728) 602925.*

Christchurch Mansion, Ipswich

HALESWORTH Halesworth & District Museum, The Almshouses, Steeple End: Two rooms in 17th century almshouses plus former fire engine shed adjacent to library and under art gallery. Local geology and archaeology including fossils, prehistoric flint and medieval finds from recent excavations. Farming, rural life and local history exhibitions. *1 May-30 Sept; Wed, 1030-1230, 1400-1630; Sat, 1030-1230; Sun & Bank Hol, 1400-1630. Tel: (0986) 873030.*

IPSWICH

◎ **Christchurch Mansion**, Christchurch Park: Fine Tudor Mansion built between 1548 and 1550, later additions. Good collection of furniture, panelling and ceramics, clocks and paintings from 16-19th century. New Suffolk Artists' gallery, lively temporary exhibition programme in Wolsey Art Gallery. *All year, Tue-Sat, 1000-1700; Sun, 1430-1630; Closes at dusk in winter;*

Open Bank Holiday Mon; closed 1 Apr, 24-28 Dec, 1 Jan. Tel: (0473) 253246. &

◎ **Ipswich Museum and Gallery**, High Street: Roman Suffolk galleries, Peoples of the world. Suffolk geology, Ogilvie Bird Gallery, Victorian Natural History Gallery. *All year, Tue-Sat, 1000-1700; closed 24-28 Dec, 1-3 Jan. Tel: (0473) 213761.* &

◎ **Tolly Cobbold Brewery**, Cliff Road: Victorian Brewery built in 1896 containing working equipment from original Brewery of 1723. Still producing beers. Contains exhibits, memorabilia, cooperage, steam engine, videos. *All year, Sat,Sun, 1130 and 1430, May-Sep, daily, 1130. Closed Christmas, Bank Holidays and New Year. £2.75. Tel: (0473) 231723*

◎ **LAVENHAM Guildhall of Corpus Christi**, Market Place: Impressive timber framed building dating from 1520s. Originally hall of Guild of Corpus Christi, now local museum with information on medieval wool trade. *26 Mar-30 Oct, daily, 1100-1700; closed 1 Apr. £2.40/free. Tel: (0787) 247646.*

LOWESTOFT

Lowestoft and East Suffolk Maritime Museum, Sparrows Nest Park, Whapload Road: Models of fishing and commercial ships old and new, shipwrights tools and fishing gear. Lifeboat display and gallery. Drifter's cabin with models of fishermen. *1 May-30 Sep, daily, 1000-1700. 50p/25p/25p.* &

Royal Naval Patrol Service Association Museum, Sparrows Nest: A complete mock up of a trawler wheelhouse and bridge with model officers on bridge. Photographs and memorabilia, books with details of various ships logs. A shrine to Lt/Cmd Stannard V C. Honours board of all officers and crews with DC, DSM, MD and VC. Posters used during World War II and articles of equipment used in that period, also a souvenir shop. *1-4 Apr, 9 May-31 Oct, Mon-Fri, 1000-1200, 1400-1630; Sun, 1400-1630; Tel: (0502) 586250.*

MILDENHALL and District Museum, 6 King Street: Local voluntary museum housed in early 19th century. Cottages with modern extensions. Exhibitions on RAF Mildenhall, Fenland and Breckland. Includes local archaelogy. *Feb-24 Dec; Wed, Thu, Sat & Sun, 1430-1630; Fri, 1100-1600. Tel: (0638) 716970.* &

Aldeburgh Moot Hall

Lowestoft and East Suffolk Maritime Museum

◎ **NEWMARKET National Horse Racing Museum**, 99 High Street: 5 permanent galleries of fine paintings, bronzes, memorabilia and trophies relating to the development of horseracing. Temporary exhibitions to supplement the permanent exhibition. Two galleries of works, the property of the British Sporting Art Trust. Equine tours by arrangement to studs, racing yards and training facilities. *29 Mar-4 Dec, Tue-Sat and Bank Holiday Mon, 0900-1700; Sun, 1400-1700. £2.50/75p/£1.50. Tel: (0638) 667333.* ⅋

ORFORD Dunwich Underwater Exploration Exhibition, Orford Craft Shop: Exhibits showing progress in the underwater exploration of the former city and underwater studies off the Suffolk coast. *Open all year, daily, 1100-1700. Closed 25/26 Dec. 40p. Tel: (0394) 450678.*

◎ **SIZEWELL, Sizewell Visitors Centre**, Sizewell B Power Station: Visitor centre giving details about all aspects of electricity generation. *All year, Oct-Mar, Mon-Sat, 1000-1600, Apr-Sep, daily, 1000-1600. Closed Christmas week. Tel: (0728) 642148.* ⅋

SOUTHWOLD

Southwold Lifeboat Museum, Gun Hill: RNLI models, photographs of lifeboat, relics from old boats. *31 May-30 Sep, daily 1430-1630. Tel: (0502) 722422.*

Southwold Museum, Bartholomew Green: Local history, archaeology and natural history. Exhibits relating to Southwold railway, and Battle of Sole Bay. Domestic bygones. *1 Apr-30 Sep, daily, 1430-1630. Tel: (0502) 723925.* ⅋

Southwold Sailors Reading Room, East Cliff: Building of character where retired seamen have a social club and reading room. Maritime exhibits and local history. *All year, daily, 0900-2100.*

STOWMARKET Museum of East Anglian Life: Nature walk, conservation lab and workshop with viewing windows for public. Working water mill and wind pump. Social history, agricultural history, craft and industrial displays. *27 Mar-30 Oct, Tue-Sun and Bank Holiday Mon; Jul & Aug, daily, 1000-1700. £3.50/£1.60/£2.50 (93). Tel: (0449) 612229.* ⅋

◎ **SUDBURY Gainsborough's House**, 46 Gainsborough Street: Gainsborough's House is a well established arts centre in the birthplace of Thomas Gainsborough RA (1727-88). The Georgian fronted town house, with an attractive walled garden, displays more of the artist's work than any other British Gallery. The collection is shown together with 18th century furniture and memorabilia in chronological sequence following the artist's career. Varied programme of exhibitions throughout the year. Fine art, photography, craft, printmaking, in particular highlighting the work of East Anglian artists. *All year, Tue-Sat, 1000-1700, Sun and Bank Holidays, 1400-1700; 1 Nov-31 Mar, closes 1600. Closed Christmas-New Year. £2.50/£1.50/£2.00. Tel: (0787) 372958.* ⅋

WOODBRIDGE Museum, 5 Market Hill: Sutton Hoo, Burrow Hill, Woodbridge Worthies, Edward Fitzgerald, Thomas Seckford, and other exhibits. *2 Apr-30 Oct, Thu-Sat, 1000-1600, Sun 1430-1630, Bank Hol Mon, 1000-1600; closed Christmas and New Year. 50p/20p/50p. Tel: (0394) 380502.*

WOOLPIT Bygones Museum, The Institute: 17th century timber framed building with one permanent display of brickmaking and other displays changing yearly depicting life of a Suffolk village. *2 Apr-25 Sep, Sat, Sun, Bank Holidays, 1430-1700; Tel: (0359) 40822.*

Gainsborough's House, Sudbury

Prices are in the order Adults/Children/Senior Citizens. Where prices are not available at the time of going to press, the 1993 (93) price is given. If no price is given, admission is free. See Touring Maps on pages 119-124 for locations of places to visit.

BEDFORDSHIRE

Melchbourne Bird Gardens, Vicarage Farm, Melchbourne, Riseley: A visit to Melchbourne Bird Gardens can give an insight into the diverse and beautiful families of birds. Situated in the peaceful village of Melchbourne, the Bird Gardens are home to a fine collection of pheasants. *All year, Mon-Fri, 1200-1700, Sat, Sun, Bank Holidays 1000-1700; closed 25 Dec. £2.50/£1.50/£1.50. Tel: (0234) 708317.* &

Stagsden Bird Gardens, Stagsden. Breeding centre for over 200 species of birds including owls, birds of prey, cranes, pheasants, waterfowl and poultry. Rose gardens. *All year, daily, 1100-1800, dusk if earlier; closed 25 Dec. £2.50/£1.00/£2.00. Tel: (0234) 822745.* &

◎ **Toddington Manor**, Toddington: Large working farm with rare breeds centre. Vintage tractor collection. Gardens with large herbaceous borders. Extensive walks all round woods and lakes. *2 Apr-30 Sep, daily, 1000-1700; closed 4-10 Jul. £2.50/£1.00/£1.50. Tel:(0525) 873566.* &

◎ **Whipsnade Wild Animal Park**, Zoological Society of London, Dunstable: Conservation centre for rare and endangered species as well a home to chimps, bears, zebras penguins and tigers. Animals are housed in spacious paddocks providing a near natural environment. Daily events include Birds of Prey, Sealions and Elephants at work demonstrations. Children's Farm, Runwild Playcentre, BP Bear Maze and Great Whipsnade Railway. Special events. *Mar-Oct, Mon-Sat, 1000-1800; Sun & Bank Hol Mon,* 1000-1900; Nov-Feb, daily, 1000-1630; closed 25 Dec. £6.95/£5.45/£5.95. Tel: (0582) 872171. &

◎ **Woburn Safari Park** , Woburn Park, Woburn: Drive-through safari park and leisure area (inclusive in admission price), boating lake, pets corner and parrot and sea lion show. *Jan & Feb safari only subject to weather, Sat & Sun, 1100-1500; Mar-Oct, daily, 1000-1700. £7.00/£4.50/£4.50 (93). Tel: (0525) 290407.* &

◎ **Woodside Farm & Wildfowl Park**, Mancroft Road, Slip End: 6 acre park with farm shop, poultry centre, arts and crafts centre, wildfowl collection, rare breeds centre, farm animals, childrens play area and coffee shop. *All year, Mon-Sat, 0800-1730, Closed 25,26 Dec, 1 Jan. £1.50/£1.15/£1.15. Tel: (0582) 841044.* &

CAMBRIDGESHIRE

Grays Honey Farm, Cross Drove, Warboys: Bee and honey exhibition showing rural and modern beekeeping around the world. Beekeeping video. Bees can be seen at work in the different observation hives. A Black Forest model railway layout shows how bees talk to each other. Make your own beeswax candles. No heat required. Picnic area includes guinea piggery and aviary. *31 Mar-24 Dec, Mon-Sat, 1030-1800. 95p/50p/95p. Tel: (0354) 693798.*

Hamerton Wildlife Centre, Hamerton: Lemurs, marmosets, meercats, wallabies, unique bird collection with rare and exotic species from around the world. Also gibbons, sloths, wildcats, otters. Adventure playground. Gift shop and covered picnic area. *Jan-Mar 1030-1600; Apr-Oct, 1030-1800; Nov, Dec, 1030-1600; Closed 25 Dec. £3.00/£1.50/£2.50 (93). Tel: (0832) 293362.* &

Home Farm, Wimpole Hall, Arrington: 19th century thatched farm building with farm museum, video loft, rare breeds of cattle, sheep and pigs . Suffolk Punch horse wagon rides. *2 Jan-11 Mar and Nov-Dec, Sat and Sun, 1100-1600; 12 Mar-30 Oct, Tue, Wed, Thu, Sat, Sun and Bank Holiday Mon, 1030-1700; closed Christmas and New Year. £3.50/£1.80. Tel: (0223) 207257.* &

Linton Zoo, Hadstock Road, Linton: Big cats, lynx, servals, llamas, toucans, parrots, reptiles, tarantulas, binturong giant tortoises plus many other animal set in 16 acres of gardens. *All year, daily, 1000-1800 or dusk if earlier; closed 25 Dec. £3.50/£2.50/£3.00. Tel: (0223) 891308.* &

White headed duck, Peakirk

Peakirk Waterfowl Gardens Trust, Peakirk: Flock of Chilean flamingos and some 112 species of duck, geese and swans in 17 acres of water gardens. Refeshment room and shop. *All year, daily, 0930-dusk, except 1 Mar-31 Oct, 0930-1830; closed 24,25 Dec. £2.50/£1.25/£1.50. Tel: (0733) 252271.* &

Ramsey Raptor Rescue, 490 Hern Road, Ramsey St Mary: Bird of prey rescue hospital founded only by donation. Wide range of species. Tea room, wildlife art gallery. *All year, daily, 1030-1700; closed 25,26 Dec, 1 Jan. Donations welcome. Tel: (073 129) 266.* &

◎ **Sacrewell Farm and Country Centre**, Sacrewell, Thornhaugh: Childrens play area with maze and trampolines. 500 acre farm, with working watermill, farmhouse gardens, shrubberies farm, nature and general interest trails, 18th century buildings, displays of farm, rural and domestic bygones. *All year, daily, 0900-2100 including Christmas and New Year. £2.00/£1.00/£1.50. Tel: (0780) 782222.* &

White-naped cranes, Stagsden Bird Gardens

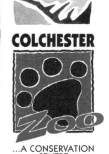
Please mention East Anglia Guide when replying to advertisements

46

Touching a snake, Colchester Zoo

Stags Holt Farm Park, Stags Holt, March: Victorian farm buildings set in ancient parkland. Suffolk Punches, traditional farm animals and farming bygones. Tea room. picnic area and play area. *All year, 1 Apr-3 Sep, Tue-Sun, Bank Holiday Mon, 1030-1700; closed 25 Dec. £2.30/£1.20/£1.75. Tel: (0354) 52406.* &

Willersmill Wildlife Park/Sanctuary/Fish Farm, Station Road, Shepreth: The Willersmill Wildlife Sanctury was started in 1979 by Terry Willers to care for injured animals or unwanted pets. The wildlife park houses wolves, monkeys, owls, otters, pinemartins, very large carp and koi feed from your hands. *All year; summer, 1000-1800; winter, 1000-1700. £2.95/£1.50/£2.25. Tel: (0763) 262226.* &

Wood Green Animal Shelters, King's Bush Farm, London Road, Godmanchester: 50 acre site housing mostly unwanted dogs and cats but also field and small animals. Approximately 9000 unwanted, neglected and injured animals admitted a year. Restaurant, bar and coffee shop, pet care centre and gift shop, small nursery. College of animal welfare. Special events programme. *All year, daily, 0900-1500. Donations welcome. Tel: (0480) 830014.* &

ESSEX

Ada Cole Memorial Stables, Broadlands, Broadley Common, Harlow: Stable yard and fields. Rescues horses, ponies, donkeys and mules. Often young foals. Shop. *All year, daily, 1400-1700, closed 25 Dec. Tel: (0992) 893841.* &

Basildon Zoo, London Road, Vange: Birds of prey, patting pens, baby animals, cafe and gift shop. *All year, daily, 1000-1800 (dusk in winter); closed 25,26 Dec. £2.50/£1.25 (93). Tel: (0268) 553985.* &

⊛ **Colchester Zoo**, Stanway Hall, Maldon Road, Colchester: 150 species present set in 40 acres of natural parkland. Daily presentations include meet the elephants, snake handling, sealion, seal, parrot, penguin and falconry displays. Childrens pet area, two adventure play areas, amusements, and road train. Restaurant, take away snack and ice cream kiosks, gift shops. *All year, daily, Apr-Jul, 0930-1800, Aug 0930-1830, Sep 0930-1800, Oct-Apr, 0930-1 hour before dusk; Closed 25 Dec. £5.50/£3.00/£4.00. Tel: (0206) 330253.* &

⊛ **Dedham Rare Breed Farm,** Mill Lane, Dedham: Dedham rare breeds farm is situated on 16 acres of land in the Dedham Vale. The animals are displayed in open paddocks and in buildings. Childrens play area and paddock where they can touch the animals. Wide walk ways separate the field and pond, all of which are safely fenced. There is a large car park and picnic area, all set near the river Stour and only a short way from Flatford Mill. *1 Mar-31 Dec, daily, 1000-1730 - or 1 hour before dusk; Closed 25 Dec. £2.50/£1.50/£2.00. Tel: (0206) 323111.* &

Epping Bury Farm Centre, Upland Road, Epping: Open farm centre with rare breeds of pigs, sheep, cattle goats and poultry. All accessible to children and disabled. Nature trail with lake and stream, picnic sites and childrens play area, including barn straw jump. Separate admission to childrens adventure barn, a safe, soft play area for children. Ball pond, nets, ladders and slides for tots to teens. No admission charge to pets corner. Café. *All year, daily, 0930-1800, closed 25,26 Dec. £2.50/£1.50. Tel: (0992) 578400.* &

Hayes Hill Farm, Stubbins Hall Lane, Crooked Mile, Waltham Abbey: Traditional farmyard - farm animals in pens and paddocks. Working commercial dairy and arable farm. Viewing at milking. Guided tours bookable in advance. *All year, daily; Mon-Fri, 1000-1630; Sat, Sun & Bank Holidays, 1000-1800. £2.00/£1.50/£1.50. Tel: (099 289) 2291.* &

Jakapeni Rare Breeds Farm, Lillyville Farm, Burlington Gardens, Hullbridge: Working organic smallholding specialising in rare breed farm animals and poultry. Pets corner, picnic area, country walk, refreshments. *1 Apr-31 Oct, Suns and Bank Hols, 1030-1730; Weekdays by appt only. £1.50/75p. Tel: (0702) 232394.* &

⊛ **Layer Marney Tower,** Layer Marney: Tallest Tudor Gatehouse in the country. Formal gardens and deer in surrounding fields. Rare Breed Farm Park allowing a chance to meet the animals. *1 Apr-2 Oct, Sun-Fri, 1400-1800, Bank Holidays 1100-1800. £3.00/£1.50/£3.00. Tel: (0206) 330202.* &

Marsh Farm Country Park, Marsh Farm Road, South Woodham Ferrers: Farm centre with beef cattle, sheep, pig unit, free range chickens, and milking demonstrations. Adventure play area, nature reserve, walks, picnic area and pets corner. *14 Feb-1 Nov, Mon-Fri, 1000-1630, Sat, Sun, Bank Holidays and school summer holidays 1030-1730; 2 Nov-11 Dec by appointment only. Christmas shopping weekends 14,15,21,22,28,29 Nov, 5,6,12,13 Dec. £1.95/£1.45/£1.45. Tel: (0245) 321552.* &

Mistley Place Park Environmental and Animal Rescue, New Road, Mistley: 25 acres of woodlands, pastures and lakeside walks. Horses, sheep, goats, pigs, peacocks, turkeys, geese, ornamental fowl, rabbits and guinea pigs roam freely (where practical and safe) around the site. Nature trail and maze. Tearoom and shop. Majority of animals rescued from ill treatment, neglect or slaughter. *All year, daily, 1000-dusk (or 1800). £2.00/£1.00/£1.00. Tel: (0206) 396483.*

Please mention East Anglia Guide when replying to advertisements

Kingdom of the Sea, Hunstanton

◎ **Mole Hall Wildlife Park**, Widdington: Otters, chimps, guanaco, lemurs, wallabies, deer. owls, waterfowl etc. Butterfly pavilion. Attractive gardens. Picnic, play areas and pets corner. Park is in gardens and fields adjoining the fully moated Manor. House of Mole Hall has records dating back to 1287. *All year, daily, 1030-1800; closed 25 Dec. £3.50/£2.25/£2.75. Tel: (0799) 40400.*

◎ **Southend Sea Life Centre**, Eastern Esplanade, Southend-on-Sea: The very latest in marine technology brings the secrets of the mysterious underwater world closer than ever before. An underwater tunnel allows an all round view, culminating in an interactive shark encounter. Discover hundreds of fascinating native marine species displayed in natural surroundings. Follow the Quiz Trail, explore the Touch Pool. Childrens play area. *All year, daily, 1000-1800; during school holidays 1000 -2100; closed 25 Dec. £4.35/£3.25/£3.45 (93). Tel: (0702) 601834.* &

LINCOLNSHIRE

◎ **Butterfly and Falconry Park**, Long Sutton: One of Britain's largest walk through butterfly houses. Hundreds of exotic butterflies. Insectarium. Gift shop, gardens, adventure playground, pets corner and picnic areas. In the attractive surroundings of the Park the Falconer gives two displays every day with eagles, owls and falcons. *13 Mar-30 Oct, daily, 1000-1800, Sep & Oct, 1000-1700. £3.40/£2.20/£3.00 Tel: (0406) 363833.* &

NORFOLK

◎ **Banham Zoo**, The Grove, Banham: Set in over 25 acres of landscaped countryside, this zoological park is the ideal setting for the care and conservation of a wide selection of rare and endangered species. Snow leopards, ocelots, maned wolves and an extensive collection of primates including chimpanzees, gibbons, lemurs amd marmosets. Deer park, reptile house, World of Penguins, Monkey Jungle Island, Bird Garden plus one of the best collections of owls in the country. Activity and Information Centre featuring a soft play area and storyroom.

Appleyard Shopping Courtyard. *All year, 1 Jan-31 Dec, daily, 1000-1830 or dusk if earlier. Closed 25,26 Dec. £5.50/£3.50/£4.00 (93) Tel: (0953) 887771.* &

Cranes Watering Farm, Rushall Road, Starston: This is a working farm, not a farm park, therefore it is very much a 'take us as you find us' sort of place. Some days there is a lot happening, other times a tour of the buildings/machinery may be all there is to offer. Wellies advisable. Pigs and cows always on site. Sheep and lambs in the spring. Milking daily at 1600. Farmshop. Picnic lawn. Written guides and childrens quiz, free. *1 Feb-24 Dec, Tue-Sat, 1000-1700, Sun 1000-1200; Small charge for groups which must pre-book and will be given a guided tour. Tel: (0379) 852387.*

Equine Rest and Rehabilitation Centre, Anne Colvin House, Snetterton: Stables and paddocks with horses, ponies and donkeys looked after by the International League for the Protection of Horses. Picnic area. *All year, Wed, Sun, 1430-1600; closed 25,26 Dec. Tel: (0953) 498682.* &

Equine Rest and Rehabilitation Centre, Overa House Farm, Larling: Stable yard and paddocks. Horses, ponies and donkeys can be seen. *All year, Wed,Sun, 1430-1600; closed 25,26 Dec Tel: (0953) 498682.*

◎ **Kingdom of the Sea**, Southern Promenade, Hunstanton: A display of British marine life. Stroll around over 20 settings as you view over 2,000 fish from 200 different species. The environments have been specifically designed to recreate their natural habitats. 50,000 gallons of water surround you in the ocean tunnel with creatures of the deep only inches away. Observe both resident seals and pups in the process of being rehabilitated for their release back to the wild, in the seal pools. *All year, daily, 1000-1700; Closed 25,26 Dec. £3.99/£2.99/£2.99. Tel: (0485) 533576.* &

◎ **Kingdom of the Sea**, Marine Parade, Great Yarmouth: Walk underwater tropical reef shark tank; sand tank with Ray fish and British sharks, plus 25 themed displays depicting British Marine Life and local settings. Amazing Green Submarine display of tropical reef fish. *All year, daily, 1000-dusk; closed 25,26 Dec. £3.99/£2.99/£2.99. Tel: (0493) 330631.* &

Living Jungle and Butterfly Farm, Marine Parade, Great Yarmouth: 5000 square yards of tropical gardens under glass with free flying butterflies, humming birds, tarantulas, scorpions, iguana and terrapins. Souvenir shop. *1 Mar-31 Oct, daily, 1000-1800. Closed Christmas. £3.00/£1.50/£2.50. Tel: (0493) 842202.*

Norfolk Rare Breeds Centre, Decoy Farm house, Ormesby St Michael, Great Yarmouth: Rare breeds of domestic farm animals, cattle, sheep, pigs, goats, poultry, donkeys, heavy horses and rabbits. Incubator and brooder on display. Information area, shop and farm museum. *1 Apr-30 Sep, Sun-Fri, 1100-1700. £2.50/£1.25/£2.00. Tel: (0493) 732990.* &

◎ **Norfolk Shire Horse Centre**, West Runton Stables, West Runton: Shire horses demonstrated working twice daily. Native ponies, bygone collection of horse drawn machinery. *1 Apr-end Oct, Sun-Fri (open Sat when Bank Holiday weekends) 10-5. £3.50/£2.00/£2.50. Tel: (0263) 837339.* &

Zebra at Banham Zoo

Scarlet Ibis, Pensthorpe Waterfowl Park

Norfolk Wildlife Centre and Country Park, Great Witchingham: The Park has one of the largest collections of European and British wildlife, exhibited in large open natural enclosures in 40 acres of parkland. The park's unique team of trained reindeer take carts around the park most afternoons, giving free rides to children.

Woodland Steam Railway, Clearwater Carp Pool, Pets Corner and Model farm; tame rare breeds Rabbit & Guineapig Village and adventure play areas. *1 Apr-31 Oct, daily, 1030-1800 or sunset if earlier. £3.50/£2.00/£3.00. Tel: (0603) 872274.* &

Otter Trust, Earsham: Large collection of British Otters. The Trust is the only place breeding the British Otter regularly in captivity and releasing young animals into the wild every year, in conjuction with English Nature in order to save the otter from extinction in lowland England. *1 Apr-31 Oct, daily, 1030-1800. £3.50/£2.00/£3.00. Tel: (0986) 893470.*

Park Farm & Norfolk Farmyard Crafts Centre, Snettisham: 329 acre genuine working farm. Gigantic adventure playground. Safari ride to see red deer herd. Pigs, calves, cattle, sheep centre - over 40 different breeds. Four farm trails, visitor centre provides farm gift shop, woolroom and tearoom. Newly opened craft workshops including pottery, wood carving, leathercraft, dried flowers, terrariums, candles; book binding, hand made cards, decoupage, paintings, glass engraving. Norfolk Brass Rubbing Centre. *Mid Mar-31 Oct, daily, 1015-1700, 1-4 Apr, daily 1030-1700. Price on application. Tel: (0485) 542425.* &

Pensthorpe Waterfowl Park, Pensthorpe, nr Fakenham: Wild and exotic waterbirds, many endangered species. Heated wildlife observation gallery. Children's adventure playground. Woodland, meadow, lakeside and riverside nature trails. 200 acre nature reserve. Licenced restaurant, conservation gift shop. Water Gardens.

Jan-15 Mar, Sat, Sun, 1100-1700; 16 Mar-31 Dec, daily 1100-1700; closed 25 Dec. £3.75/£1.75/£3.25. Tel: (0328) 851465. &

Redwings Horse Sanctuary, Hill Top Farm, Hall Lane, Frettenham: Visitors are able to meet the rescued horses and ponies. Stalls, craft shops, bric-a-brac and refreshments. *Easter-mid Dec, Sun & Mon, 1400-1700. £2.00/£1.00/£1.00. Tel: (0603) 737432.* &

Thrigby Hall Wildlife Gardens, Thrigby Hall, Filby: Wide selection of Asian mammals, birds and reptiles, including tigers, crocodiles and storks. 250 year old landscaped garden. Play area. New Swamp House for large crocodiles and other tropical swamp dwellers. Willow-pattern garden. *All year, daily, 1000-1800 or dusk in winter. £4.00/£2.50/£3.50. Tel: (0493) 369 477.* &

The Tropical Butterfly Gardens, Long Street Nursery, Great Ellingham: Landscaped gardens heated to a year round 24 degrees celcius, containing tropical trees and flowers. The gardens contain several hundred exotic tropical butterflies flying freely around the visitors. Garden Centre. Gift shop and coffee shop. *All year, Mon-Sat, 0900-1800 (1700 in winter), Sun and Bank Holidays 1000-1800 (1700 in winter); closed 25 Dec-1 Jan. £2.25/£1.25/£1.95. Tel: (0453) 453175.* &

Wroxham Barns, Tunstead Road, Hoveton: Junior farm where visitors can take part in feeding times, stroke the animals and collect eggs. Part of a craft complex with workshops, craft shop, tea room and traditional funfair. *May-Oct, daily 1000-1800; Nov-Apr, 1000-1700. £1.50/£1.50/£1.50. Tel: (0603) 783762.* &

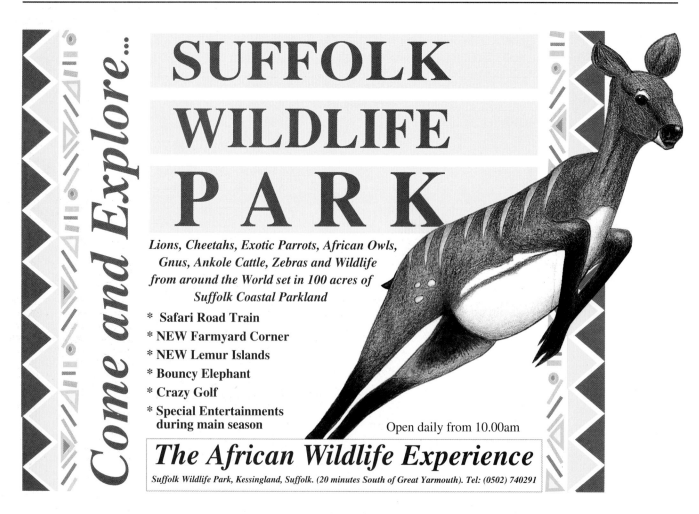
Please mention East Anglia Guide when replying to advertisements

Tropical Butterfly Gardens, Great Ellingham, Norfolk

Pentlow Farm, The Childrens Farm, Cavendish: The Childrens Farm, is a unique experience for children of all ages. Lots of farm and baby animals are easily accessible and feeding time can be shared by all our visitors. *1 Mar-31 Aug, Sun, 1200-1700; Whitsun and school summer holidays, Mon-Fri, 1430-1630. Adm charge for groups which must pre-book. Tel: (0787) 280194.*

⊛ **Rede Hall Farm Park**, Rede Hall Farm, Rede: Working farm based on agricultural life of the 1930's-1950's including working Suffolk horses, use of agricultural implements and wagons. Management of cattle and sheep of the era. Working farrier shop. Cafeteria and gift shop. Childrens pets corner and play area. Nature trail, cart rides. Bygones and working displays of seasonal farm activities. *1 Apr-30 Sep, daily, 1000-1730. £3.00/£1.50/£1.75. Tel: (0284) 850695.* ₺

⊛ **Suffolk Wildlife Park**, Kessingland: The African Wildlife Experience - 100 acres of wild life, picturesque lake and waterfowl. Safari road train, large childrens play area. Gift shop, indoor and outdoor picnic areas. Cafeteria with patio seating; baby changing/nursing facilities. Walk around the park in the footsteps of one of the great African explorers, by following one of the three signed routes. Childrens entertainment every afternoon during July and August (except Saturday and Wednesday). Every Wednesday there is a bird of prey demonstration. *All year, daily, 1000-1830 (or dusk if earlier); Closed 25, 26 Dec. £5.00/£3.00/£4.00 (93). Tel: (0502) 740291.* ₺

Valley Farm Camargue Horses, Wickham Market: Britain's only herd of breeding Camargue horses from the south of France. Also white animal collection including Gobi the Arabian camel. *All year, Thu-Tue, 1000-1600; closed 25,26 Dec, 1 Jan. Donations welcome. Tel: (0728) 746916.*

SUFFOLK

Cow Wise, Meadow Farm, West Stow: A modern working dairy farm with Friesian and Jersey cows, calves, goats, lambs, and free range hens. Visitors can see the cows milked from a specially constructed gallery. Touch table, freshwater life, sense boxes. *6 Mar-10 Jul, Sun & Bank Holiday Mon, 1400-1700. £1.80/£1.30. Tel: (0284) 728862.* ₺

⊛ **East of England Birds of Prey and Conservation Centre**, St Jacobs Hall, Laxfield: Large selection of birds of prey in aviaries. Three flying displays per day. *Apr-Oct, daily 1000-1730; Nov-Mar, Sat, Sun, 1000-1730. Closed 25 Dec. £3.30/£2.00. Tel: (0986) 798844.* ₺

⊛ **Easton Farm Park**, Easton, Wickham Market: Victorian farm setting for many species of farm animals including rare breeds. Modern milking unit, Victorian dairy, Suffolk horses. Farm trail. Food and farming exhibition. *20 Mar-2 Oct, daily, 1030-1800. £3.85/£2.10/£3.00. Tel: (0728) 746475.* ₺

⊛ **Kentwell Hall**, Long Melford: Mellow red brick Tudor Manor house surrounded by moat. Rare breed domestic farm animals in tranquil setting around timber framed farm buildings. *For full opening details see Historic House entry. Moat House, gardens and farm only £2.40/£1.60/£2.00. Tel: (0787) 310207.*

Thrigby Hall Wildlife Gardens, near Great Yarmouth

Prices are in the order Adults/Children/Senior Citizens. Where prices are not available at the time of going to press, the 1993 (93) price is given. If no price is given, admission is free. See Touring Maps on pages 119-124 for locations of Places to Visit.

ANCIENT MONUMENTS

BEDFORDSHIRE

◉ **Bushmead Priory,** Colmworth: Small Augustinian priory founded c1195. Magnificent 13th century timber roof of crown-post construction. Medieval wall paintings and stained glass. *Apr-Sep, Sat, 1000-1800, Sun, 1400-1800. £1.20/60p/90p. Tel: (023062) 614.*

◉ **De Grey Mausoleum**, Flitton: Remarkable treasure house of sculptured tombs and monuments from the 16th to 19th century, dedicated to the de Grey family of nearby Wrest Park. *All year, Sat, Sun, key may be obtained from key-keeper at 3 Highfield Road, Flitton - access through Flitton church. Tel: (0536) 402840.*

◉ **Houghton House**, Ampthill: Reputedly the inspiration for 'House Beautiful' in Bunyan's 'Pilgrim's Progress', the remains of this early 17th century mansion still convey elements which justify the description, including work attributed to Indigo Jones. *Any reasonable time. Tel: (0536) 402840.* ♿

CAMBRIDGESHIRE

Buckden Towers, Huntingdon: Complex of buildings, mainly 15th century, including the Great Tower, Kings Room and Inner Gatehouse of formerly moated ecclesiastical palace of the Bishops of Lincoln. Catherine of Aragon was imprisoned here. *Church and courtyard open during daylight hours, buildings and grounds by appointment only. Donations welcome. Tel: (0480) 810344.*

Cambridge American Military Cemetery, Coton: Visitors reception building for information, graves area and Memorial Chapel. *16 Apr-30 Sep, 0800-1800; 1 Oct-15 Apr, 0800-1700; Tel: (0954) 210350.*

◉ **Denny Abbey**, Ely Road, Chittering: Remains of 12th century church and 14th century dining hall of religious house. Run as hospital by Knights Templar. Became Franciscan nunnery in 1342. *Summer, daily; Winter, Sun only; 1000-1600. £1.20/60p/90p. Tel: (0223) 860489.* ♿

◉ **Duxford Chapel**, Whittlesford: 14th century chapel once part of the hospital of St John. *Contact Regional Office. Tel: (0223) 455515.*

◉ **Ely Cathedral**, Chapter House, The College, Ely: One of England's finest Cathedrals. The Octagon is the crowning glory. Guided tours and tower tours available in summer. Brass Rubbing and Stained Glass Museum. *British Summer Time, daily, 0700-1900; Winter, Mon-Sat, 0730-1800, Sun, 0730-1700; No facilities available (shop, guided tours or refreshments) on 1 Apr, 25,26 Dec. £2.60/free/£2.10. Tel: (0353) 667735.* ♿

◉ **Flag Fen Bronze Age Excavations**, Fourth Drove, Fengate: Unique in Britain - Bronze Age remains on timber platform timber "island". Reconstruction at one tenth life size of Flag Fen

King's College Chapel, Cambridge

3,000 years ago. Accurate reconstruction of Bronze Age countryside - with fields, live animals and buildings. Play area for under 8 year olds. New visitor centre housing hundreds of splendid bronzes and other fascinating finds. *All year, daily, 1100-last entry 1600; Guided tours, Easter-end Oct. Closed 25,26 Dec. £2.80/£1.95/£2.55 (93). Tel: (0733) 313414.* ♿

◉ **Isleham Priory Church**, Isleham: Remains of Norman church with much "herringbone" masonry. *Any reasonable time.*

Kings College Chapel, Kings College, Cambridge: The exhibition in Northern side chapels shows why and how the chapel was built in pictures, works of art and models. *All year, Mon-Sat, 0930-1630, Sun, 0930-1800; with occasional variations when there are rehearsals and concerts. £2.00/£1.00/£2.00. Tel: (0223) 350411.* ♿

◉ **Longthorpe Tower**, Thorpe Road, Longthorpe: 14th century tower of a manor house. The wall paintings form the most complete set of domestic paintings of the period, in England. Exhibitions are held from time to time by local artists. *Apr-Sep, weekends only, 1000-1800. £1.20/60p/90p. Tel: (0733) 268482.*

◉ **Peterborough Cathedral**, 14 Minster Precincts, Peterborough: Norman cathedral. Early English West Front. 13th century painted nave ceiling. Former grave of Mary Queen of Scots. Grave of Katherine of Aragon. Saxon sculpture. *Jan-Apr, Mon-Sat, 0730-1815, Sun 0745-1700;*

Peterborough Cathedral

May-Aug, Mon-Sat 0745-2000, Sun, 0800-1730; Sep-Dec, Mon-Sat, 0730-1815, Sun, 0745-1700. Tel: (0733) 897337. &

Ramsey Abbey, Ramsey. 12th century Lady Chapel and Tudor house with early and mid 19th century additions. *1 Apr-31 Oct, Sun, 1400-1700, Thu during term time, 1500- 1700. Tel: (0487) 813285.*

Ramsey Abbey Gatehouse, Abbey School, Ramsey: Ruins of 15th Century gatehouse. *2 Apr-31 Oct, daily, 1000-1700. Tel: (0263) 733471.*

Saint Ives Bridge Chapel, Bridge Street, St Ives: St Ives Bridge and Chapel was built in the 1420's. It is a superb example of a very rare kind of building, with the midstream chapel rising directly from the waters of the Great Ouse, and views all round of the river and the historic St Ives Quay. The hatches through which bridge tolls were passed into the chapel can still be seen, as can the rebuilt arches on the south side of the bridge, a relic of the Civil War when the bridge was broken and replaced with a drawbridge, to defend the line of the river against attack by the Royalists. *All year, any time, key from Norris Museum or local shops, displayed. Tel: (0480) 465101.* &

Thorney Abbey Church, Thorney, Peterborough: Norman nave (c1100). Fine church organ originally built in 1787-1790. *All year, daily, 0800-dusk. Tel: (0733) 270388.*

ESSEX

Chelmsford Cathedral, Cathedral Office, Guy Harlings, Chelmsford: Medieval church, reordered in 1984 blending old and new. Modern sculpture and tapestry. *All year, daily, 0815-1730, depending on services. Tel: (0245) 263660.* &

Cressing Temple, Witham Road, Braintree: Site of Knights Templar settlement from 1137. Two magnificent timber-framed barns survive from that period. The Barley Barn circa 1200 and the Wheat Barn circa 1250. The site has connections with many of the great moments of England's past, sacked during the Peasants Revolt (1381) and threatened again during the English Civil War. Tudor walled garden in process of restoration. Tudor Court Hall and Granary building also on show. *May-Sep, Mon-Fri, 0900-1630, Sun, 1400-1730; Mon-Fri, £1.00/50p/50p; Sat, Sun £2.00/£1.00/£1.00. Tel: (0376) 584903.* &

Hedingham Castle

Murals, Cathedral and Abbey Church of St Alban

Grange Barn, Coggeshall: Restored 12th century barn. Earliest surviving timber framed barn in Europe. *27 Mar-9 Oct, Tue, Thu, Sun and Bank Holiday Mon, 1300-1700. £1.10/55p. Tel: (0376) 562226.*

Hadleigh Castle, Hadleigh: Familiar from Constable's picture, the castle stands on a bluff overlooking the Leigh Marshes. Single large bailey 50 feet high. 13th and 14th century remains. *Any reasonable time. Tel: (0702) 555632.*

Harwich Redoubt, Main Road, Harwich: Anti Napoleonic circular fort commanding harbour. *All year, Sun 1000-1200, 1400-1700; 1 Jul-31 Aug, daily, 1400-1700; Closed 29 May, 25 Dec. £1.00/free/£1.00. Tel: (0255) 503429.*

Hedingham Castle, Castle Hedingham: Splendid Norman keep built in 1140 by the famous de Veres, Earls of Oxford. Approached by a lovely Tudor bridge built in 1496 to replace the drawbridge, visited by King Henry VII, King Henry VIII and Queen Elizabeth I, and besieged by King John. Magnificent Banqueting Hall with Minstrels' Gallery and fine Norman arch. Beautiful grounds, peaceful woodland and lakeside walks. Beside medieval village and Norman church. *1 Apr-31 Oct, daily, 1000-1700; closed 25 Dec, 1 Jan. £2.50/£1.50/ £2.25. Tel: (0787) 60261.*

Leez Priory, Hartford End, Chelmsford: Scheduled ancient monument comprising 13th century priory ruins and 16th century redbrick Tudor mansion and tower. 15 acres of parkland, lakes , walled gardens and extensive Tudor tunnels. Oak panelled great hall and other public rooms available for private parties. *3 Apr-25 Sep, Sun and Bank Holidays, 1200-1800. £3.50/£2.00/£2.00. Tel: (0245) 362555.* &

Mistley Towers, Mistley: Two towers designed by Robert Adam in 1776. Key available from 18 Stour View Close, Mistley. *Any reasonable time.*

Mountfitchet Castle, Stansted Mountfitchet: Re-constructed Norman Motte and Bailey Castle and village of Domesday period. Grand hall, church, prison, siege tower and weapons, domestic animals roam site. *13 Mar-13 Nov, daily, 1000-1700; £3.50/£2.50/£3.00. Tel: (0279) 813237.* &

Priors Hall Barn, Widdington: One of the largest surviving medieval barns in South East England. Representative of type of aisled barn in NW Essex. *Apr-Sep, Sat, Sun, 1000-1800. Tel: (0799) 410470.*

Saint Botolphs Priory, Colchester: Remains of 12th century priory near town centre. Nave with impressive arcaded west end, of the first Augustinian priory in England. *Any reasonable time. Tel: (0536) 402840.*

ANCIENT MONUMENTS

Saint Osyth's Priory

Saint Osyth's Priory, St Osyth: 12th century abbey, flint flush gatehouse, later Tudor buildings. Art collection contains paintings by Stubbs. Extensive gardens. *1-4 Apr, 1 May-30 Sep, garden and monument, daily, 1000-1700; Art Collection, 1030-1230, 1430-1630; 20 Jul-20 Aug art collection only 1100-1300, 1400-1600. £3.00/75p/£1.50. Tel: (0255) 820492.* &

⊛ **Tilbury Fort**, No. 2 Office Block, The Fort, Tilbury: One of Henry VIII's coastal forts. Remodelled and extended in the 17th century in French style. The development of fortifications over the following 200 years can be seen. Exhibitions, the powder magazine and bunker-like 'casemates' show how the fort protected London from seaborne attack *All year, daily, 1000-1800. £1.70/85p/£1.30. Tel: (0375) 858489.* &

Waltham Abbey Church, Highbridge Street, Waltham Abbey: Norman church. Reputed site of King Harold's tomb. Lady chapel with crypt. Crypt houses exhibition of history of Waltham Abbey. Shop. *All year, British SummerTime, Mon, Tue, Thu, Fri, Sat, 1000- 1800, Wed 1100-1800, Sun 1200-1800; Winter, Mon, Tue, Thu, Fri, Sat, 1000-1600, Wed 1100-1600, Sun 1200-1600; 1 Apr, 1500-1800; Closed 25 Dec after morning service. Tel: (0992) 767897.* &

HERTFORDSHIRE

⊛ **Cathedral and Abbey Church of St Alban**, St Albans: Abbey church of a Benedictine monastery founded by King Offa in 793 on the site of execution of St Alban, first British martyr (died c209). The present church was built 1077 using Roman brick from nearby Verulamium. At the dissolution of the monastery in 1539 the building became the parish church of St Albans. Saved from imminent collapse by the Victorians, the Abbey Church became a cathedral in 1877. Saints chapel contains the newly restored ecumenical shrine of St Alban. Many medieval wall paintings. Shop, refectory restaurant. *Winter, daily, 0900-1745; summer, daily, 0900-1845. Guided tours, 1500, (Sat 1400) or prebooked. £2.00 donation suggested.* &

⊛ **Royston Cave**, Melbourn Street, Royston: A unique bell shaped chamber cut from the chalk below Melbourn street, of unknown origin but the carvings are clearly medieval and most have religious and historical significance. Believed to have been used by the Knights Templar before their proscription by the Pope in the 14th century. *2 Apr-25 Sep, Sat, Sun, Bank Holiday Mon, 1430-1700. 50p/10p/10p. Tel: (0763) 245484.*

NORFOLK

⊛ **Baconsthorpe Castle**, Baconsthorpe: Guide books and postcards on sale at Baconsthorpe Post Office. 15th century semi-fortified house. The remains include the inner and outer gatehouse and curtain wall. *Any reasonable time.*

Beeston Regis Priory, Beeston Regis Common, Sheringham: Extensive ruins of Priory with interpretation on site. *Any reasonable time.*&

⊛ **Binham Priory**, Binham: Remains of early 12th century Benedictine priory. *Any reasonable time.*

⊛ **Blakeney Guildhall**, Blakeney; Remains of 14th century Guildhall. *Any reasonable time. .*

⊛ **Burgh Castle**, Church Farm, Burgh Castle, Great Yarmouth: One of the few monuments in private ownership. Can only be approached on foot. Information and tearoom available only Easter to October. Remains of Roman fort, overlooking the River Waveney. *Any reasonable time.*

Burnham Norton Friary, Burnham Norton: Remains of Carmelite Friary Gatehouse. Founded in c 1240. Two storeys with flush work

Saint Botolph's Priory, Colchester

panelling. Early 14th century moulding and vaulted ceiling in gatehouse. *All year, daily. Tel: (0603) 222709.*

⊛ **Caister Roman Town**, Great Yarmouth: Remains of Roman commercial port. Footings of walls. *Any reasonable time.*

⊛ **Castle Acre Castle**, Castle Acre: Remains of a Norman manor house, which became a castle. *Any reasonable time.*

⊛ **Castle Acre Priory**, Castle Acre: Impressive ruins of Cluniac priory by William de Warenne, c. 1090. Church and decorated 12th century West front, 16th century gatehouse and priors lodging. *All year, daily, 1000-1800. £2.00/£1.00/£1.80.*

⊛ **Castle Rising Castle**, Castle Rising: Fine mid 12th century keep with notable history. Set in the centre of a massive earthwork. Remains include bridge and gatehouse. *All year, daily, 1000-1800. £1.20/60p/90p.*

⊛ **Creake Abbey**, Burnham Market: Remains of an abbey church dating from 13th century, including presbytery and north transept with chapels. *Any reasonable time.*

⊛ **Grimes Graves**, Lynford: Site exhibition. Neolithic flint mines 4000 years old. First excavated in 1870s. Over 300 pits and shafts. One pit open to the public. 30 ft deep - 7 radiating galleries. *Closed 24,25 Dec but open at all other times. £1.20/60p/90p. Tel: (0842) 810656.*

⊛ **Nelson's Monument,** Great Yarmouth: Monument erected in honour of Nelson in 1819: 144 feet high, 217 steps to the top. *3 Jul-28 Aug, Sun, 1400-1700; 21 Oct (Trafalgar Day), 1000-1700. 60p/30p/40p. Tel (0493) 855746.*

New Buckenham Castle, New Buckenham: Norman Motte and Bailey Castle and chapel with remains of later additions. A solid thick keep surrounded by an earthwork bailey 40 ft high. *Any reasonable time, provided key is available. Key from Castle House or Garage opposite. Closed 25 Dec. £1.00/30p. Tel: (0953) 860251.*

North Elmham Chapel, High Street, North Elmham: The remains of a Norman chapel later converted into a house and enclosed by earthworks. *Any reasonable time.*

Walsingham Roman Catholic Shrine

⊛ **Norwich Cathedral**, 62 The Close, Norwich: Norman Cathedral (1096). 14th century. Roof Bosses depicting bible scenes from Adam and Eve to resurrection. Saxon Bishop's throne and the largest Monastic cloisters in England. Cathedral Close. Shop and buffet. *Mid May-mid Sep 0730-1900, mid Sep-mid May 0730-1800; Shop and buffet closed 3 Apr , Dec 25,26. Tel: (0603) 764385.* ♿

Roman Catholic Cathedral of St John The Baptist, Unthank Road, Norwich: St John's was built at the expense of Henry, Duke of Norfolk in the late 19th century. It is a fine example of nineteenth century Gothic architecture, with unique stained glass and many other features. *All year, Sun, 0830-1930, Mon-Fri, 0730-1600, Sat, 0730-1900 24 Dec, 0800-0000; 25 Dec, 0800-1200. Tel: (0603) 624615.* ♿

Saint Benets Abbey, (Parish of Horning), Ludham: Ruins of monastery founded 1020 AD by King Canute. Gatehouse with interesting carvings. 18th century windmill tower. Perimeter wall round 34 acres. Fishpond. *All year, daily.*

Saint Peter Mancroft Church, Haymarket, Norwich: Norman foundation (1075) New (present) church consecrated in 1455. Perpendicular font (1463). Flemish Tapestry (1573) East Window & Thomas Browne memorial. *All year, Mon-Fri, 0930-1630, Sat, 1000-1230; Closed on Public Holidays. Tel: (0603) 610443.* ♿

Shrine of our Lady of Walsingham, Holt Road, Walsingham: Pilgrimage church containing Holy House standing in extensive grounds. *All year, daily, 6.30-dusk. Tel: (0328) 820266.*

Slipper Chapel - Catholic National Shrine, Friday Market, Walsingham: Now Roman Catholic National Shrine of Our Lady. Small 14th century Chapel connected with ancient shrine in Walsingham (latter now destroyed). New shrine complex including tea room, Repository and Chapel of Reconciliation. *All year, daily, winter 0800-1600, Summer 0800-1900; Shrine open 1 Apr-1 Nov. Tel: (0328) 820495.*

Thetford Priory, Thetford: Custodian on duty selling literature at weekends from Good Fri-30 Sep. Founded by Norman warrior Roger Bigod. Henry VIIIs natural son Duke of Richmond formerly buried here. *Any reasonable time. Tel: (0842) 756127 .*

Castle Acre Castle

Framlingham Castle belongs to English Heritage

Thetford Warren Lodge, Thetford: Ruins of a small two-storey hunting lodge. Can only be viewed from the outside. *Any reasonable time.*

⊛ **Weeting Castle**, Weeting: Remains of moated castle. *Any reasonable time.*

SUFFOLK

Bungay Castle, Bungay: Twin towers and massive flint walls are all that remain of original Norman Castle. Saxon mounds. *All year, daily, 0900-1800; key must be collected from choice of nearby locations. Tel: (0986) 893148.* ⅃

⊛ **Bury St Edmunds Abbey**, Bury St Edmunds: Remains of Abbey in beautifully kept gardens. The two great gateways are the best preserved buildings. *Opening time same as park opening hours, contact Borough Council, Tel: (0284) 764667.*

⊛ **Framlingham Castle**, Framlingham: 12th century curtain walls with 13 towers and Tudor brick chimneys. Built by Bigod family, Earls of Norfolk. Wall walk. 17th century almshouses. Home of Mary Tudor in 1553. *1 Apr-30 Sep,*

daily, 1000-1800; 1 Oct-31 Mar, daily, 1000-1600. Closed 24-26 Dec & 1 Jan. £1.80/90p/£1.35. Tel: (0728) 723330.

⊛ **Leiston Abbey**, Leiston: Remains of 14th century abbey including transepts of church and range of cloisters. *Any reasonable time.*

⊛ **Orford Castle**, Orford: Magnificent 90 foot high keep with views across River Alde to Orford Ness. Built by Henry II for coastal defence in 12th century. Local topographical display. *1 Apr-30 Sep, daily, 1000-1800; 1 Oct-31 Mar, Wed-Sun, 1000-1600. Closed 24-26 Dec & 1 Jan. £1.80/90p/£1.35. Tel: (039 44) 50472.*

Saint Edmundsbury Cathedral, The Cathedral Office, Angel Hill, Bury St Edmunds: 16th century Nave (was St James Church, made Cathedral in 1914) East End added post-war, completed late 1960. North Side built 1990. *Services; Sun 1000, Sung Eucharist Sun 1130; Choral Matins of Communion Evensong Tue, Wed, Thu, 1700, Fri, 1900, Sun 1530. 1 Jun-30 Aug, 0830-2000; Other British Summer Time 0830-1800; Winter 0830-1730. Tel: (0284) 754933.* ⅃

Saint James's Chapel, Lindsey: Small medieval chapel once attached to nearby castle. *Any reasonable time.*

⊛ **Saint Olaves Priory**, Herringfleet: Priory remains with early 14th century undercroft with brick vaulted ceiling (see also nearby windmill). Key to undercroft available from Miss Rutley at the Priory House. *Any reasonable time.*

Sutton Hoo Archaeological Site, Sutton Hoo, Woodbridge: A group of low, grassy burial mounds overlooking the river Deben. Excavations in 1939 brought to light the richest burial ever discovered in Britain - an Anglo Saxon ship containing a magnificent treasure. It is thought to have been the grave of Raedwald, one of the earliest English kings known, who died in 624/5 AD. The Sutton Hoo treasure has become one of the principal attractions of the British Museum, but its discovery raised many questions about the site which remain unanswered. *1 Apr-31 Aug, Sat, Sun, 1400-1600. £1.50/50p.*

⊛ **West Stow Country Park and Anglo Saxon Village.** West Stow: Reconstruction on its original site of 6 pagan Anglo Saxon buildings, built using the original tools and techniques available to the Anglo-Saxons. Visitor Centre. Taped guides with sound effects and music bring the village to life. *All year, daily, 1000-1615. Closed 25,26 Dec. £2.50/£1.50/£1.50. Tel:(0284) 728718.* ⅃

Prices appear in the order Adults/Children/Senior Citizens. Where prices are not available at the time of going to press, the 1993 (93) price is given. If no price is given, admission is free. See Touring Maps on pages 119-124 for locations of places to visit.

COUNTRYSIDE

LONG WALKS AND DISTANCE PATHS

BEDFORDSHIRE

Greensand Ridge Walk, 40 mile footpath from Leighton Buzzard to Gamlingay. Well signposted and waymarked. *Details from Bedfordshire County Council.*

Upper Lea Valley Walk, Follows the valley of the River Lea from Leagrave Common, via Luton town centre to East Hyde. *Details from Bedfordshire County Council.*

CAMBRIDGESHIRE

Bishops Way: 7-9 miles circular route on ancient tracks north of Ely. *Details available from Cambridgeshire County Council, leaflet 40p.*

Clopton Way: 10 mile linear walk from Wimpole to Gamlingay via the prehistoric trackway and deserted medieval village of Clopton. Links in with the Wimpole Way and Greensand Ridge Walk. *Details from Cambridgeshire County Council, leaflet 40p.*

Devil's Dyke: 7 1/2 mile long defensive fortification ditch dating from 500 AD, running from open chalklands and undrained fenland north of Reach to thick woodland south of Stechworth. *Leaflet available from Bedfordshire & Cambridgeshire Wildlife Trust, Maris Lane, Trumpington, Cambridge, Tel: (0223) 846363.*

Grafham Water Circular Ride: A circular ride of 13 miles around the reservoir. The route includes ancient woodlands, medieval granges and excellent views across the water. *Details from Cambridgeshire County Council, free leaflet.*

Nene Way: 10 miles, from Peterborough to Wansford along the valley of the River Nene. *Details from Ferry Meadows Country Park, Ham Lane, Peterborough. Tel: (0733) 234443.*

Ouse Valley Way: Long distance river valley walk along the Great Ouse from Eaton Socon to Earith. Total length 26 miles. *Information pack available from Huntingdon Tourist Information Centre, £1.00. Tel: (0480) 425831.*

Three Shires Way: A long distance ride of 45 miles from Grafham Water into Bedfordshire and Buckinghamshire to link with the Swan's Way. *Details from Cambridgeshire County Council, free leaflet.*

Wimpole Way: 13 miles through woodlands and fields from Cambridge to Wimpole Hall. *Details from Cambridgeshire County Council, leaflet 40p.*

ESSEX

Epping Forest Centenary Walk: 15 miles through Epping Forest from Manor Park to Epping (links Essex Way to outskirts of London). *Booklet £1.50 plus p&p from Epping Forest Information Centre, High Beach, Loughton.*

Essex Way: 81 mile walk from Epping to Harwich. *Booklet £1.74 (inc postage) from West Essex Ramblers Association, "Glenview", London Road, Abridge, Essex, Tel: (0992) 813350.*

Flitch Way (Disused Braintree to Bishops Stortford Railway): 15 mile route through NW Essex. Some sections suitable for cyclists and horseriders. Ranger service.

Forest Way: 25 miles of gentle walking along footpaths and ancient green lanes between the forests of Epping and Hatfield. *Booklet £2.50 from Essex County Council Planning Department, County Hall, Chelmsford. Tel: (0245) 437647*

Harcamlow Way: 140 miles in the form of a "figure-of-eight" footpath walk from Harlow to Cambridge and back. *Booklet £2.50 (inc postage) from West Essex Ramblers Association (address above).*

St Peters Way: 45-mile walk from Chipping Ongar to ancient chapel of St Peter-on-the-Wall at Bradwell-on-Sea. *Booklet £1.44 (inc postage) from West Essex Ramblers Association (address above).*

Three Forests Way: 60 miles circular walk linking the forests of Epping, Hatfield and Hainault. *Booklet £1.24 from West Essex Ramblers Association (address above).*

NORFOLK

Angles Way: A 70 mile walk along the Waveney and Little Ouse valleys. *Free leaflet from Norfolk County Council (SAE please).*

Around Norfolk Walk: A 220 mile walk following the Peddars Way, Coast Path, Weavers Way and Angles Way, taking in most of Norfolk's varied scenery. *Free leaflet from Norfolk County Council (SAE please).*

Great Eastern Pingo Trail: 8 mile walk, partly along disused railway line, taking in Breckland scenery. *Leaflet 58p (inc p&p) from Norfolk County Council.*

Marriott's Way: 20 mile footpath and bridleway between Norwich and Aylsham along former railway line. *Free leaflet from Norfolk County Council (SAE please).*

Norfolk Bridle/Cycle routes: Circular routes (15-25 miles) centred around the villages of Poringland, Reepham, Hockwold, Swaffham and Massingham. *Booklet from Norfolk County Council (SAE please).*

Peddars Way and Norfolk Coast Path with Weavers Way: Official long distance footpath of 93 miles, between Knettishall Heath and Holme, then along the coast to Cromer. Through heath and Breckland woods and varied coastal scenery. Plus Norfolk County Council Recreational Path from Cromer to Great Yarmouth of 56 miles. *(Guide which includes accommodation list, £1.80 plus 28p p&p from East Anglia Tourist Board or Peddars Way Association, 150 Armes Street, Norwich NR2 4EG. Official guide available from HMSO £8.99 plus postage.*

Wash Coast Path: A 10 mile route between Sutton Bridge Lighthouse and West Lynn giving spectacular views of the saltmarshes and the Wash. *Free leaflet from Norfolk County Council (SAE please).*

Weavers Way: 57 mile walk from Cromer to Great Yarmouth via Blickling and Stalham. *Free leaflet from Norfolk County Council, (SAE please).*

Walkers at Snape in Suffolk

COUNTRYSIDE

SUFFOLK

Constable Trail: A 9 mile walk through the landscape and villages associated with the artist's childhood and life. Four shorter walks available. *Booklet £1.25 inc postage from Peddar Publications, Croft End, Bures, Suffolk CO8 5JN. Tel: (0787) 227823.*

Gipping Valley River Path: Located along the 17 mile long former tow path between Ipswich and Stowmarket alongside the River Gipping. *Free leaflet from Suffolk County Council (SAE please).*

Painters Way: 28 mile walk along the valley of River Stour, from Sudbury to Manningtree through countryside which inspired Gainsborough, Constable and Munnings. *Booklet £1.25 inc postage from Peddar Publications, Croft End, Bures, Suffolk, CO8 5JN. Tel: (0787) 227823.*

Suffolk Coast Path: 45 mile path along coast from Bawdsey to Kessingland. *Leaflet, 20p from Suffolk County Council (SAE please).*

Suffolk Way: A long distance walk of 106 miles passing through heathland Suffolk from Flatford in Constable Country to Lavenham, Framlingham and Walberswick, following the coast to Lowestoft. *Booklet £2.85 (inc. postage) from Footpath guides, Old Hall, East Bergholt, Colchester CO7 6TG.*

ICKNIELD WAY

A long distance path following mainly broad green lanes and easy tracks in seven counties, linking the Peddars Way to the Ridgeway. *Three free leaflets may be obtained from Suffolk County Council; horseriders leaflets also available (SAE please).*

SHORTER WALKS

BEDFORDSHIRE

Circular Walks: 13 circular walks throughout the county, which are clearly waymarked and vary in length from between 2 1/2 to 11 miles. *Further information from Bedfordshire County Council.*

Guided Walks: Led by the County Council's experienced staff all year round. Tel: (0234) 228310 for a free copy of the latest walks' programme. *£1.00/50p/50p each walk.*

Pond dipping at High Woods Country Park, Colchester

CAMBRIDGESHIRE

Coe Fen and Paradise Trails, Cambridge: Nature trails on common land next to River Cam. *Guide books from Bedfordshire & Cambridgeshire Wildlife Trust, Maris Lane, Trumpington, Cambridge, Tel: (0223) 846363.*

Ely Easy Access Trail: A 2 mile trail along the river and nature trail in Ely. Accessible to people of all ages and abilities. Paths are not surfaced so access will deteriorate in winter. *Leaflet from Cambridgeshire County Council, (SAE please).*

Giants Hill, Rampton. 12th century moat and castle mound, and grassland. Interpretative boards. *Leaflet from Cambridgeshire County Council (SAE please).*

Peterborough: 19 circular walks in rural Peterborough of between 3-11 miles through landscapes including undulating farmland, ancient woodland, riverside scenery and a variety of wildlife. *"Country Walks around Peterborough Volumes I and II". Available from TIC, 45 Bridge Street, Peterborough. Tel: (0733) 317336.*

Roman Road Walk: (Linton-Hildersham). 6 1/2 mile circular walk, along a Roman trackway and the historic villages of Linton and Hildersham. *Details from Cambridgeshire County Council, leaflet 40p.*

Roman Road Circular Walk: (Stapleford-Wandlebury). 6 mile circular waymarked walk, passing from Stapleford along the River Granta up to Copley Hill, along the Roman Road and back through Wandlebury. *Details from Cambridgeshire County Council, leaflet 40p.*

Shepreth Riverside Walk: Attractive tree-fringed meadows alongside River Cam between Shepreth and Barrington. Walk now available through to Malton Lane. Walking, picnics, nature study, small car park. *Further details from Cambridgeshire County Council.*

Wandlebury Country Park Nature Trails: 3 short trails around hilltop crowned by the Wandlebury Ring-an Iron age fort. Mainly woodland with some chalk grassland, fine views.

Wicken Walks: Walks through cross section of Fen Landscape. *Leaflet 40p . Details from Cambridgeshire County Council.*

Woodman's Way: Circular waymarked walk of 6 miles passing through the once wooded islands of March and Wimblington. *Details from Cambridgeshire County Council, leaflet 40p.*

ESSEX

Backwarden Nature Reserve Nature Trail, Danbury: 1 1/2 mile trail through heath and woodland. Blackthorn thickets, pools, marsh and bogland. *Leaflet 25p (inc p&p) from Essex Wildlife Trust, Tel: (0206) 729678.*

Basildon Greenway: A series of circular footpaths and connecting linear walks in and around Basildon countryside. *Leaflet 50p from Pitsea Hall Country Park. Tel: (0268) 550088.*

Crays Hill Circular Walk: 5 mile waymarked circular walk centred on the old village of Crays Hill. *Leaflet 50p from Pitsea Hall Country Park, Pitsea. Tel: (0268) 550088.*

◉ **Lee Valley Park Circular Walks:** *Further information from Lee Valley Park Countryside Centre, Tel: (0992) 713838.*

Maldon Trail: Historic route through Maldon, passing many buildings dating from 15th, 16th, 17th centuries. *Leaflet available from Maldon Tourist Information Centre, Tel: (0621) 856503.*

Maldon Maritime Trail: Leaflet showing varied walks around the Blackwater estuary and up to Beeleigh Falls, available from *Maldon Tourist Information Centre, Tel: (0621) 856503.*

Norsey Wood Trail: Walk through woodland of archaeological and conservation importance which is still managed by traditional methods. *Further information from Norsey Wood Nature Reserve. Tel: (0277) 624553*

North Blackwater Trail: Leaflet describing picturesque route along the riverside, passing marshes and through villages, available from *Maldon Tourist Information Centre, Tel: (0621) 856503*

Plotland Trail and Museum, Dunton, Basildon. Trail through former plotland area. *Further information available from the Warden Tel: (0268) 419095.*

Please mention East Anglia Guide when replying to advertisements

Ramsden Crays Circular Walk: Approx 3 mile waymarked walk. *Leaflet 50p from Pitsea Hall Country Park, Pitsea. Tel: (0268) 550088*

Wildside Walks: 6 walks to help you discover the Country Parks of Essex. *Wildside walking Pack, £2.50 from Essex County Council.*

NORFOLK

Bacton Wood Forest Walks: 3 forest walks 2km, 3km and 4km through gentle hilly woodland east of North Walsham. Some 30 species of trees grow here.

Burlingham Woodland Trails: 3 woodland walks (1, 2 and 3 miles) through the Burlingham estate, 8 miles east of Norwich. *Booklet £1.50 (inc postage) from Norfolk County Council.*

⚫ **Felbrigg Lakeside and Woodland Walks** (National Trust): These walks are in the grounds of Felbrigg Hall. Dogs are not allowed on the Lakeside walk. *All year, daily, dawn to dusk, ex 25 Dec.*

Harrold Odell Country Park, Bedfordshire

Kelling Heath Nature Trail: 2 1/2 mile woodland nature trail with conservation lake and other points of interest, magnificent views. Historic sites. Adjacent to North Norfolk Steam Railway. *Leaflet, parking and information from Kelling Heath Caravan Park. Weybourne. Tel: (026370) 224.*

⚫ **Mannington Walks:** Waymarked walks and trails through woodlands, meadows and farmland. Information Centre. *Car Park £1.00*

Marriott's Way Circular Walks: A series of walks based on the Marriott's Way. *Booklet with maps from Norfolk County Council .*

Norfolk Guided Walks: 2-3 mile walks throughout Norfolk. *Details of times, locations and subjects from Department of Planning and Transportation, Norfolk County Council.*

Parish Walks: A series of leaflets, describing short circular walks centred on villages throughout Norfolk. Recent additions - Filby, Southrepps, Winterton and Thurning. *Leaflets 50p each (inc p&p) from Norfolk County Council.*

South Norfolk Footways: Circular walks in the parishes of Diss, Framlingham Earl, Hingham, Long Stratton, Loddon, Mulbarton, Poringland, Pulham, Shotesham and Wymondham. *Free leaflet (send SAE) from TIC, Meres Mouth, Mere Street, Diss, IP22 3AG. Tel: (0379) 650523.*

The Great Eastern Pingo Trail: 8 mile circular walk from Thompson Common near Watton. *Leaflets 60p (inc postage) from Norfolk County Council.*

Walks around Pretty Corner: Approx 250 acres of woodlands for fine and easy walks. Starting from Pretty Corner Main Car Park at the A148 near Sheringham.

Weavers Way Circular Walks: 6 walks based on the Weavers Way. Booklet with maps from *Norfolk County Council, £2.50 (inc postage).*

SUFFOLK

Countryside Walks: A series of well signposted circular walks. *Further details of walks and leaflets, 20p each, from Suffolk County Council (SAE please).*

Gipping Valley: 8 circular walks, waymarked, linked to River Path. 3-7 miles. *Laminated walk-cards from Suffolk County Council, £1.50.*

Lavenham, Long Melford and Sudbury Walks: 1-4 mile walks along dismantled railway lines through beautiful countryside. *Leaflet 20p from Suffolk County Council.*

Orford Walks: 4 walks in and around Orford. One suitable for wheelchairs. *Leaflet 20p from Suffolk County Council.*

Rendlesham Forest, Phoenix Trail (E Woodbridge off B1084): Series of waymarked forest walks to suit a range of abilities including wheelchairs. Picnic site and toilets.

St Cross Farm Walks, South Elmham Hall, St Cross, Harleston: Self guided trails around farm and deer park. *£1.00 per car.*

Shotley Peninsula Walks: Walks of about 6 miles include Shotley Gate, Erwarton, Pin Mill, Woolverstone, Holbrook, Freston, Brantham and Bentley. *Further details and free leaflets from Babergh District Council, Planning Department, Council Offices, Corks Lane, Hadleigh, Suffolk. Tel: (0473) 822801.*

Stour Valley Countryside Walks: Arger Fen Woodland (Nayland) and from Bures (2-4 miles). *Free leaflet from Suffolk County Council (SAE please).*

Thornham Walks (off A140, 3m SW Eye): 12 miles of footpaths through the woodlands and farmlands around Thornham Magna. Trail leaflets

50p. 1/2 mile path suitable for wheelchairs. Picnic area. *Guided walks £1.50/75p. Admission £1.00/free.*

Walberswick Walk: Circular walk starting from the village green, along the seashore, river estuary, through marshes and across heathland. *Leaflet 20p from Suffolk County Council (SAE please).*

COUNTRY AND LEISURE PARKS

BEDFORDSHIRE

Dunstable Downs, Beds County Council: Highest point in the county with superb views over the county and the Vale of Aylesbury. Watch the gliders and walk among the chalk downland flora. Visitors Centre.

Harrold Odell Country Park, Beds County Council: Landscaped lakes attract many wildfowl varieties. Extensive reedbeds, river meadows and riverbanks. Visitors Centre.

Priory Country Park, Barkers Lane, Bedford: 228 acres of open country, 80 acres of which are water. Wildlife conservation areas, angling, sailing and Visitor Centres.

Stewartby Lake Country Park, Beds County Council: Disused clay pit, now the largest expanse of water in the county. Attracts many birds in autumn and winter. Water sports.

Stockgrove Country Park, Beds County Council: Parkland, oak woodland, coniferous plantations, lake and diverse wildlife. Visitors Centre.

Sundon Hills Country Park, (Upper Sundon, Luton) Beds County Council: 250 acres of rolling chalk downland with excellent views of surrounding area.

CAMBRIDGESHIRE

Ferry Meadows Country Park, Nene Park, nr Peterborough (off A605 2m W of city centre): Sailing, windsurfing, hire craft available at Watersports Centre. Fishing, miniature steam railway, boating, picnicking, walking, nature reserve, visitor centre, conservation garden.

Grafham Water (5m SW Huntingdon off B661): This 2 1/2 sq mile man-made reservoir has fishing and sailing facilities and many water birds. 3 Nature Trails, 2 bird hides (one with facilities for disabled), pleasure boat trips. Picnic sites, restaurant, cafe, free parking, public footpaths, toilets (disabled facilities), cycle hire and visitor/exhibition centre.

Hinchingbrooke Country Park: 156 acres of woods, lakes and meadows. Watersports, countryside events, walks and displays at the Visitor Centre. Facilities for the disabled. Ranger Service.

Wandlebury (3m SE Cambridge off A1307): Parkland with Iron Age hill fort, picnics, woodland walks and nature trail. Dogs on leads.

⚫ **Wimpole,** (National Trust) nr New Wimpole: Walks in park landscaped by Bridgeman, Brown and Repton, surrounding Wimpole Hall.

ESSEX

Belhus Woods (1m N Aveley), Essex County Council: 158 acres. Woodlands, lakes and open areas for walking and picnicking. Fishing from 0800 to dusk. Proposed horse-ride. Visitor Centre. Ranger Service.

⚫ **Brentwood Park,** Warley Gap: Ski centre, golf range, woodland walk. Health club and leisure facilities. Tel: (0277) 211994.

Please mention East Anglia Guide when replying to advertisements

COUNTRYSIDE

Chalkney Wood, Earls Colne, Essex County Council: Ancient woodland site of 63 acres.

Cudmore Grove, East Mersea, Essex County Council: Access to a pleasant beach and grassland for picnics. 35 acres. Information Room. Ranger Service.

Danbury (5m E Chelmsford), Essex County Council: 41 acres. Danbury Country Park is set in the former pleasure gardens of the mansion and provides for quiet enjoyment of the lakes and exotic trees and shrubs. Ranger Service.

Epping Forest: 6,000+ acres, mostly within Essex, owned by the Corporation of the City of London. Much of it is SSSI and includes ancient woodlands of beech, oak and hornbeam, grasslands and attractive water areas. Two Iron Age earthworks visible. Epping Forest Centre at High Beach.

Garnetts Wood, Barnston, nr Dunmow, Essex County Council: Ancient woodland of 62 acres.

Grove Woods, Rochford District Council: 40 acres of recent woodland between Eastwood and Rayleigh. Walks among old orchards and overgrown ruins of small holdings. Waymarked circular route, surface suitable for wheelchairs. Permissive way marked horse route.

Hadleigh Castle Country Park, Essex County Council, Southend and Castle Point Borough Councils. 450 acres of downland, woodland and marshes. Wildlife area. Horseride. Ranger Service.

Hainault Forest Country Park, London Borough of Redbridge: 902 acres of open space, playing fields, lakes, golf course and ancient woodland. Foxburrows Farm contains rare breeds of farm animals.

Harlow Town Park: Fully landscaped 164 acre park with scenic walks and views. Pets corner, pitch n putt, adventure playground, paddling pool. Cafes and riverside complex.

Hatfield Forest (4m E Bishop's Stortford): 1,000 acres of wooded medieval landscape and nature reserve with lake. Miles of peaceful woodland walks including 1 1/4 mile waymarked nature trail. *£2.40 per car.*

High Woods Country Park, Colchester Borough Council: 330 acres of attractive woodland, grassland, farmland and wetland. Numerous footpaths. Visitors Centre, bookshop and toilets.

Hockley Woods, Rochford District Council: 260 acres of ancient coppice woodland, the largest in Essex. Pleasant walks and a horse trail. Picnic and play area. 2 waymarked routes.

Langdon Hills (1m SW Basildon), Essex County Council: Divided into two parks, Westley Heights and One Tree Hill, the Country Park overlooks the Thames estuary and has a range of scenery including open grassland, deciduous woodlands, and sandy heaths. Horse ride through park. Information at One Tree Hill plus AA viewpoint. Ranger Service.

Lee Valley Regional Park: Stretches 23 miles along the Lee Valley from London's East End, through Essex and to Ware in Hertfordshire. Parkland, picnic sites, angling, camping, sports centres, marinas, bird watching and a farm. *Countryside Centre at Abbey Farmhouse, Crooked Mile, Waltham Abbey. For further information, Lee Valley Information Line, Tel: (0992) 700766.*

Maldon Promenade: 100 acres of formal and informal parkland adjoining River Blackwater. Riverside walks, picnics, children's play areas.

Marks Hall Estate, Coggeshall. Country estate with ornamental grounds, lakes, parkland, woodland and waymarked walks. Visitor centre in restored Essex barn. *Easter-Oct, daily, closed Mon (ex Bank Hol Mon). £2.00 per car. Tel: (0376) 563040.*

Marsh Farm Country Park, South Woodham Ferrers, Essex County Council: 320 acres of country park operating as a modern livestock farm. Country walks round the sea wall, farm tracks and nature reserve. Visitor Centre. Picnic areas. *See also Animal Collections.*

Pitsea Hall Country Park, Pitsea: Country park with an emphasis on conservation and natural history. Attractions include a marina, craft workshops, National Motorboat museum and relocated historic buildings.

Programme of Ranger Guided Activities: Talks can be arranged. Further details from the Ranger Service, Weald Country Park, South Weald, Brentwood. Tel: (0277) 261343.

Thorndon (2m S Brentwood), Essex County Council: 540 acres. Thorndon North is almost totally woodland with pleasant walks and a horse ride. Thorndon South has woodland walks, fishing and some extensive views of the Thames estuary. Ranger Service. Countryside Centre.

Weald (1m NW Brentwood), Essex County Council: 428 acres of woodland, lakes and open parkland open to the public for informal recreation. Fishing and horse riding. Visitor Centre, Ranger Service.

NORFOLK

Fritton Lake (6m SW Gt Yarmouth on A143): 250 acres of wood, grassland and formal gardens. Lake, rowing and fishing. 9 hole golf, putting. Adventure playground. Cafe, shop and craft workshops. Falconry centre.

Holt Country Park (1m S Holt on B1149): Conifer wood and heathland with walks, nature trail. Car parking, picnic areas and toilets. 98 acres woodland and 113 acres heathland.

Lynford Aboretum: 1m E Mundford off A1065: A collection of over 200 trees species in an attractive parkland setting with walks around an ornamental lake and into the forest.

Sandringham (7m NE King's Lynn on A149): Wood and heathland. Nature trail. 650 acres.

Sheringham Park (National Trust), Sheringham (car access off A148 Cromer to Holt road): Rhododendrons, woodland, spectacular views of park and coastlines. *Car park £2.30.*

Thetford Forest Park: 50,000 acres of pine forest straddling Norfolk and Suffolk. Waymarked walks and trails lead from the car parks into the forest. Forest Office, Santon Downham, Tel: (0842) 810271. High Lodge Forest Centre, 2m E Brandon. Tel: (0842) 810271

Wolterton Park: 340 acres of historic parkland with marked trails. Orienteering, adventure playground, Hawk and Owl Trust exhibition. Special events programme. Toilets. *Car Park £2.00.*

SUFFOLK

Alton Water, Holbrook Road, Stutton, nr Ipswich: Water park with walks, nature reserves and picnic areas. Cycle tracks and cycle hire. Watersports centre offering sailing and windsurfing. Coarse angling, day tickets available. Visitor Centre serving snacks.

Brandon (1/2m S Brandon): Lake, lawns, tree trail, orienteering course, Victorian walled garden, Visitor Centre, toilets, woodland picnic areas and forest walks. 32 acres.

Clare Castle, Clare, nr Sudbury: Ruins of Clare Castle and baileys. A former railway station with visitor centre, water-fowl, nature trail, history trail, walks, picnic areas, toilets. 25 acres.

Ickworth Park, (National Trust) Horringer (3m SW Bury St Edmunds, on A143): Walks through woodland and by canal. Leaflet available from machine at car park 50p. *£1.00/50p payable on entrance to park.*

Knettishall Heath (5m E Thetford): Attractive Breck landscape, heather, grass heath and mixed woods, Peddars Way long distance footpath starts at W end. Angles Way, the Broads to the Breks path finishes at E end. Toilets and extensive picnic area. 400 acres.

West Stow Country Park (6m NW Bury St Edmunds, off A1101): Grassland, heathland, lake and river with many pleasant walks. Also reconstructed Anglo-Saxon village (see Ancient Monuments section for full details). 125 acres. Children's play area. Visitor centre, car parking, picnicking and toilet facilities.

East Carlton Countryside Park, Rockingham Forest Tourism

ADJOINING COUNTIES

Rockingham Forest Tourism - Can help you discover Northamptonshire's countryside. Stately homes, where to stay, leisure drives, list of guides, walks, what's open. For further information contact c/o Civic Centre, George Street, Corby, Northants NN17 1QB, Tel: (0536) 407507.

USEFUL ADDRESSES

Leisure Services, Bedfordshire County Council, County Hall, Bedford. Tel: (0234) 228671.

Rural Group, Department of Property, Cambridgeshire County Council, Shire Hall, Castle Hill, Cambridge. Tel: (0223) 317445.

Planning Department, Essex County Council, County Hall, Chelmsford. Tel: (0245) 492211.

Department Planning and Transportation, Norfolk County Council, County Hall, Martineau Lane, Norwich. Tel: (0603) 222776.

Planning Department, Suffolk County Council, County Hall, Ipswich. Tel: (0473) 265131.

NATURE RESERVES

Ordnance Survey grid references have been provided for some of the reserves which are less easy to locate. For further details please contact the Naturalists' Organisations, addresses and telephone numbers on page 64.

BEDFORDSHIRE

Cooper's Hill, nr Ampthill [TL 028376] (Ampthill Town Council/BCWT): One of the best examples of Heathland in Bedfordshire, supporting populations of characteristic insects and lizards.

Felmersham Gravel Pits, nr Felmersham [SP 991584] (BCWT): Disused gravel workings composed of open water, marsh, grassland, hedges and developing woodland with rich plant life. Excellent site for damselflies and dragonflies.

Flitwick Moor, off Flitwick-Maulden road, turn off by Folly Farm [TL 046354] (BCWT): Once valley fen and heath; now contains a variety of habitats including damp birch woodland, open water, unimproved grassland and sphagnum moss.

The Lodge, RSPB Headquarters (1m E Sandy off B1042): Mature woodland, pine plantations, birch and bracken slopes with a remnant of heath and an artificial lake. 4 nature trails. Formal gardens. Many breeding birds, muntjac deer are often seen. *Reserve and gardens, daily 0900-2100 or sunset when earlier. £1.50 (free RSPB members).*

Totternhoe Knolls, nr Dunstable [SP 986216] (BCWT): A long, partly wooded chalk ridge, subject to quarrying since Saxon times. Plants include kidney and horseshoe vetch, clustered bellflower and wild thyme.

CAMBRIDGESHIRE

Fowlmere, E of A10 Cambridge to Royston road, nr Shepreth (RSPB): Reedbeds, pools, watercress beds. Kingfishers, turtle doves, water rails. *Access at all times from reserve car park. Non members £1.00. Warden: Mike Pollard, 19 Whitecroft Road, Meldreth, Royston, Cambridgeshire.*

Hayley Wood, nr Gamlingay [TL 294534] (BCWT): Ancient woodland of tall oak standards forming a canopy above the mixed coppice and smaller trees of field maple, ash, hazel and hawthorn. Bluebell, oxlip and other spring flowers.

Nene Washes, nr Whittlesey, 5 miles E Peterborough (RSPB): Wet meadows and marshland with breeding waders and wintering ducks and swans. *Entry by permit from warden: C Kitchen, 31 Pinewood Avenue, Whittlesey, nr Peterborough.*

Ouse Washes, nr Manea reached from A141 Chatteris-March road (RSPB/BCWT): Extensive wet meadows. Breeding black-tailed godwits. The most important inland site in Britain for wintering ducks and swans. Observation hides, information centre and toilets. *Access free at all times from reserve car park. Warden: C Carson, Limosa, Welches Dam, Manea, March.*

Wildfowl & Wetlands Trust, Welney Centre, Welney: Year round reserve with numerous hides and a large observatory overlooking some 900 acres of the Washes. Around 3,500 wild swans and many thousands of wildfowl in winter, in summer notable for waders and other birds and pleasant walks in the unique washland habitat. *All year, daily 1000-1700 (except 24/25 Dec). Nov-Feb, special evening visits to watch the swans under floodlights, pre-booking essential Tel: (0353) 860711. £2.95/£1.50/£2.20/family £7.40 (93).*

Wicken Fen (NT): Practically the last remaining undrained fen with general access; especially interesting for plant and insect life, waterfowl in winter and breeding marsh birds in summer. Display. *All year, daily (ex 25 Dec), dawn-dusk. Parties must book in advance, Tel: (0353) 720274. £2.50/£1.25.*

ESSEX

Abberton Reservoir, nr Colchester (EBWS): Special protected area for wild duck, swans and other water birds. Visitor centre with panoramic views. 2 nature trails and 5 bird hides. Access to perimeter road restricted to EBWS permit holders, although visible from roads. *All year, daily ex Mon (open Bank Hol Mon), 0900-1700, closed 25 & 26 Dec.*

Chigborough Lakes, 3m E Maldon, off B1026 (EWT): Former gravel pit with 4 lakes, one of which has dried up. Willow swamp scrub, grassland and water birds; wildfowl in winter.

Colne Estuary, (EN) East Mersea; foreshore, beach and marshes.

Fingringhoe Wick Nature Reserve 3m SE Colchester (EWT): 125 acres of woodland and lakes by the Colne estuary. Nature trails, observation tower and 8 hides. Conservation Centre. *All year, daily ex Mon, 0900-1700 (open until 1800 in summer). Closed 25/26 Dec.*

John Weston Reserve, Walton-on-the-Naze (EWT): Small reserve forming part of a much larger complex of cliffs, rough grassland, scrapes and saltings which form the Naze. Nature trail.

Langdon Nature Reserve, SW Basildon (EWT): 460 acres of woodland, flower

Broadland Conservation Centre at Ranworth

meadows, lakes and former plotland gardens, including the ancient woodlands of Marks Hill.

Leigh: (EN/EWT) Mudflats, saltmarsh and part island. Access to footpaths and nature trail.

Roding Valley Meadows, from Oakwood Hill, off Rectory Lane, Loughton (EWT): Largest water meadows left in Essex with flower rich meadows and marsh alongside the River Roding. Variety of birds including kingfisher and good insects.

Stour Wood and Copperas Bay, off B1352 road from Manningtree to Ramsey (RSPB): Mixed woodland and mudflats on Stour estuary. Ducks, geese and waders numerous in autumn and winter. Nightingales and woodpeckers can also be seen. Access at all times to hides overlooking estuary from reserve car park. Donations welcome. *Warden: R Leavett, 24 Orchard Close, Great Oakley, Harwich.*

Wildside Walks: 6 walks to help you discover the nature reserves of Essex. *Wildside walking pack £2.50 from Essex County Council Planning Department, County Hall, Chelmsford.*

NORFOLK

The Norfolk Coast

Blakeney Point (NT): Shingle spit, sand dunes, seals, shop and display in Lifeboat House. Access for disabled. Hides. Access by boat from Morston or Blakeney. *Morston and Blakeney car park charge.*

Cley Marshes (NNT): Fresh water and salt marshes, large number of rare migrants which appear each year. Visitor Centre built on high ground with magnificent views; displays on conservation and history of the Cley area. Gift shop. No dogs please. *Visitor Centre Apr-Oct, Tue-Sun, 1000-1700. Closed Mon, open Bank Hols. Marshes all year, access by permit available from Visitor Centre or Watchers's cottage in winter. Adm charge for non-members.*

Holkham (EN): Sand and mud flats, salt marsh, sand dunes with Corsican pines.

Holkham Hall Lake: Freshwater 1 mile in length on which moorhen & coot, grebes, cormorants, swans, geese and ducks can be seen. *Advance notice to Estate Office for large groups please, Tel: (0328) 710227.*

Holme Bird Observatory Reserve (NOA): 6 acres. Permanent warden. 300 species. Hides. Nature trail. *Visitors welcome all year, permits available on the spot.*

Scolt Head Island (EN): Island reserve with extensive salt marshes and sand dunes. Nature Trail. *Access by ferry from Brancaster Staithe and Burnham Overy Staithe, Apr-Sep.*

Snettisham, signposted from A149 road from King's Lynn to Hunstanton (RSPB): Gravel pits on the Wash. Spectacular flocks of waders at high tides, breeding terns, ducks. Observation hides. Information centre. *Access at all times from public car park at beach. Warden: P Fisher, 13 Beach Road, Snettisham, King's Lynn.*

Titchwell, off A149, W of Brancaster (RSPB): Reedbeds, lagoons, saltmarsh and sandy beach. Nesting avocets, marsh harriers and bitterns. Good variety of birds throughout the year. Access at all times along the west bank. Observation hides, visitor centre, shop, toilets. *£2.00 car park charge for non members. Warden: N Sills, Three Horseshoes Cottage, Titchwell, King's Lynn.*

Winterton Dunes (EN): Large sand dune area with coastal plants and birds.

Holkham Beach on the North Norfolk Coast

Broadland

Berney Marshes and Breydon Water, nr Great Yarmouth (RSPB): Flooded grazing marsh and estuary mudflats. Waders and wildfowl present throughout the year. No road access. Norwich-Great Yarmouth train stops at Berney Arms halt. Also reached by foot along Weaver's Way or by boat from Breydon Marine or Great Yarmouth, bookable in advance with the warden: *D Barrett, RSPB, Ashtree Farm, Breydon Marina, Butt Lane, Burgh Castle, Great Yarmouth.*

Broadland Conservation Centre, Ranworth (NNT): A floating gallery for bird watching moored on Ranworth Broad; displays on conservation and the history of the Broads approached by a 350 metre nature trail through woodland to the waters edge. No dogs please. *1 Apr-31 Oct, Sun-Thu 1030-1730; Sat 1400-1700. Non members adm charge to centre.*

Bure Marshes (EN): Extensive fen, broads, fen woodland and Hoveton Great Broad; nature trail can only be reached by boat, upstream from Salhouse Broad. *Early May-mid Sep (ex weekends).*

Cockshoot Broad (NNT): Boarded walkway (3/4 mile) along River Bure and Cockshoot dyke leading to bird hide overlooking the Broad. No dogs please.

Hickling Broad (EN, NNT): Large Broad, open reed and sedge beds, oak woodland. Passage waders in large numbers in spring and autumn; bittern, heron and bearded tit in summer. Stronghold of swallowtail butterfly. Boats may pass along the public channels. No dogs please. *Visitor Centre, Stubb Rd, Hickling, 1 Apr-30 Sep, daily, 1000-1700. Reserve all year, daily, 1000-1700, £2.00/NNT members free. Water trail 2 1/2 hr trip in boat: May & Sept, Tue, Wed, Thu; Jun, Jul & Aug, Mon-Fri; depart 1030 and 1430 from Pleasure Boat Inn. Advance booking essential. Tel: (069261) 276.*

Horsey Mere (NT): Winter wildfowl, with occasional swans; extensive reed beds and proximity to sea give it a special attraction to birds of passage. *Restricted access by boat.*

How Hill, Wildlife Water Trail, Broads Authority: Water trail by small electric launch. Trail covers river and dykes through marshes and fens of the How Hill Nature Reserve. Guide describes area, walk to bird hide. *1 Apr-31 May & 1-31 Oct, Sat, Sun, Bank Hols & Half Term week, 1100-1500. 1 Jun-30 Sep, daily, 10-5. £2.50/£1.50.*

Strumpshaw Fen, signposted from Brundall off A47 Norwich to Great Yarmouth road (RSPB): Broads, reedbeds and woodland with many birds including marsh harriers and kingfishers. Wild flower meadows, dragonflies and butterflies also notable. Information centre, observation hides and toilets. *All year 0900-2100 or sunset when earlier. Non members £2.50/£1.50. Warden: M Blackburn, Staithe Cottage, Low Road, Strumpshaw.*

Surlingham Church Marsh, north of A146 Norwich-Lowestoft road (RSPB): Former grazing marsh with dykes and pools. Nesting little ringed plovers and common terns. Circular walk of 1 1/2 miles starting by Surlingham church. Observation hides. Wellingtons or boots advisable. *Access at all times. Warden: Pete Bradley, 2 Chapel Cottages, The Green, Surlingham.*

Inland Norfolk

East Wretham Heath (NNT): Grassland heath with some woodland. Typical Breckland country, which in other areas has been much altered by recent afforestation. Sandy soil supports many continental plants unusual in England. *All year (ex Tue, Christmas and New Year) 1000-1700.*

East Winch Common, off the A47 at East Winch (NNT): One of the few large remnants of heathland in the county. Plants include heather, purple moor grass, sundew and beautiful marsh gentian. Dragonflies, damselflies and a variety of birds. Nature trail. No dogs please.

NATURE RESERVES

Minsmere Bird Sanctuary belongs to the RSPB

Foxley Wood, 6m NE East Dereham (NNT): Largest ancient woodland in the county. Wide rides benefit butterflies and the site is rich in wildflowers in the spring and summer. No dogs please. *Closed Thu.*

Honeypot Wood, from the A47 W East Dereham take the road to Wendling (NNT): Honeypot wood is a remnant of the ancient woodland that once covered Norfolk, there are rare plants and wild flowers in abundance. Concrete rides enable wheelchairs to get about the wood with comparative ease. No dogs please.

Lolly Moor, Westfield village, 3m S East Dereham (NNT): A small site with damp grassland, fen and wet woodland, actively managed for the Trust by local conservationists. The public are welcome to enter the reserve and there is a short nature trail. No dogs please.

Narborough Railway Line, 1m S Narborough village (NNT): A disused railway embankment composed of chalk ballast and supporting one of the best examples of chalk grassland in the county. The site is being managed jointly with Norfolk Branch of the British Butterfly Society. No dogs please.

Thompson Common, 4m S Watton via B111 (NNT): A mosaic of grasslands, pingos (shallow ponds formed during the ice age), scrub and woodland. Shetland ponies and roe deer graze the common. Nature trail. No dogs please.

Wayland Wood, 1m SE Watton, access from A1075 (NNT): An ancient and historic wood, still managed in the traditional way as coppice with oak standards. Wayland is mentioned in the Domesday book. Its name is derived from the Viking name of the wood "Wanelund", meaning sacred grove. No dogs please.

SUFFOLK

Bonny Wood, [TM 076520] Barking Tye, nr Needham Market (SWT): Ancient woodland with marvellous spring flowers. Leaflet available.

Bradfield Woods [TL 935581] 5m SE Bury St Edmunds (SWT): Outstanding ancient woodland coppiced since medieval times. Visitor Centre. Leaflet available. *Guided walks for groups by arrangement with the warden Tel: Rattlesden 7996.*

Bromeswell Green, [TM 296504] nr Melton (SWT): Variety of woodland, estuary and meadow habitats. Nature trail.

Carlton Marshes [TM 508918] nr Lowestoft (SWT): Grazing marsh and fen; Wetland birds. Visitor Centre. *Guided walks for groups by arrangement with the warden. Suffolk Broads Wildlife Centre on site. Tel: (0502) 564250.*

Cavenham Heath (EN): Area of heathland supporting wide range of birds. Access to area south of Tuddenham-Icklingham track only. Parking at Temple Bridge.

Cornard Mere, [TL 887388] nr Sudbury (SWT): Wetland important for birds and flowers.

Darsham Marshes [TM 420691] (SWT): Marsh, fen and woodland. Excellent birdlife and flora. Leaflet available.

Dunwich Heath (NT): One mile of sandy beach and gravel cliff with 214 acres of heathland. Exhibition, tea room, shop and holiday flats. *All year. Car park £1.00 (£1.50 Jul & Aug).*

Framlingham Mere [TM 284638] (SWT): Wet meadows and large shallow mere. Near castle. Circular walk. Good water birds.

Groton Wood, [TL 976428] nr Sudbury (SWT): Superb broadleaved wood, with large ancient small leaved lime grove. Bluebells and orchids. Leaflet available.

Havergate Island, Orford (RSPB): Britain's largest colony of avocets also breeding terns. Many wading birds in spring and autumn. Short boat crossing by permit in advance from *The warden J Partridge, 30 Munday's Lane, Orford, IP12 2LX (please enclose SAE). Members £2.50, non-members £5.00 payable on arrival.*

Lackford [TL 803708] 6m NW Bury St Edmunds (SWT): Award winning large gravel pits restored for wildlife. Much to see in summer and winter. Hides. Leaflet available.

Landguard, [TM 285315] nr Felixstowe (SWT): Wonderful coastal flora. Migrant and coastal birds. Leaflet available.

Martins Meadows, [TM 227573] nr Monewden (SWT): One of the finest hay meadows in Britain. Keep to edges of meadows.

Minsmere, nr Westleton (RSPB): 2,000 acres of marsh, lagoon, reedbed, heath and woodland. Immense variety of birds including bitterns,

marsh harriers and avocets. *All year, daily (ex Tue) 0900-2100 or sunset when earlier. Closed 25 & 26 Dec. Non-members £3/£1.50/£2. Access at all times from Dunwich cliffs to free public hides on beach. Warden: G Welch, Minsmere Reserve, Westleton, Saxmundham, Suffolk.*

Newbourne Springs [TM 271433] (SWT): Woods, fen, heath and reedbed with abundant songbirds in spring, including nightingales. Visitor Centre. Leaflet available.

North Warren, off B1122 one mile N Aldeburgh and from Aldeburgh-Thorpeness coast road (RSPB): Heathland, fen and grazing marshes. Breeding waders, heathland birds. *Access at all times. Warden: R Macklin, Firethorn Cottage, Rectory Road, Middleton, Saxmundham.*

Redgrave & Lopham Fen [TM 046797] (SWT): Large sedge and reed bed at source of rivers Waveney and Little Ouse. Boardwalk accessible for the disabled. Leaflet available. Reserve office Tel: (037988) 618.

Reydon Wood [TM 476790] (SWT): Ancient woodland and green lane. Nature trail provided. Leaflet available.

Trimley Marshes [TM 263532] (SWT): Marshes good all year, near estuary. Visitor Centre. 1 mile walk to hides.

Walberswick and Westleton Heaths, nr Saxmundham (EN): Extensive area of heathland and coastal habitats supporting a varied flora and fauna. *Access by public footpaths only.*

Wolves Wood, beside A1071 2m E Hadleigh (RSPB): Mixed deciduous wood with nightingales, woodpeckers and hawfinches. Observation hide and information centre. Access at all times from car park. Donations welcome. *Warden: c/o Stour Wood Reserve, 24 Orchard Close, Great Oakley, Harwich.*

NATURALISTS' ORGANISATIONS

(with abbreviations as used in text).

Broads Authority, 18 Colegate, Norwich, Norfolk. Tel: (0603) 610734.

BCWT: Beds & Cambs Wildlife Trust, Enterprise House, Maris Lane, Trumpington, Cambridge. Tel: (0223) 846363.

EBWS: Essex Birdwatching Society, The Saltings, 53 Victoria Drive, Great Wakering, Southend-on-Sea, Essex.

EWT: Essex Wildlife Trust, Fingringhoe Wick Nature Reserve, nr Colchester, Tel: (0206) 729678.

NT: The National Trust, Blickling, Norwich, Norfolk, Tel: (0263) 733471.

EN: English Nature (East Region), 60 Bracondale, Norwich, Tel: (0603) 620558.

NNT: The Norfolk Naturalists' Trust, 72 Cathedral Close, Norwich, Tel: (0603) 625540.

NOA: Norfolk Ornithologists' Association, Aslack Way, Holme-next-the- Sea, nr Hunstanton, Tel: (048525) 266.

RSPB: Royal Society for the Protection of Birds, Headquarters: The Lodge, Sandy, Beds, Tel: (0767) 680551. East Anglia Office, Stalham House, 65 Thorpe Road, Norwich, Tel: (0603) 661662.

SWT: Suffolk Wildlife Trust, Brooke House, The Green, Ashbocking, Ipswich. Tel: (0473) 890089.

PEOPLE TO HELP YOU EXPLORE THE AREA

EAST ANGLIA Registered GUIDE

GUIDED TOURS BY REGISTERED BLUE BADGE GUIDES

Each registered Guide has attended a training course sponsored by the East Anglia Tourist Board and can be identified when wearing the "Blue Badge". Regional Blue Badge Guides are further qualified to take individuals or groups around the region for half day, full day or longer tours if required. For a list of these Guides and an information sheet on Guiding Activities, please contact the East Anglia Tourist Board. The 10 towns/cities listed below support registered Guides. *Please contact the Tourist Information Centre (see pages 116-117) in the town/city for further information unless otherwise indicated.*

BURY ST EDMUNDS

Regular Town Tours: Tours lasting 1 1/2 hours leave from the Tourist Information Centre on Tue and Thu afternoons Jun-Sep and also Sun mornings Jul-Sep. Tickets can be purchased in advance, or on the day.
Tours for Groups: Guides can also be arranged for groups at any time. Please give at least one week's notice.

CAMBRIDGE

Regular Walking Tours: Individual visitors may join tours which leave the Tourist Information Centre daily and up to 5 times a day in summer. Colleges are included as available, generally not those which charge admission.
City Centre Tours: These tours do not go into the colleges, but explore the street scenes and the historic past of the city. Evening drama tours take place during mid summer.
Group Tours: Guides are available at any time for private groups. Each tour lasts about 2 hours. One guide can escort up to 20 people. Guides for the whole of East Anglia also available. Tel: (0223) 463290.
College Tours for Groups: All parties of 10 or more who intend to tour the colleges must be accompanied by a Cambridge registered Blue Badge Guide. Colleges which charge admission are only included on request (cost added to tour price). Most colleges are closed to the public during examination time, mid Apr-end Jun.
Fitzwilliam Museum, Trumpington Street. Regular tours take place during the summer and last about 1 1/4 hours. Groups may also book tours during museum opening times. Tel: (0223) 332900.

COLCHESTER

Regular Town Tours: Individuals may join the tours leaving the Tourist Information Centre daily during the summer, Mon-Sat 1400, Sun 1100. The tour takes about 1 3/4 hours.
Group Tours: May be booked at any time of year. Please give at least four days notice.

ELY

Cathedral & City Tours: Guides are available for pre-booked groups all year and tours may include the Cathedral and city, or just the city.

Cathedral Only Tours: Groups may book a special guided tour of Ely's magnificent Cathedral. Contact The Chapter Office, Tel: (0353) 667735 Mon-Fri, 0900-1600.
Regular Tours: Individuals may join these tours on Thu and Sat in Jul and Aug. Tours include the city and either the Cathedral or Oliver Cromwell's House.
Oliver Cromwell's House Tours: available for pre-booked groups all year round. The tour may be combined with a city tour.
Theme Tours: Tours can be arranged on a particular theme as required. For example, local pubs, ghosts, haunted places, the fens drainage story, photographic spots. By appt only.

IPSWICH

Regular Town Tours: Individuals may join the tours which leave the Tourist Information Centre, May-Sep, Tue 1415. Tours take about 1 hour.
Group Tours: Tours can be arranged for groups all year. Please give at least one week's notice.

KING'S LYNN

Regular Town Tours: Individuals may join the tours which leave the Tourist Information Centre May-Sept, Wed & Sat; Sun in Aug and each afternoon during Festival Week at 1400. The tour takes about 1 hour.
Group Tours: Guided tours can be arranged for groups by contacting the King's Lynn Town Guides Tel: (0553) 671925, 1800-2100 weekdays.

NORWICH

Regular City Tours: Historic Norwich walking tours leave from the Tourist Information Centre, lasting 1 1/2 hours: Easter Sun & Mon, 1030; Apr, May & Oct, Sat 1430; 23 May-30 Sep, Mon-Sat, 1430; Aug only 1030 & 1430; Jun-Sep, Sun 1030. Bank Hol tours, 1030.
Group Tours: Walking tours can be arranged for groups all year on a variety of themes all year. Please give at least one week's notice.
Coach Tours for Groups: Guides can be arranged to accompany a day or half day coach tour of East Anglia and Norwich. Assistance with itineraries.

PETERBOROUGH

Group Tours: Guides are available for city and cathedral tours at any time for private groups, each tour lasts approx 1 1/2 hours. Please give at least one week's notice.

SAFFRON WALDEN, DUNMOW & UTTLESFORD DISTRICT

Guided walking tours of Saffron Walden on Sun, 1500, leaving from the museum. Specialist tours by arrangement. Tel: (0799) 510445.

WALSINGHAM

Regular Tours: 31 Mar-end Sep, Wed 1100, Thu 1100; Jul and Aug also Thu 1430; Oct, Wed 1100. Tours last approx 2 hours. Tel: (0328) 820250.
Group Tours: All year by appt.

Cambridge and East Anglia Guided Tours - Half, full day or short break tour itineraries. Also specialist tours arranged to order. All tours accompanied by East Anglia Blue Badge Guides. Contact the Tours Organiser, Tourist Information Centre, Wheeler Street, Cambridge CB2 3QB. Tel: (0223) 463290/322640, Fax (0223) 463385.
Cycle Hire Centre. Byways Bicycles has a choice of cycles for hire, to suit all ages. Follow a planned route showing you local places of interest, pubs, tea rooms or picnic places, or choose your own. Cycling holidays also arranged. Byways Bicycles, Darsham, Nr Saxmundham, Suffolk IP17 3QD, Tel: (0728) 688764. Open Easter and May-Oct, 1000-1800 (at other times by appointment). Closed Tue.

Minsmere Cliffs

Just Pedalling. Well known for their cycling holidays. Also day or weekly hire of 3 speed and mountain bikes. Conveniently situated in the Broads area where cycling is easy and interesting. Open all year. Contact: Alan Groves, Just Pedalling, 9 Church Street, Coltishall, Norfolk NR12 7DW. Tel: (0603) 737201.
The National Stud, Newmarket. The 75 minute conducted tours will delight all animal lovers. The 8 horse stallion unit and up to 100 mares and foals are included in the visit. The guides give a full insight in to the workings of a modern thoroughbred stud. Open late Mar-Oct. Booking essential Tel: (0638) 663464.
Newmarket Equine Tours/National Horseracing Museum. Tour historic Newmarket with an expert guide. Watch racehorses exercising on the gallops and in the swimming pool. Visit a training yard and The National Stud. Combine old and new at the museum. Booking essential. Charges on request. Tel: (0638) 667333.
Rockingham Forest Tourism - Can help you discover Northamptonshire's countryside. Stately homes, where to stay, leisure drives, list of guides, walks, what's open. Contact them at: c/o Civic Centre, George Street, Corby, Northants NN17 1QB. Tel: (0536) 407507.
Windmill Ways Walking and Cycling Holidays in Norfolk. Leisurely breaks to suit individual tastes. Start and finish when you choose; travel at the pace you wish; complete personal service. Accommodation booked in quality guesthouses and hotels; maps, routes and local information provided; baggage transported; excellent touring, mountain or tandem bikes with back-up service. Colour brochure available. Windmill Ways, 50 Bircham Road, Reepham, Norfolk NR10 4NQ. Tel: (0603) 871111.

Beautiful Bury St Edmunds

Bury St Edmunds is an attractive mediæval market town situated in rolling Suffolk countryside.
The town has much to offer the visitor, including a theatre, art gallery, museums, 16th century Cathedral, attractive shops and magnificent gardens.
The West Stow Anglo-Saxon village is close by.
For details, contact the Tourist Information Centre, St Edmundsbury Borough Council, 6 Angel Hill, Bury St Edmunds, IP33 1UZ. Tel. 0284 764667.

St Edmundsbury Cathedral

Bury St Edmunds, Suffolk (next to the Abbey Gardens)

The Mother Church of Suffolk dating from 15th Century

Renowned for its warm and welcoming atmosphere

1000 needlepoint kneelers on display

Guided tours by arrangement

Tasteful Coffee Shop

Friendly Gift Shop

Tel: 0284 754933

BEAUTIFUL SOUTH SUFFOLK

Inspiration to Constable, Gainsborough and Munnings, this lovely part of Suffolk has much to offer.

For free visitor information, please contact:

**TOURISM DEPT. REF. EAG
BABERGH DISTRICT COUNCIL
CORKS LANE
HADLEIGH
IPSWICH
IP7 6SJ
Tel: (0473) 825846**

SOUTH SUFFOLK TOURISM

ESSEX

Heritage

Coast

Countryside

For further information, details of where to stay, places to visit and events, please contact the Essex Tourist Information Centre, County Hall, Chelmsford, Essex CM1 1GG, or phone (0245) 283400 (24 hrs.).

HERITAGE TOWNS

AMPTHILL

Ampthill, one of Bedfordshire's finest historic towns lies 8 miles south of Bedford. Radiating out from its crossroads are picturesque narrow streets lined mainly with Georgian houses, many of which were restored in the early 1950's by the former president of the Royal Academy, the architect and writer, Sir Albert Richardson. There are also many interesting Tudor buildings, and a cross now marks the spot where the 15th century castle stood, where Catherine of Aragon was sent while Henry VIII arranged the annulment of their marriage. Market day Thursday. Early closing Tuesday. *Further information from TIC.*

BEDFORD

The ancient county town of Bedford dates back to before Saxon times. The River Great Ouse flows through the town on its journey to the Wash. Since Victorian times the river has been cherished and attractive gardens, water meadows and riverside walks line the banks. The Embankment is one of the country's finest river settings with its graceful suspension bridge and bandstand, which today still plays host to concerts throughout the summer. The Bedford River Festival is held in May, in even numbered years. Held annually in May is the town's regatta which attracts oarsmen from all over the country. Bedford is internationally famous as the home of John Bunyan, author of The Pilgrim's Progress. His life story is portrayed in the Bunyan Museum, and the 16th century Moot Hall at Elstow. The town is dominated by fine buildings, which include the Bedford Museum and award winning Cecil Higgins Art Gallery and Museum. Market days Wednesday and Saturday. Early closing Thursday. *Further information from TIC.*

BUNGAY

An unspoilt market town standing on Suffolk's border with Norfolk, on the banks of the River Waveney. The Domesday Book noted 5 churches in Bungay and of these 2 remain. Bungay Castle, rebuilt in about 1300, stands as a reminder of the town's turbulent past. Largely rebuilt after the Great Fire in 1688, the town has many fine Georgian buildings. The Market Place contains

the Butter Cross, on top of which is the figure of Justice. There is wide variety of shops, all within easy walking distance of the Market Place. The town is encompassed by a well-signed footpath walk, the Bigod Way, providing a range of country walks 2 to 10 miles in length. *For free Tourist Guide, Tel: 0986 893243.*

BURNHAM-ON-CROUCH

The largest town in the area known as the Dengie Hundred, a peninsula abutting into the North Sea, bounded northward by the River Blackwater and southward by the River Crouch, dates back to prehistoric times. Throughout its history it has maintained a strong maritime flavour culminating today in its title "Pearl of the East Coast", evocative of the beautiful views across the River Crouch with its numerous yachts. There are various attractions including a large yacht harbour, two museums, a sports centre, pleasant shopping area and a good selection of pubs and restaurants. Early closing Wednesday. *Further information from Maldon TIC.*

BURY ST EDMUNDS

An ancient market town, full of history and Suffolk charm, and ideally situated for touring East Anglia. Cambridge, Ely and the Suffolk coast are within easy reach, as are Ickworth House, Clare Priory and Euston Hall. The country park at West Stow features a unique reconstructed Anglo-Saxon village and there are country parks at Clare and Nowton on the outskirts of the town. Bury St Edmunds has a wealth of historic buildings. The boards are still trodden at the Theatre Royal, a Regency theatre designed by William Wilkins,

and the Market Cross Art Gallery was designed by Robert Adam. Moyse's Hall Museum in the Market Place is a Norman building which houses local history collections and the Manor House is a brand new museum of fine arts and time keeping. There is a leisure centre with indoor swimming pools, a cinema and open air markets on Wednesday and Saturday. The Bury festival takes place each May. Early closing Thursday. *Tourist Information Packs (£2 inc postage) from TIC.*

CAMBRIDGE

The river, and the Roman road, made Cambridge an important settlement and market from early times. The Saxon tower of St Benet's Church, the mound built by William the Conqueror for his castle, and several medieval churches all survive. The Folk Museum (Castle Street) and the University Museum of Archaeology and Anthropology (Downing Street) have interesting items from the city's past. The University was established in the 13th century, and the first college, Peterhouse, was founded in 1284. The later medieval colleges, including King's and Trinity, were all built in or beside the existing town. The more modern colleges are scattered over west Cambridge, with the new faculty buildings. (Individual visitors may generally walk through the college grounds, but party organisers must

67

CAMBRIDGE

When in Cambridge make the most of your visit.

Join a Walking Tour, accompanied by a Blue Badge Guide.

Tours leave the Tourist Information Centre daily throughout the year.

For further information or details regarding the special arrangements necessary for groups, please contact:

The Tourist Information Centre, Wheeler Street, Cambridge CB2 3QB

Tel: (0223) 322640/463290
Fax: (0223) 463385

Please mention East Anglia Guide when replying to advertisements

contact the Tourist Office preferably well before their visit.) The Fitzwilliam Museum is one of the principal museums of fine and applied arts in Britain. Market days Mon-Sat. *Leaflet and Guide from TIC.*

COLCHESTER

Colchester is a marvellous mix of the old and new. Centuries old streets blend in with modern shopping centres. Large stores, small specialist shops - we have them all. Away from the shops, Colchester's famed history is everywhere to be seen. Parts of the original Roman wall can still be seen and Balkerne Gate near the Mercury Theatre is one of the largest surviving monuments of Roman Britain. The Norman castle, built on Roman foundations displays the town's magnificent archaeological collections. The Natural History museum just opposite has been re-displayed to reflect both current environmental concerns and the wonders of the natural world. The new leisure centre has a two level pool with falling rapids, sauna world and 24 lane bowling alley; there is also a 1200 seater hall. Other attractions well worth a visit are St Botolph's Priory and St John's Abbey gate house. Colchester is also home to the University of Essex which contributes considerably to the town. Local personalities who have lived in Colchester include John Ball, one of the leaders of the peasants' revolt of 1381, and William Gilberd, physician to Queen Elizabeth I. Daily walking tours of the town in the summer months. Market day Saturday. Early closing Thursday. *Further information from TIC.*

DEDHAM

Dedham Vale is described as 'Constable Country', and it was this countryside which inspired John Constable's paintings. A footpath leads along the edge of the River Stour to Flatford Mill and Willy Lott's cottage, the scene of his famous 'Hay Wain'. The village has a charm fitting with the mellow countryside. The grammar school which the young painter attended still exists although it now stands as 2 private houses. St Mary's Church commands the central position in the village, the building of which was financed by the wool merchant Thomas Webbe. South of the village the road passes Castle House, the home of the painter Sir Alfred Munnings. Early closing Wednesday. *Further information from TIP, Duchy Barn.*

DISS

Diss is a thriving market town set in the Waveney valley. It still retains much of its picturesque old world charm despite seeing a certain amount of modern development. The older part of the town is found around its market place and the site of the six acre mere – a lake which is a haven for ducks. St Mary's church is a fine imposing building which dominates the market place and has watched history pass it by for seven centuries. The streets leading from the church, the market place and mere feature a wealth of interesting architecture, and a variety of specialist shops and restaurants. Market and auction day Friday. Early closing Tuesday. *Further details from TIC.*

DUNSTABLE

At the junction of the 4000 year old Icknield Way and Roman Watling Street lies Dunstable, created early in the 12th century by Henry I. An Augustinian priory was founded here in 1131, and was later chosen by Henry VIII for the trial of his first wife, Catherine of Aragon. Very fine Norman work remains from the priory, including the nave arcade and the west front. The town is on the edge of the highest point in Bedfordshire, the Dunstable Downs, which offer stunning views over the county and are rich in wildlife. Market days Wednesday, Friday and Saturday. Early closing Thursday. *Further information from TIC.*

ELY

Ely Cathedral is a superb architectural achievement of the Middle Ages and is a dominating feature of the Fenland skyline. The Octagon is an engineering masterpiece and the Lantern above it is one of the finest examples of 14th-century carpentry. The great Lady Chapel (1321) retains the beauty of its carvings and tracery. It has a fine long Nave and the choir has 14th century stalls. Stained glass museum in North Triprium. Nearby is Oliver Cromwell's House which houses a themed tourist information and visitor centre. The Ely museum occupies one of the many old monastic buildings which surround the Cathedral. Along and near the Riverside Walk are interesting old houses and the attractive Maltings public hall. Antique and craft market Saturday, general market Thursday. Early closing Tuesday. *Mini-guide available from TIC.*

EPPING

Epping, now a busy little market town, dates from the 13th century and was once an important coaching centre. Some of the old coaching inns still survive along the attractive main street. Epping's long High Street follows the line of one of the 'purlieu banks' that marked the edge of the forest, which today, extends for some 270 acres north of the town. The Forest, almost 6,000 acres in total, is famous for its beautiful hornbeam trees. Market day Monday. Early closing Wednesday. *Book of maps of District (75p) and free guide from Council Information Desk, Civic Offices, High St. Tel: (0992) 560000.*

EYE

Retains the peaceful atmosphere and character of a small 18th century market town resting in the heart of the Suffolk countryside. The first definite evidence of a settlement dates from Roman times. The castle mound, which dates back to 1156, affords panoramic views of Eye and its surrounding countryside. The Church of St. Peter and St. Paul, founded in the 12th century with its magnificent tower and rood screen is particularly worth a visit. Town trail available. Early closing Tuesday. *Further information from Stowmarket TIC.*

FRAMLINGHAM

A quiet market town with many attractive buildings. The striking 12th century castle, built by Roger Bigod, is mainly intact and marvellous views may be seen from its battlements. The Lanman Museum in the castle grounds provides a valuable insight to the lives of the town's people. The Church of St. Michael contains historic tombs and effigies. It has close links with the Mowbrays and Howards, two important medieval families. The town has an interesting shopping centre and good sports centre. Market day Saturday. Early closing Wednesday. *Further information from Aldeburgh TIC.*

HADLEIGH

This busy market town in the valley of the River Brett is of special historical and architectural importance. At one time a Viking Royal Town, it later rose to become the 14th most prosperous town in the country through its wool trade during the 14th century and 15th century. The medieval heart of Hadleigh, St Mary's Church, the Deanery Tower and the Guildhall bears witness to its historical importance. Today the long High

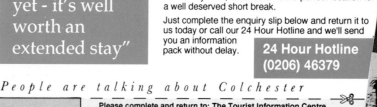
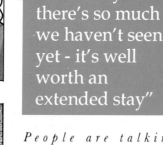
Please mention East Anglia Guide when replying to advertisements

70

Street has a wide variety of shops offering personal and friendly service. Hadleigh offers free parking. Market days Friday and Saturday. Early closing Wednesday. *Leaflet and accommodation list from TIC.*

HARWICH AND DOVERCOURT

Harwich still has a strong flavour of the medieval sea-faring township it once was. Christopher Jones, master of the Mayflower was married here, and Charles II took the first pleasure cruise from Harwich. During the time Samuel Pepys was MP for the town Harwich was the headquarters of the King's navy. Now, lightships, buoys and miles of strong chain are stored along the front and passengers arriving on the North Sea ferries at Parkeston Quay see the nine-sided High Lighthouse as the first landmark. Southwards along the coast is Dovercourt, with its new indoor swimming pool, the residential and holiday suburb of Harwich. Market day Friday. Early closing Wednesday. Holiday guide to the Essex Sunshine Coast from *Council Offices (EDU), Thorpe Road, Weeley, Clacton on Sea, Essex, CO16 9AJ. Information also from Harwich TIC. Tel: (0255) 256161.*

HOLT

A small, attractive country town just inland from the coast and nestling in undulating North Norfolk countryside. The main street is lined by Georgian buildings mainly built after the fire of 1708. The town has many picture galleries and bookshops. Holt is well known for the public school Greshams, founded in 1555. The North Norfolk Steam Railway has its terminus on the outskirts of the town, connecting Holt with the seaside resort of Sheringham. Market day Friday. Early closing Thursday. *For a free guide write to: Coast and Countryside, Dept EG94, Brochure Despatch Centre, Unit 28, Mackintosh Road, Rackheath Industrial Estate, Norwich, Norfolk NR13 6LH. Tel: 0603 721717 (24 hours).*

HUNTINGDON

Historically significant as the birthplace of Oliver Cromwell, popular as a National Hunt Racing venue, and now famous as the busy market town at the heart of John Major's Parliamentary constituency, Huntingdon was originally the old county town of one of England's smallest rural shires. The town grew up around a river crossing on the Great Ouse and by Norman times it was a provincial town with no less than 16 churches. The Black Death put an end to the town's early prosperity and it did not really return until the 18th century when improved roads saw the town gain importance as a staging post for coaches travelling on the Great North Road. Huntingdon's most famous son is Oliver Cromwell (born 1599). The Cromwell Museum now houses an interesting collection of personal items and portraits which once belonged to Cromwell and his family. Hinchinbrooke House on the outskirts of Huntingdon is the ancestral home of the Cromwell family. It opens to the public on Sunday afternoons. Market day Saturday. Early closing Wednesday. *Further information from TIC.*

IPSWICH

Ipswich is England's oldest heritage town. As Suffolk's county town it is a major commercial and shopping centre. Set in beautiful parkland Christchurch Mansion (1548), furnished as a country house contains the finest collection of Constable and Gainsborough paintings outside London. Within the Mansion is the Wolsey Art Gallery with an extensive programme of temporary exhibitions. Ipswich Museum contains replicas of the Sutton Hoo and Mildenhall Treasures and a Roman Villa display. The Ancient House has the country's finest example

of pargeting. Ipswich has 12 medieval churches, one of which has been designated the new TIC. The Tolly Cobbold brewery is well worth a visit for a guided tour. Sport and leisure facilities are excellent including the award winning Crown Pools. Most indoor and outdoor sports are available. Ipswich Town Football Club provides Premier Division football, with speedway and stock car racing just outside the town. First class live entertainment is provided by The Corn Exchange, the Wolsey Theatre and the Regent Theatre. There are 7 cinema screens, 2 nightclubs and a wide variety of restaurants. Market days Tuesday, Friday and Saturday. Early closing Wednesday. *Regular guided tours and a (sigposted) Town Trail from TIC. A tourist and accommodation guide (free) is available.*

KERSEY

Kersey church on its hilltop site dominates the village which runs steeply down The Street to a water-splash where ducks rest peacefully. Some call it the "prettiest village in England" and it certainly lives up to this. Many fascinating historic buildings line the main street, large merchants houses, weavers cottages and a medieval pub. Kersey's past prosperity as a settlement important for the manufacture of Kersey cloth, is reflected in the magnificence of the 14th century St Mary's Church. *Further information from Hadleigh TIC.*

KING'S LYNN

King's Lynn entertained King John before his last journey to Newark Castle, where he died. His baggage-train, following after him, badly miscalculated the tide and was lost crossing the Wash. People still look for the treasure and Lynn makes visitors believe in treasure trove. Medieval streets run down to the quays, merchant's houses with their private warehouses still present an aspect of considerable wealth and two guildhalls still function. One is the Town Hall, now housing Tales of the Old Gaol House, a new crime and punishment attraction as well as the splendid civic treasures, including a magnificent set of Charters dating right back to the days of King John (access through TIC) and the other is the King's Lynn Arts Centre home of the King's Lynn Festival (held the last two weeks of July). There are three museums including the Town House Museum of social history and True's Yard, a museum of King's Lynn's fishing quarter, two market places (with markets on Tuesday,

Friday and Saturday), many fine buildings to visit, plus Lynnsport and Leisure Park, East Anglia's newest and largest sports and leisure complex, and a cinema. The surrounding countryside is attractive, and contains several historic houses open to the public, including Sandringham, as well as a variety of other attractions. Early closing Wednesday. *Brochure from TIC.*

LAVENHAM

A beautifully kept example of a Suffolk wool town with superb ancient buildings. The church of Peter and St Paul stands proud to the south of the village with its 141 ft tower. The manufacture of various kinds of cloth and the preparation of wool and yarn were the main source of Lavenham's wealth for at least 500 years. The 16th century Guildhall is one of the finest Tudor half-timbered buildings in the country. Overlooking the market place it now contains an exhibition of local history items and the woollen cloth industry. *Further information from TIC.*

LEIGHTON BUZZARD

Situated on the Grand Union Canal, Leighton Buzzard has in modern times become famous for sand. It is essentially a market town and has a wide Georgian High Street with mews shops, an ancient street market and a fine parish church, which dates from 1277. It has a 190 foot spire, medieval graffiti and 13th century ironwork. The 15th century pentagonal market-cross at the centre of the town, has played host to witch trials, horse auctions and the calling of marriage banns. The Leighton Buzzard Narrow Gauge Railway was built in 1919 to carry sand from the quarries, but now offers passenger trips around the town. Market days Tuesday and Saturday. Early closing Wednesday. *Further information from South Bedfordshire District Council, High Street North, Dunstable, Bedfordshire LU6 1LF. Tel: (0582) 474014.*

LITTLE WALSINGHAM

A busy pilgrimage centre since the middle ages. The high street opens out into a square in the centre of which is a 16th century octagonal pump-house. Many of the religious buildings can still be seen including the Abbey and hostels used by the pilgrims over the centuries. There is an Anglican shrine built in 1931 which may be visited and a few miles away at Houghton St Giles is the Slipper Chapel. *Further information*

available from TIC. For a free guide write to: Coast and Countryside, Dept EG94, Brochure Despatch Centre, Unit 28, Mackintosh Road, Rackheath Industrial Estate, Norwich, Norfolk NR13 6LH. Tel: 0603 721717 (24 hours).*

LUTON

The fortunes of Luton were largely founded on the straw hat industry, which grew in the 17th century throughout the south of the county. Luton is proud of this tradition and tells the history of the industry in its museum. In recent years it has become a centre for modern industry, including car manufacturing. The Mossman Collection is a unique and nationally important collection of horse-drawn vehicles. The collection is located in Stockwood Park, together with the Stockwood Craft Museum and the Hamilton Finlay Sculpture Garden. Market days Monday to Saturday. Early closing Wednesday. *Further information from TIC.*

MALDON

The attractive town of Maldon lies on the Rivers Chelmer and Blackwater and is an important yachting centre and home of Thames sailing barges which can be seen by the Hythe quay. The town, granted a Royal Charter in 1171, has many interesting old buildings, including the 15th century Moot Hall, 17th century Plume library, riverside and canal walks and between the main streets run the attractive lanes and "chases" which are such a feature of the town. Fishing and sailing facilities. Market days Thursday and Saturday. Early closing Wednesday. *Explore the town or the surrounding district by obtaining various free publications, including the ETB Mini-Guide, from the TIC.*

MARCH

Occupying an island in the fens, March has a known history of 1,400 years. The old course of the River Nene winds its way through the centre past a beautiful park and picturesque riverside walks. The town is an oasis in the flatlands and

has a good shopping centre, ideal for river tourists. The medieval church of St Wendreda treasures a stunning 15th century double hammerbeam angel roof which displays 118 oak angels in full flight. A medieval stone base of a calvary cross stands by the wayside leading to the church. Market days Wednesday and Saturday. Early closing Tuesday. *Further information from Fenland District Council Tel: (0394) 54321 ext 311.*

NEEDHAM MARKET

A small town in the Gipping Valley with many pleasant country and riverside walks. It boasts Mid Suffolk's most popular recreation site, Needham Lake, with its fishing and picnic facilities. There are many attractive buildings in the town and of particular interest is the church interior with its dramatic hammerbeam roof. Craft and antique shops add further interest. Early closing Tuesday. *Further information from Stowmarket TIC.*

NEWMARKET

James I was the first king to visit Newmarket, primarily because the hunting was so good, but it was his Scottish nobles who introduced racing to England and found the heath at Newmarket so ideal for the matches which were then run usually between two horses at a time. Charles II was single-minded in his devotion to racing from the first, and Newmarket became during the racing season, in fact if not in name, the alternative court to Whitehall. The Rowley Mile racecourse takes its name from his hack Old Rowley. Nell Gwynn's cottage can still be seen, having escaped the fire of 1683 which consumed most of old Newmarket. The town became firmly established as the centre of horse racing and breeding a position which it still maintains, embodied in the handsome buildings of the Jockey Club in the High Street. The National Horse Racing Museum and the National Stud are well worth a visit. Market days Tuesday and Saturday. Early closing Wednesday. *Further information from TIC.*

NORWICH

It was George Borrow who wrote of Norwich "A fine old city, truly, view it from whatever side you will; but it shows best from the east." Indeed from St James' Hill on Mousehold Heath on a warm day in summer when the sky is blurred with heat, the view down on the city seems to come from an illustration to a medieval Book of Hours. The 33 medieval churches within the old walls, the course taken by the walls themselves, and the impregnable arm of the River Wensum describe the old city very much as it must have been. Descending into the town, the Norman Castle keep assumes a dominance it does not have viewed from above, and the delicate height of the Cathedral spire assumes its true proportions. The old Guildhall looks out on to the market place, a patchwork of stall awnings known locally as "tilts", which offers local produce in profusion. Narrow flint-cobbled streets, such as Elm Hill, lead past elegant town houses. Alleys and courtyards invite exploration. On the edge of the city the modern University includes the award winning Sainsbury Centre for Visual Arts. In addition to the Castle Museum, with its excellent Art Gallery, there are several other museums and galleries. Shopping facilities include many fascinating specialist shops and the new Castle Mall precinct. The ancient capital of East Anglia, Norwich is an ideal base from which to explore the region's wealth of market towns and villages, the many medieval churches, the unique Broads, and the coastline with its tranquil harbours, nature reserves, fishing villages and traditional seaside. Market days Monday to Saturday. Early closing Thursday. *Information pack available from TIC.*

ORFORD

A thriving port when Henry II had a castle built there in 1165. At that time the shingle spit separating the river from the sea ended near the quay. Since then the spit has extended 5 miles to the south west resulting in the port's decline, but not affecting the village's beauty. The river crossing to Orford Ness is now a place for mooring pleasure boats. The 90ft keep, all that remains of the castle, provides excellent views of the brick and timber cottages below and across to the marshes beyond. Good restaurants and walks. Car park by harbour. Early closing Wednesday. *Further information from Aldeburgh TIC.*

PETERBOROUGH

Peterborough combines the best elements of past and present with a perfect blend of thousands of years of history enhanced by a wealth of new facilities. At the heart of the city stands the great Norman cathedral which has dominated the city for over 750 years. Further evidence of Peterborough's past can be found at Flag Fen Bronze Age excavation and the Museum and Art Gallery. Steam enthusiasts can travel back in time on the Nene Valley Railway through Ferry Meadows Country Park to central Peterborough. For the lovers of historic buildings, you can choose to visit Longthorpe Tower with its collection of medieval wall paintings, or enjoy the grace of Burghley House. Combining these elements with first class leisure facilities, a riverside theatre, multi screen cinema, a 17th Century farm, waterfowl gardens and stone built villages - Peterborough is the ideal city. Market days daily except Sunday and Monday. *Various guides and leaflets available from TIC.*

ROYSTON

Royston lies at the crossing of the ancient Icknield Way and Ermine Street, and is said to have been named after the Lady Roysia who placed a cross set in stone to mark this crossing. The town has several interesting houses and inns, and an unusual bell shaped cave, thought to be pre Roman. There is a small local history museum. Market days Wednesday and Saturday. *Further information from Royston Town Hall, Royston, Herts SG8 7DA. Tel: (0763) 245484.*

SAFFRON WALDEN

The ancient town of Saffron Walden has revolved around its market for many generations. The medieval market rows are well preserved and timber-framed buildings abound, many decorated by pargeting. The church, reputed to be the largest in Essex, dominates the town and nearby are the remains of the Norman Castle. On the Common is a rare earth maze, also a restored hedge maze at Bridge End Gardens. The Museum is known for its ethnographic department and also houses a large collection of local interest including many Saxon finds. The Saffron Crocus can be seen flowering outside the Museum in the autumn. It has never been proved that Cromwell's headquarters were in the Sun Inn but Henry Winstanley was certainly born in the town. Nearby is the Jacobean mansion of Audley End. Market days Tuesday and Saturday. Early closing Thursday. *Town Trail leaflet from TIC.*

ST IVES

An attractive riverside market town, St Ives grew up on the site of a busy Easter Fair at a river crossing on the Great Ouse near the old Saxon village of Slepe. In its heyday in the 13th century, the fair was one of the 4 biggest in the country, and merchants from all over Western Europe came to buy cloth on Huntingdonshire looms. The most notable landmark in St Ives today is the 15th century stone bridge and bridge chapel in the town centre. At that time in England there were many such chapels but now only 3 remain. These chapels provided a retreat for travellers, and it is believed they also served as toll houses. Oliver Cromwell is St Ives most famous resident. His short residence is marked by the impressive statue in the market place, which was erected in 1901 to mark the 300th anniversary of his birth. Market days Monday and Friday. Early closing Thursday. *Further information from Huntingdon TIC.*

ST NEOTS

Standing proudly on The River Great Ouse, St Neots grew up around a 12th century Benedictine Priory. A market charter was granted in 1130 and the town flourished. The old Priory was finally closed and demolished during the Dissolution of the Monasteries (1536-1539). In the 17th and 18th centuries there was much rebuilding in the town. The river was dredged, and sluices were built enabling goods to be brought in by water. Today the importance of the town's position on the Great North Road can be seen in the handsome rectangular market place and the town's surviving coaching inns and hostelries. On fine summer days visitors and residents alike make their way to the Riverside and Priory Parks to boat or fish, enjoy a picnic, listen to a band concert or simply take in the natural beauty.

HERITAGE TOWNS

Walking enthusiasts can join the Ouse Valley Way in Riverside Park or set off on the Town Trail from the Market Square. The 15th century parish church of St Mary is a well known local landmark with its 130ft church tower and splendid perpendicular architecture. Market day Thursday. Early closing Thursday. *Further information from Huntingdon TIC.*

STOWMARKET

Stowmarket is a busy market town and an important shopping centre for the surrounding countryside. During the 17th and 18th centuries, the town was a noted centre of the woollen trade and the River Gipping was canalised between Stowmarket and Ipswich to carry the town's trade. A walk can be taken along the former towpath through the woods and meadows by the river. Stowmarket's Museum of East Anglian Life is worth a visit. Market days Thursday and Saturday. Early closing Tuesday. *Further information available from TIC.*

SUDBURY

Sudbury is a thriving market town, very much the centre of the smaller villages and communities which surround it. Mentioned in the Domesday Survey of 1086, Sudbury stands on the River Stour which winds round three sides of the town. River meadows surrounding the town provide excellent walking. Sudbury still retains many ancient and interesting buildings. The weaving industry here dates back to the 13th century, and even today the finest silk, including that used in the Princess Royal's wedding dress, is woven in Sudbury. The present main centre is the Market Hill, dominated by St Peter's church, no longer used for regular worship, but now the home for concerts and exhibitions. Before the door stands the bronze statue of Thomas Gainsborough, the town's most famous son. Gainsborough's House, where the famous painter was born, is now preserved as a delightful museum with an exhibition gallery. Market days Thursday and Saturday. Early closing Wednesday. *Leaflet and accommodation list from TIC.*

SWAFFHAM

First-time visitors to Swaffham are always impressed at the extent of the triangular-shaped market place which gives the town an air of expansive tranquillity, transformed every Saturday by the famous open-air market and lively public auction. Around the market place are many fine Georgian buildings. Close by stands the majestic church of St Peter and St Paul, one of the finest of the medieval churches in East Anglia. It has a magnificent hammerbeam roof, with carved angels. Swaffham is an ideal touring

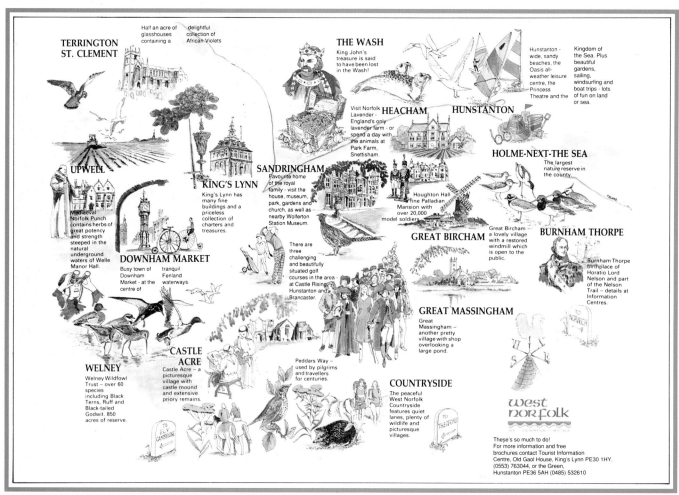

Please mention East Anglia Guide when replying to advertisements

centre for the many attractions of North West Norfolk. Craft market Wednesday. Early closing Thursday. *Further information and free brochure from Swaffham TIP.*

THAXTED

Thaxted has been a community since Saxon times, with its greatest days in the 14th and 15th centuries when it prospered because of its cutlery industry. It was at this time that the Guildhall was built and that the present shape of the town grew up, with little houses, some white, some colourwashed or half timbered, winding down the hill past the church into Town Street. The tall spire of the church is one of the landmarks of Thaxted, soaring 181 feet above the town. The other well-known sight is the windmill built in 1804 by John Webb. From the top floor the view of the town and surrounding countryside is quite outstanding. Market day Friday. Early closing Wednesday. *Further information from Saffron Walden TIC.*

THETFORD

Thetford has been a thriving market town since before the Norman Conquest, and many traces of its fascinating past remain, from the IronAge ramparts surrounding the Norman castle mound, to the stately priory ruins and the fine buildings of the town centre's Conservation area. 1000 years ago Thetford was one of the largest towns in the country, archaeological digs have revealed important Roman, Saxon and Iron Age finds. Thetford is a wonderful centre for river and forest walks. It has an excellent little museum in the picturesque 15th century Ancient House, just a few yards from the birthplace of Thomas Paine, "Father of the American Revolution". The Charles Burrell Museum tells the story of this once world famous manufacturer of steam traction engines. There is a good Sports Centre and a thriving Arts Centre, with year-round arts and crafts exhibitions and workings. Thetford offers the best of both worlds a lively town in lovely countryside. Market days Tuesday and Saturday. Early closing Wednesday. *Further information available from Ancient House Museum, White Hart Street, Thetford. Tel: (0842) 752599.*

WISBECH

The present day character of Wisbech is mainly that of a prosperous Georgian market town. Indeed, the North Brink, the Crescent and Museum Square must be among the finest examples of Georgian street architecture in the country. The town grew up around its port, trading from medieval times but flourishing commercially with the draining of the Fens in the 17th century. The years 1700-1850 witnessed tremendous growth, which established the fine buildings seen today. Whilst the port has declined in importance, Wisbech remains the market centre for a large agricultural and horticultural area. Of particular note in the town are buildings including Elgood's historic brewery, Peckover House and Gardens, the Old Market, the Market Place and the Crescent area (including the Wisbech and Fenland Museum). Octavia Hill, one of the founders of the National Trust, lived at No. 8 South Brink. The Angles Centre presents theatre and exhibitions all year. Two modern shopping centres complement the traditional retail areas. Auctions of plants and produce Monday to Friday, 1600 at Cattle Market Chase and household effects and bygones on Wednesday and Saturday, 1000. Market days Thursday and Saturday. Early closing Wednesday. *Free Town Trail, Accommodation and Visitor Guide from TIC.*

WOBURN

A small and beautifully preserved Georgian town, acknowledged as one of the most important historic towns in Britain. Woburn Abbey, home of the Dukes of Bedford for over 300 years is set in a magnificent 3000 acre deer park. The house was rebuilt in the mid 18th century and contains an extensive art collection. Britain's largest drive through safari park, Woburn Wild Animal Kingdom is home to a variety of species. The Heritage Centre is housed in old St Mary's church, combining a museum of Woburn's history with Tourist Information. *Further information from Woburn Heritage Centre or Ampthill TIC.*

WOODBRIDGE

Built on the banks of the Deben, it is not hard to believe this quiet, mainly Georgian town has a history of shipbuilding and sail-making. The name 'Woodbridge' derives from the Saxon language meaning Woden's town, and in later years

people have been searching for centuries to find the wooden bridge after which the town was supposedly named! Its famous Elizabethan Statesman, Thomas Seckford has left his mark on the town. His endowment of almshouses in Woodbridge and investment in properties in London means the Seckford Foundation is still in being today. The Shire Hall on Market Hill was built by him, and the Seckford family home is now a hotel outside Woodbridge. The famous Tide Mill has been restored to full working order and is open to the public. From the quay enjoy a walk along the sea wall path. St Mary's church has a large 15th century West tower with strange buttresses that change shape as they ascend. *Tourist information from: Council Offices, Melton Hill (0394) 383789.*

WYMONDHAM

Wymondham (pronounced "Win-dum") retains all the character of a historic market town. The recently restored ancient octagonal timber framed Market Cross dominates the Market Place. The Green Dragon public house is the oldest inn. It has a fine half timbered facade with a gabled dormer window and a carved head of a bearded man supporting the jetty. Wymondham Abbey, founded in 1107 is dominated by its two tall towers which appear against the skyline from whatever side one approaches. The interior is very impressive with its ranks of arches and windows soaring up to the beautiful hammerbeam roof. The local museum tells the story of the town, which was once an important weaving centre. Opened in 1845 the railway station once served an important junction. It has been beautifully restored and now houses a museum of railway memorabilia. Market day Friday. Early closing Wednesday. *Further details from TIP.*

ALDEBURGH

The wide High Street, with its cottages and shops, runs north-south just a stone's throw from the shingle beach where the lifeboat is always ready. Fishermen draw up their boats on to the beach and sell their fish. The Moot Hall, the Tudor centre of the town, stands exposed only yards from the sea, which over the centuries has whittled away the shoreline. Benjamin Britten and Peter Pears began the Aldeburgh Festival in 1948 and it has developed into a year-round programme of music and arts, shared between Aldeburgh and Snape Maltings concert hall. The Aldeburgh Festival is in June, the Maltings Proms in August. Thorpeness village, a seaside village created in 1910 is just two miles up the coast. Winner of the Tidy Britain Group Premier Seaside Award for cleanliness of beach and water. *TIC*.

BRIGHTLINGSEA

Once an important fishing town, Brightlingsea is now a yachting centre with one of the best stretches of sailing on the East Coast. Superb walks along the banks of Brightlingsea Creek and the River Colne offer the naturalist a chance to study birdlife on the saltings. *Holiday guide to the Essex Sunshine Coast from Council Offices (EDU), Thorpe Road, Weeley, Clacton-on-Sea, Essex, CO16 9AJ. Tel: (0255) 256161.*

CLACTON-ON-SEA

Clacton-on-Sea's south facing seven mile long sandy beach forms the sunshine holiday coast of Essex. It is a strikingly clean town with tree-lined streets and colourful gardens. An everyday holiday programme of entertainments, events, leisure centre, sports and recreation, also coastal

trips and coach excursions, is planned to provide a variety of interests to suit most tastes. The town is an ideal centre for visiting a number of historic houses and castles. The beach has gently sloping sand. The Princes Theatre and West Cliff Theatre, pier, and various amusement centres provide a wide range of exciting attractions. *TIC. Holiday guide to the Essex Sunshine Coast from Council Offices (EDU), Thorpe Road, Weeley, Clacton-on-Sea, CO16 9AJ. Tel: (0255) 256161.*

CROMER

Dominated by its parish church the town of Cromer stands in a cliff top setting, with wide sandy beaches running down to the sea. It is famous for its fishing boats that still work off the beach and offer freshly caught crabs. The town boasts a fine pier theatre, museums and lifeboat station along with the usual seaside attractions. A week not to be missed is carnival week held in August. *TIC. For a free guide write to Coast and Countryside, Dept EG94, Brochure Despatch Centre, Mackintosh Road, Rackheath Industrial Estate, Norwich, Norfolk, NR13 6LH. Tel: (0603) 721717 (24 hours).*

FELIXSTOWE

A popular resort town between the estuaries of the rivers Deben and Orwell on the Suffolk coast. It is popular as a family resort with a playground, boating lake, model yacht pond, miniature railway, amusement park and the beach itself which is safe at all states of the tide and is a mixture of sand and shingle. The Spa Pavilion Theatre presents a lively and wide-ranging programme of entertainment throughout the year and the Leisure Centre has three swimming pools and a sauna, fitness area and lounge bars. Felixstowe is justly proud of its cliff gardens which provide a floral welcome all year. The resort is an ideal centre from which to tour the lovely and historic Suffolk countryside. Sea and river cruises, and ferries across the River Orwell to Harwich. Events: May Folk Festival, Championship Driving Tests, Drama Festival; July High Season Entertainment at Spa Pavilion begins, East of England Lawn Tennis Championships, Deben Week Regatta; Aug Felixstowe Carnival; Nov Fishing Festivals. *Guided tours in season. TIC.*

FRINTON-ON-SEA AND WALTON-ON-THE-NAZE

Frinton, sited on a long stretch of sandy beach, is quiet, secluded and unspoilt. Its main shopping street has been named the "Bond Street of East Anglia". Summer theatre and other open-air events take place during the season. A variety of attractive hotels and guest houses face the magnificent greensward on the clifftop. Frinton also has excellent golf and tennis clubs. Walton is more fun of the fair. It is a jolly, quaint little resort which focuses on the pier with all its attractions. The sea front has good sand and to the rear of Walton are the Backwaters, a series of saltings and little harbours leading into Harwich harbour. Indoor swimming pool on the seafront and new multi-purpose hall called the Columbine Centre. *TIP. Holiday guide to the Essex Sunshine Coast from Council Offices (EDU), Thorpe Road, Weeley, Clacton-on-Sea, CO16 9AJ. Tel: (0255) 256161.*

GREAT YARMOUTH

Is one of Britain's most popular seaside resorts with wide sandy beaches and the impressive Marine Parade which has colourful gardens and almost every imaginable holiday attraction and amenity. The award-winning multi-million pound leisure complex, the Marina Centre, offers a huge variety of all-weather sports and entertainment facilities, including a swimming pool with waves! Gorleston has a wide promenade lined with flower gardens and old streets dating from the days when it was an important sea port. The sandy beaches outside the town are unspoilt. Great Yarmouth is also an interesting historical centre, sections of the old walls remain and there are numerous museums and other places of

Please mention mention East Anglia Guide when replying to advertisements

78

historic interest to be explored. Boating: Yacht Station and Port of Yarmouth Marina; day cruises to the Broads, Broads sailing and day boats for hire. Entertainment: Huge variety, including star-name live shows at various theatres and venues - Britannia Theatre (Tel: 0493 842209), July-mid Sept. Gorleston Pavilion (Tel: 0493 622832) early June-end Sept. Hippodrome (Tel: 0493 844172), early July-Sept. Wellington Pier Theatre (Tel: 0493 844945 or 842244), early June-mid Sept. Winter Garden (Tel: 0493 844945), early June-late Sept, variety family entertainment. Royalty Theatre (Tel: 0493 842043), early July-mid Sept, summer show and latest film presentations. St Georges Theatre (Tel: 0493 858387) June-Sept, summer show; remainder of year, concerts, recitals, plays etc. Marina Centre Piazza (Tel: 0493 851521) entertainment nightly, late June-late Sept. Also horse racing and numerous other holiday attractions including 'Kingdom of the Sea' Sealife Centre, Ripley's 'Believe it or Not' exhibition, 'Treasure World' underseas exhibition and a huge Pleasure Beach with all the latest rides. *Full details of all facilities and accommodation included in Holiday Guide available from TIC, price 50p (in advance by post, free).*

HUNSTANTON

Hunstanton possesses two quite distinct physical features: it is famous for its striped cliffs, made of successive layers of carr stone, red chalk and white chalk; and unlike any other resort in East Anglia, the town faces west. Winner of the European Blue Flag and Tidy Britain Group Premier Seaside Award for cleanliness of beach and water. Hunstanton's wide sandy beaches are excellent for bathing, and it is also popular with boating, windsurfing and water-skiing enthusiasts. Hotels and guest houses are bounded to the south by well laid out caravan sites and holiday centres and to the north, cliffs slope away to the dunes and quiet sandy beaches. The focal point of the town is the large, open greensward known as "The Green", and there are the lovely Esplanade Gardens sloping gently down to the sea. The Oasis all weather leisure centre, Princess Theatre, Jungle Wonderland and the Kingdom of the Sea are favourite attractions for visitors. *Free brochure from TIC.*

LOWESTOFT AND OULTON BROAD

Lowestoft successfully combines its role as a leading holiday resort with that of a modern fishing and commercial port. Lowestoft South Beach is winner of the Tidy Britain Group Seaside Award for cleanliness of beach and water. Oulton Broad, one of the finest stretches of inland water in England, offers the chance to get afloat in a range of craft from modern cruiser or day boat to sailing dinghy or rowing boat. Add to the natural amenities such facilities as theatre, the East Point Pavilion indoor tourist centre, indoor and outdoor swimming pools, attractive parks, putting and bowling greens, tennis courts,

boating lakes, sports centre, American theme park, museums, high speed motor boat racing, and concerts, naturist beach, and you have the making of an ideal family holiday. The staff of the tourist information centre in the East Point Pavilion will do all they can to make your stay a happy one. They will offer help in finding accommodation, and suggest things to do and places to visit, and arrange a tour of the fishing industry or book a theatre seat. Lowestoft and Oulton Broad is a fine holiday centre where a warm welcome is assured. *TIC. Free Waveney Guide available from Room 2, District Technical & Leisure Services Dept, Mariners Street, Lowestoft NR32 1JT. Tel: (0502) 565989 (answerphone).*

SHERINGHAM

Sheringham is a mixture of Victorian and Edwardian houses which has grown up around its fishing traditions. The original village is still the haunt of seafarers who carry on the brave tradition of manning the lifeboat. Sandy beaches and a range of amusements and activities are to be found in and around Sheringham. Attractions include the North Norfolk Steam Railway, museums, theatre and the Splash Fun Pool. *TIC. For a free guide write to Coast and Countryside, Dept EG94, Brochure Despatch Centre, Unit 28, Mackintosh Road, Rackheath Industrial Estate, Norwich, Norfolk, NR12 6LH. Tel: (0603) 721717 (24 hours).*

SOUTHEND-ON-SEA

Re-discover this Thames side resort, with seven miles of beach lined promenades, fringed with pretty parks, elegant esplanades and lively amusements. Winners of the Tidy Britain Group Seaside award for cleanliness of beach and water at East Beach, Shoeburyness and Three Shells Beach. A visit to the town is never complete without walking on the longest pleasure pier in the world (1.33 miles), or ride on the unique pier trains. The High Street shops, boutiques and street markets provide excellent shopping. Relax for a while in one of the many parks and gardens, Britain in Bloom Regional Award and National Finalist, or take the shuttle train from the Sea Life Centre along the sea front up through Cliff gardens to the Cliffs Pavilion, the family entertainment

centre. Along with the many attractions, there are lots of special events taking place throughout the year. *TIC. For a free guide and events list contact: Marketing Department, PO Box 6, Southend-on-Sea, SS2 6ER. Tel: (0702) 355120.*

SOUTHWOLD

Southwold is an elegant and attractive town standing on the cliff top facing the sea, with its mixture of sand and shingle beach. Winner of the European Blue Flag and Tidy Britain Group Premier Seaside Award for cleanliness of beach and water. Fishermen's cottages, pleasant old streets and green open spaces give it much character. Discreetly fashionable as a Victorian bathing place, there is still an atmosphere of old-fashioned charm. Trade with northern Europe has left its mark on many buildings in Southwold, which show a marked Dutch influence, although the battle of Sole Bay between the Dutch and English fleets was just off the coast here (and commemorated in the local brewery's Broadside Ale). *TIC. Free Waveney Guide available from Room 2, District Technical & Leisure Services Dept, Mariners Street, Lowestoft, Tel: (0502) 565989 (answerphone).*

WELLS-NEXT-THE-SEA

A small but busy port for coasters and the local whelk and shrimp boats. Wells is a town of narrow streets and flint cottages with interesting shops. There are two steam railways, a small line runs from the quay to the Pinewoods Caravan Park which offers pitch and putt, a canoeing lake and the beach beyond; or you can enjoy a ride on the narrow gauge railway to Walsingham. Sandy beaches, nature reserves and miles of footpaths make Wells-next-the-Sea an ideal holiday town. Winner of the Tidy Britain Group Seaside Award for cleanliness of beach and water. *TIC. For a free guide write to Coast and Countryside, Dept EG94, Brochure Despatch Centre, Mackintosh Road, Rackheath Industrial Estate, Norwich, Norfolk, NR13 6LH. Tel: (0603) 721717 (24 hours).*

GOOD BEACH GUIDE

On the north Norfolk coast there are wonderfully big beaches where the sea goes out for miles and where it is possible to get away from everything. On the East Coast beaches tend to be narrower, and shelve steeply. Suffolk beaches are always safer and more attractive at low tide when there is normally a strip of clean sand and the beaches shelve less steeply. (Tide tables can always be found in the East Anglian Daily Times.) At Hunstanton the high tide comes right up to the promenade as it does at Clacton, ensuring a clean beach but restricted space as high water approaches. Beware undercurrents particularly where beaches shelve steeply, and remember that the current flows south on the flood and north on the ebb and can run quite strongly, especially when the wind is in the same direction. Although East Anglia has more sunshine than most parts of the country there can be onshore easterly winds so a windbreak can be useful. Groynes constructed to stop erosion also make useful shade and shelter for picnics. Beware of strong offshore winds; these take effect 50 to 100 metres from the beach, air beds and small inflatables are very vulnerable.

Dunwich beach, Suffolk

NORFOLK

1 Hunstanton
Winner of the European Blue Flag and Tidy Britain Group Premier Seaside Award (Resort Beach category). Sandy beaches make an ideal playground for children, whilst windsurfers find the Wash an excellent location for their sport. To the north there are red and white cliffs and then sand dunes and a quieter beach at Old Hunstanton. The beach is very gently shelving and when the tide goes out it makes a pleasant walk for a swim. Deck-chairs. Pony rides. Pitch and putt and crazy golf courses. Specially designed route for wheelchairs along the seafront. Car parking. Toilets. Dog Ban. TIC.

2 Holme-next-Sea
A long unspoilt sandy beach with a wild area of dunes and marshes at Gore Point. Nearby 400-acre nature reserve. Approached via Holme village (approx 2 miles). Car parking. Toilets.

3 Brancaster
Very quiet broad sandy beach with dunes. Approached by lane leading north from the village.

The tide retreats for more than a mile to the east, but not so far to the west. Car parking. Toilets.

4 Holkham
A huge private sheltered sandy beach with dunes backed by pine trees. A favourite spot for picnics and swimming. The tide goes out for miles. Car parking along Lady Anne's Drive on payment of fee in summer, but free in winter.

5 Wells-next-the-Sea
The wide spacious beach is a mile from the town, and is reached across dunes, or by the narrow gauge railway. Consisting of sand and shingle, the beach has a large boating lake known as Abraham's Bosom and pine trees on one side with the harbour channel on the other side. Winner of the Tidy Britain Group Seaside Award (Resort Beach category). Car parking. Toilets. Wells is famous for its cockles, whelks and shrimps. Dog Ban. TIC.

6 Sheringham
A beach of sloping pebbles and shingle above sand. Rocks and groynes with shallow pools at low tide. Low cliffs. Fishing boats are hauled up on the beach. Amusements and refreshments. Deck-chairs. Car parking. Toilets. Dog Ban. TIC.

7 East Runton & West Runton
Gently shelving sand and shingle beaches backed by low crumbling cliffs. Groynes. Rocky at low tide. Car park. Dog ban at West Runton. Toilets.

8 Cromer
Gently shelving sandy beach with shingle and pebbles, the west beach is more shingly than the east one. Shallow pools at low tide. Cliffs. Pier with entertainment. Famous lifeboat. Crab fishing. Deck-chairs. Car parking. Toilets. Dog Ban. TIC.

9 Overstrand
Gently shelving sandy beach with pedestrian access. Groynes, pleasant cliff-top walks. Small car park. Toilets. Dog Ban.

10 Mundesley
Quiet holiday resort built in a dip in the coast line. Cliff path access to a smooth sandy beach between groynes. Deck-chairs. Car parking. Toilets. Dog Ban. TIC.

11 Winterton-on-Sea
Very wide sandy beach backed by extensive sand dunes. Pools at low tide. Nature reserve. Car park. Toilets. TIP.

12 Hemsby
Wide sandy beach scattered with stones and backed by grassy dunes. Amusements and deck-chairs. Boat trips. Car parking. Toilets. TIP.

13 Scratby/California
Low cliffs and long track down to wide sandy beach. Shallow pools at low tide. Amusements on cliff top at California. Car park at Scratby. Toilets. TIP.

14 Caister-on-Sea
Wide sandy beach which shelves steeply in some places. At the north end, towards California, there are low sandy cliffs. Low sea wall with dunes behind. Boat trips. Volunteer Lifeboat Station. Deckchairs. Car parking on Beach Road (central beach). Toilets. Picnic area. TIP.

15 Great Yarmouth
Very long sandy beach lined by the Marine Parade with its colourful gardens and countless attractions and amenities. Two piers with entertainment. Dunes at North beach. Boat trips, trampolines, and numerous refreshment stalls. Marina Centre. Deckchairs. Beach huts and tents. Car parking. Toilets. Dog Ban. TICs.

16 Gorleston
Quieter than nearby Great Yarmouth. Flat sandy beach with some pebbles. Dog ban on northern section from ravine to harbour. Pier, forming part of harbour entrance. Amusements. Low cliffs between sea wall and promenade. Beach chalets. Deck-chairs. Car parking. Toilets. Dog Ban. TIP.

17 Hopton
Flat sandy beach with some shingle beneath low cliffs. TIP.

SUFFOLK

18 Corton
Sand and shingle beach, with southern area available to naturists. Car parking in official car park. Dog Ban.

19 Lowestoft
South Beach is the sandy pleasure beach with two piers. Winner of the Tidy Britain Group Seaside Award (Resort Beach category). Punch and Judy. Deck-chairs. Amusements. The East Point Pavilion is a new indoor tourist centre. Ness Point is Britain's most easterly point. The North Beach, is somewhat quieter and sandy with cliffs and sand dunes. Car parking. Toilets. Dog Ban. TIC.

20 Pakefield
Sandy beach scattered with shingle below low grassy cliffs. Car parking. Toilets. Dog Ban.

21 Kessingland
Easy access to pebble and shingle beach with some sand. Low cliffs. River. Suffolk Wildlife & Country Park nearby. Winner of the Tidy Britain Group Premier Seaside Award (Rural Beach category). Dog Ban.

22 Southwold
Part sand, part shingle beach depending upon tides, with some dunes for sheltered picnics. Uncommercialised, but pots of tea are available on the beach. Short pier with amusements and refreshments. Deck-chairs and beach huts. Parking. Toilets. TIC. Winner of the European Blue Flag and Tidy Britain Group Premier Seaside Award (Resort Beach category). Dog Ban.

23 Walberswick

Approached over The Flats, the beach is sand and shingle with sand dunes. It becomes steeper and more shingly to the south with some pebbles. Popular with painters and birdwatchers. Stall selling fish on beach. Car parking. Toilets.

24 Dunwich

Short walk to shelving sand and shingle beach above sand. High eroding cliffs should be avoided. There is marsh, dunes and more sand to the north. Winner of the Tidy Britain Group Seaside Award (Rural Beach category). Nature reserve at nearby Dunwich Heath. Occasional underwater exploration of old submerged town destroyed by storms – they say you can hear the church bells from beneath the waves! Car parking. Toilets.

25 Thorpeness

Steeply shelving shingle beach with some sand at low tide. Dunes and low cliffs starting to the north. Curious holiday resort developed in early 1900s with varied architectural styles. Car parking limited. Toilets.

26 Aldeburgh

Quiet unspoilt resort. Long steeply shelving shingle beach with groynes. Winner of the Tidy Britain Group Premier Seaside Award (Rural Beach category). Lifeboat. Fishing boats hauled up, with stalls selling fresh fish daily. Car parking. Toilets. Dog Ban. TIC.

27 Shingle Street

As its name suggests, a steep shingle beach particularly good for bracing walks and beachcombing (sometimes you can find amber). Popular for offshore fishing. Very limited car park.

28 Felixstowe

Popular south-east facing holiday resort with Leisure Centre (three swimming pools), seafront gardens, pier, museum, amusements and entertainment. Shelving sand and shingle beach with little tidal movement. Some groynes down to pebbles and sand. Low cliffs to the north. Deckchairs and beach huts for hire. Car parking. Two-mile long promenade with public seating. Toilets. Dog Ban. TIC.

ESSEX

29 Walton-on-Naze

Traditional resort with a gently shelving sandy beach. Groynes, cliffs and dunes at The Naze a grassy area on low cliffs giving excellent views of the busy shipping lanes around Harwich and Felixstowe. Nature trail. Pier and groynes. Donkey rides, deck-chairs. Speedboat trips. Putting and tennis. Refreshment kiosks at regular intervals along the seafront. Car parking. Toilets. Dog Ban. TIC.

30 Frinton-on-Sea

Wide expanse of greensward on top of low cliffs above a wide gently shelving sandy beach. A first-class golf course plus excellent cricket, tennis and squash facilities. A resort of peace and tranquility. Deck-chairs. Toilets. Car parking. Dog Ban.

31 Holland-on-Sea

Good sandy beaches which are usually quieter and less crowded than nearby Clacton. Groynes. Deck-chairs. Adjoining is the Holland Haven Country Park. Picnicking facility. Car parking. Toilets. Dog Ban.

32 Clacton-on-Sea

Gently sloping long sandy beach. Amusements and entertainments. Pier featuring spectacular rides, roller skating rink, living ocean, fourth dimension and night spot. Magic City the latest childrens fun filled attraction. Leisure centre and children's adventure world. Pavilion Entertainment Centre. Deck-chairs. Car parking. Toilets. Dog Ban. TICs.

33 Southend-on-Sea

Seven miles of sea and foreshore with sand and shingle beach. Expanse of seaside provides walks, traditional seaside entertainment, boat trips, water sports. Longest pleasure pier in the world with pier trains, Sea Life Centre, Peter Pan's Pleasure Park, Never Never Land Fantasy Park, colour illuminations. Popular beaches include East beach at Shoeburyness which is a winner of the Tidy Britain Group Premier Seaside Award (Rural Beach category). This stretch of the coast has a wide expanse of grass, as well as a shingle beach ideal for young children to play. Additional beaches include Three Shells Beach, winner of the Tidy Britain Group Seaside Award (Resort Beach category), Thorpe Bay and Chalkwell. Look out for the colourful information boards on the seafront keeping you up to date on the bathing water quality. Restaurants, refreshment kiosks, archway cafes, deckchairs, boat trips, car parking, toilets. Dog Ban. TIC.

TIC: Tourist Information Centre

TIP: Tourist Information Point

Dog Ban: 1 May-30 Sep, dogs banned from the main beach areas. Further details from the nearest TIC.

Seaside Award logo

Premier Seaside Award logo

European Blue Flag logo

SEASIDE AWARDS/BLUE FLAG AWARDS

The Tidy Britain Group Seaside Award covers both the beach and the bathing water. The beach must be free of litter, pollution and large amounts of rotting seaweed. The water quality must meet the mandatory standard of the EC Bathing Water Directive, and a Seaside Award flag confirms this. A Premier Seaside Award is given if the water meets the higher guideline standard of the EC Directive. In addition there are a number of separate qualifications which rural and resort beaches must meet, individually.

The European Blue Flag, also administered by the Tidy Britain Group, is a European award for resort beaches only and allows comparison of standards between and within the countries of the European community.

For further details of the Seaside Awards/European Blue Flag Awards and a list of 1994 award beaches (available June), contact The Tidy Britain Group: Tel (0603) 762888.

BOAT HIRE

CRUISER HIRE

⚜ **B B Cruiser Co,** Riverside Estate, Brundall, Norfolk, Tel: (0603) 713507: 2-6 berth cruisers. Weekly hire.

⚜ **Blakes Holidays Ltd,** Wroxham, Norfolk: Cruisers, yachts and houseboats on the Norfolk Broads. Narrowboats on the Cambridgeshire waterways. Choose from a wide selection of types from 2-12 berth. Tel: (0603) 782911 (instant bookings/general enquiries). Blakes Country Cottages Tel: (0603) 783221. Free colour brochure Tel: (0603) 782141 or 783226 (Recorded message).

⚜ **Broads Tours Ltd,** Wroxham, Norfolk, Tel: (0603) 782207. Broads cruiser hire and self drive day boats. *Apr-Nov.*

⚜ **Broom Boats Ltd,** Riverside, Brundall, Norfolk, Tel: 0603 712334: 2-9 berth boats, weekly hire.

⚜ **Compass Craft,** Ferry View Estate, Hornham, Tel: (0692) 630401: 2-10 berth boats, weekly hire.

⚜ **Grebe Canal Cruises,** Pitstone Wharf, Leighton Buzzard, Beds, Tel: (0296) 661920: One 4 and one 6 berth cruiser. Day boat, regular trips and excursions.

⚜ **Greenway Marine Ltd,** Riverside, Loddon, Norfolk, Tel: (0508) 20397: 2-9 berth boats, weekly hire.

⚜ **Highcraft,** Griffin Lane, Thorpe St Andrew, Norwich, Tel: (0603) 701701: Motor cabin cruisers. Day, picnic boats and rowing boats from Norwich Yacht Station, Riverside Road.

⚜ **King Line Cruises,** Horning, Norfolk, Tel: (0692) 630297: 2-6 berth cruisers. Weekly, daily and hourly hire. Riverside cottages. Facilities for wheelchairs.

⚜ **Maffett Cruisers,** Chedgrave, Norfolk, Tel: (0508) 20344: 2-8 berth cruisers. 1 dual position steerer, traditional broads cruiser. Weekly hire.

⚜ **Stalham Yacht Services,** Stalham, Norfolk, Tel: (0692) 580288: 2-10 berth Broads cruisers,

house boats, day launches. Weekly, daily and hourly hire available.

⚜ **VIP Harvey Eastwood**, Riverside, Brundall, Norfolk, Tel: (0603) 713345: 2-8 berth cruisers, day boats.

NARROWBOAT HIRE

⚜ **Blackwater Boats,** Croft End, Bures, Suffolk, Tel: (0787) 227823: 4 berth steel narrowboats on the Chelmer and Blackwater Canal for short breaks or longer holidays. Luxurious self-drive boats or skippered cruises by arrangement.

⚜ **Fox Boats**, 10 Marina Drive, March, Cambs, Tel: (0354) 52770: 9 narrow boats, short break and weekly hire.

DAY BOAT HIRE

CAMBRIDGESHIRE

Cambridge

Scudamores Boatyards, Mill Lane, Granta Place, Tel: (0223) 359750: Punts and rowing boats for hire on "the backs" and River Granta.

Jet Ski Aquasports Ltd, 23-27 Bermuda Road, Tel: (0223) 352847: Punt and canoe hire at Quayside. Jet Ski hire at Cawcutts Lane, Impington.

Huntingdon

Huntingdon Marine & Leisure Ltd, Bridge Boatyard, Tel: (0480) 413517. Day boat hire. Boat engine, chandlery & inflatable sales.

Purvis Marine Boatyard, Hartford Road, Tel: (0480) 453628. Canoes, row boats, motor launches and day boats.

ESSEX

Dedham

D. E. Smeeth, The Boatyard, Mill Lane, Tel: (0206) 861748: Rowing boats and canoes. Evening bookings for parties. Teas, ices and snacks.

Mersea Island

Eastcoaster Sailing, 5, Prince Albert Road, Tel: (0206) 382545: Specialises in sailing holidays, sail training, charter and can also offer a unique day's sailing for business entertaining.

NORFOLK

Acle

Anchor Craft, Acle Bridge, Tel: (0493) 750500: Day launches, cruisers.

Hickling

Whispering Reeds Boatyard, Tel: (069 261) 314: Rowing boats, sailing boats, motor launches, cruisers, houseboats for hire. Slipway facilities available.

Horning

Ferry Boatyard Ltd, Ferry Road, Tel: (0692) 630392: Cruisers and day launches. Modern workshop facilities with electric hoist, boat sales and marina moorings.

Norwich

⚜ **Highcraft,** Griffin Lane, Thorpe St Andrew, Tel: (0603) 701701: Motor cabin cruisers. Day, picnic boats and rowing boats from Norwich Yacht Station, Riverside Road.

Potter Heigham

Herbert Woods, Broads Haven, Tel: (0692) 670711: All weather cabin type day launches. Some electric passenger boats make regular trips to Hickling Broad.

Wroxham

Faircraft Loynes, The Bridge, Tel: (0603) 782280: 32 all-weather cabin-type day launches. Hire cruisers available for weekly cruises. Passenger boats make regular trips to visit various Broads. Facilities on certain boats to accommodate wheelchairs.

Moore & Co, Tel: (0603) 783311: 2-9 berth modern motor cruisers and self drive day launches.

Please mention East Anglia Guide when replying to advertisements

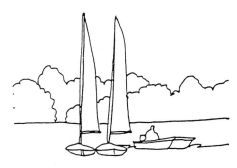

SUFFOLK

Brandon
Bridge House, Tel: (0842) 813137: Rowing boats and canoes.

Bungay
Outney Meadow Caravan Park, Tel: (0986) 892338: Rowing boats, skiffs and canoes. Hourly or daily hire.

Lowestoft
Day Launch Hire, Yacht Station, Oulton Broad, Tel: (0502) 513087: Inboard motor launches. *Easter-end Sep.*

REGULAR EXCURSIONS

ESSEX

Harwich
Orwell & Harwich Navigation Co Ltd, The Quay, Tel: (0255) 502004: Pleasure steamer M/S Brightlingsea carrying up to 150. Morning and afternoon cruises with commentary on Rivers Stour and Orwell, and Harwich Harbour. Cruises, discos, folk nights. Booking advisable. Also 12-seater covered launch available for hire. Ferry service to Felixstowe.

Harwich/Felixstowe passenger ferry

Southend-on-Sea
Pleasure cruises from Southend Pier. Regular service to Rochester, M V Princes Pocahontas, also Thames estuary cruise. Special paddle steamer trips on P S Kingswear Castle. *For details and bookings contact TIC.*

HERTFORDSHIRE

Watford
'Arcturus' Day Cruises, Cassio Wharf, Tel: (043 871) 4528: Famous Star Class, wooden boat built 1934. Public trips from Ironbridge Lock in Cassiobury Park. *Easter-Oct, Sun & Bank Hol 1430 and 1600; also Tue & Thu in Aug 1400 and 1530.*

NORFOLK

Blakeney
Colin Bishop Ferry Service, Tel: (0263) 740753: Trips to Blakeney Point and the seals.

Burnham Overy Staithe
William Scoles, The Old Rectory, Gt Snoring, Fakenham, Tel: (0328) 820597: Trips to Scolt Head Bird Sanctuary and Overy Beach.

Horning
Mississippi River Boats, The Little House, Irstead, Tel: (0692) 630262: 1-2hr Broadland trips on 100-seater double-decked Mississippi paddle boat. Bar, meals for up to 80 by arrangement. *Easter-end Sep. Apr-May party bookings only.*

Norwich
Southern River Steamers, Elm Hill & Thorpe station, Tel: (0603) 624051: Two river boats seating 84 & 92 for 1 1/2 and 3 hour Broadland river cruises and city cruises. Also available for private hire to groups.

Hunstanton
Searle's Hire Boats, South Beach Road, Tel: (0485) 534211: July-Sept: Motor launch carrying up to 60. Cruises to Seal Island viewing the seals of the Wash. Also 1/2 hour coastal cruises. Fishing trips. Speedboat rides.

Stalham
Stalham Water Tours, 28 St. Nicholas Way, Tel: (0692) 670530 answerphone: All weather luxury cruiser for 1-2 1/2 hour Broads cruises. Light refreshments. Departs Richardson's Boatyard, Stalham. Visit to How Hill Gardens, *Mon-Fri & Sun afternoons.*

Wroxham
Broads Tours Ltd, Tel: (0603) 782207: 1 1/4, 1 1/2, 2 and 3 1/2 hour Broadland tours in all-weather motor launch. Largest boat takes 170. *May-Sep.*

SUFFOLK

Orford
Lady Florence, Tel: (0831) 698298: Four hour lunch cruises on the rivers Alde and Ore. Dinner cruises in summer. Coal fire in winter. Bar.

Oulton Broad
Waveney River Tours Ltd, Mutford Lock, Bridge Road, Tel: (0502) 574903: "Waveney Princess", with licensed bar, up to 125 passengers. "Enchantress", up to 92 passengers. Light refreshments. Broads trips. *Easter, end May-end Sep.*

Snape
Snape Maltings, Tel: (0728) 688303: One hour trip on the River Alde aboard Edward Alan John, a covered boat carrying up to 70 passengers. Departure times dependent on tides. Reduction for pre-booked groups. Details and times on request.

Waldringfield
Waldringfield Boat Yard, Tel: (0473) 736260: Cruises on River Deben, morning, afternoon and evenings. Reservations must be made.

BOAT HIRE FOR GROUPS

BEDFORDSHIRE

Leighton Buzzard
Leighton Lady Cruises, Brantoms Wharf, Tel: (0525) 384563: 70 foot narrow boat. Heated passenger saloon with cushioned seats, seating up to 54. Cream teas and buffet available on request. Tel for public trips list.

ESSEX

Chelmsford
Chelmer & Blackwater Navigation Ltd, Paper Mill Lock, Little Baddow, Tel: (0245) 225520: Modern pleasure barge, with bar and refreshments. Charter for groups of up to 48. Individual trips Sun and Mon of Bank Hol weekends. *Apr-Oct.*

Maldon
Anglian Yacht Services, The Hythe, Maldon, Tel: (0621) 852290: Thames sailing barge "Reminder" for individuals or for groups of up to 12.

NORFOLK

Norwich
Norfolk Wherry Trust, 14 Mount Pleasant, Tel: (0603) 505815: The Trust owns "Albion" which may be chartered for up to 12 people. Membership available with special members' cruises.

Wherry Yacht Charter, Barton House, Hartwell Road, The Avenue, Tel: (0603) 782470: Broadland cruising on historic wherry yachts "Olive" and "Norada", and pleasure wherry "Hathor". For groups of up to 12 on each.

SUFFOLK

Ipswich
P & Q Sailing Centre & Holiday Charter, Mannings Lane, Woolverstone, Tel: (0473) 780293: Two cruising yachts for parties of up to 5 per yacht, Also sailing tuition. *Apr-Oct.*

Woodbridge
'Neljan', Ferry Quay, Tel: (0860) 907625: Two masted Dutch sailing barge built at turn of the century. 3 to 4 hour meal cruises seating 12, under engine from Felixstowe Ferry along the River Deben. May be chartered for sailing trips.

FESTIVAL PHONELINE

Further information on other festivals in the region may be obtained from the Eastern Arts Board, Tel: (0223) 215355.

Aldeburgh Festival
10-26 Jun (0728) 453543

Broxbourne Midsummer
5 Jun-3 Jul (0992) 465459

Bury St Edmunds Festival
12-28 May (0284) 769505

Chelmsford Cathedral
14-21 May (0245) 359890

Chelmsford Spectacular
26-29 Aug (0245) 490490

Clacton Jazz Festival
26-29 Aug (0245) 492211

Cressing Temple
22-24 and 29-31 Jul
(0245) 492211

East Anglian Summer Music Festival, Hadleigh
Jul-Aug (0473) 822596

Felixstowe Folk
13-15 May (0394) 274366

Festival Brentwood
Sep (0277) 218897

Haverhill
12-19 Jun (0440) 712858

Hunstanton
11-26 Jun (0485) 532722

Kings Lynn Festival
16-30 Jul (0553) 774725

Luton Carnival
30 May (0582) 30131

Norfolk and Norwich Festival
6-16 Oct (0603) 764764

Peterborough Cathedral
1-9 Jul (0733) 343342

Rickmansworth Canal Festival
May (0923) 778382

Snape Proms
Aug (0728) 453543

Southend-on-Sea Special Events
(0702) 355169

St Andrews Gorleston
29 Oct-13 Nov (0493) 664108

Swaffham
17-24 Sep (0760) 24741

Thaxted
17 Jun-10 Jul (0371) 830350

Wangford Festival
Jul (0502) 78235

Wingfield
Mar-Sep (0379) 384505

SNAPE MALTINGS

Snape Maltings Riverside Centre

This remarkable collection of old maltings buildings is set on the banks of the River Alde. Many interesting shops, galleries and restaurants offer quality products and fresh home cooked food. There is a programme of painting and craft weekends, river trips in summer and unusual self-catering accommodation.
OPEN ALL YEAR, EVERY DAY, 10-6 (5 in winter)
Snape Maltings, nr Saxmundham, Suffolk IP17 1SR
Tel: (0728) 688303/5

Snape Maltings Concert Hall

Home of year-round programme of events, including Aldeburgh Festival (10-26 June 1994), Snape Proms (1-31 August), Aldeburgh October Britten Festival and Easter, Christmas and New Year concerts. Also Britten-Pears School for Advanced Musical Studies (public master classes April - October). Guided tours for groups by arrangement.
Tel: (0728) 452935, Box Office (0728) 453543

EVENTS

This is just a selection of events in the region. Please contact the East Anglia Tourist Board Tel: (0473) 822922 for details of these and other events.

SHOWS AND DISPLAYS

3-6 Feb	Springfields Horticultural Exhibition, Spalding, Lincs
26-27 Feb	Motorbike '94, Springfield Exhibition Centre Spalding, Lincs
13 Mar	Dolls Fair, Woburn Abbey, Beds
19 Mar	National Shire Horse Show, East of England Showground, Peterborough
3-4 Apr	Medieval Jousting Tournament, Knebworth House, Gardens and Park, Herts
9-10 Apr	Thriplow Daffodil Weekend, Thriplow, Cambs
1-3 May	Spring Craft Show, Woburn Abbey, Beds
30 Apr- 2 May	Tudor May Day Celebrations, Kentwell Hall, Long Melford Suffolk
2 May	Ickwell May Day Festival, Ickwell Green, near Biggleswade, Beds
7-9 May	Spalding Flower Parade '94, Spalding, Lincs
14-15 May	Fighter Meet Air Show, North Weald Airfield, Essex
15 May	South Suffolk Show, Ingham, Bury St. Edmunds, Suffolk
21 May	Hadleigh Agricultural Show, Hadleigh, Suffolk
28-29 May	Air Fete '94, RAF Mildenhall, Suffolk
29-30 May	Braintree Country Fair and Festival, Towerlands Centre, Braintree, Essex
1-2 Jun	Suffolk Show, Suffolk Showground, Ipswich, Suffolk
11-12 Jun	East Anglian Daily Times Country Fair, Melford Hall, Long Melford, Suffolk
17-19 Jun	Essex County Show, Essex County Showground
18 Jun	Flitwick Carnival, Flitwick, Beds
18-19 Jun	Festival of Gardening, Hatfield House, Herts
19 Jun- 17 Jul	Historical Re-Creation of Tudor Life, Kentwell Hall, Long Melford Suffolk - Sat, Sun & 15 Jul.
29-30 Jun	Royal Norfolk Show, The Showground, Norwich

29 Jun- 2 Jul	Rose Fair, Wisbech, Cambs
9 Jul	Tendring Hundred Show, Manningtree, Essex
9-10 Jul	South Bedfordshire Show, Toddington, Beds
9-10 Jul	Wings n Wheels Spectacular, North Weald Airfield, Epping, Essex
19-21 Jul	East of England Show, East of England Showground, Peterborough
27 Jul	Sandringham Flower Show, Sandringham House, Norfolk
6-7 Aug	Springfields Flower Show, Springfields Garden and Exhibition Centre, Spalding, Lincs
14 Aug	National Jaguar Drivers Club Rally, Woburn Abbey, Beds
17 Aug	Cromer Carnival, Cromer, Norfolk
27 Aug	Thames Sailing Barge Race, Southend-on-Sea, Essex
28-29 Aug	Eye Show, Eye Showground, Suffolk
28-29 Aug	Classic Car Show, Knebworth House, Gardens and Park, Herts
1-4 Sep	Burghley Horse Trials, Burghley Park, Lincs
15-18 Sep	Interfire '94, East of England Showground, Peterborough

MUSICAL EVENTS

26 Feb- 5 Mar	Bedfordshire Music Festival, Market Square, Bedford
7-12 Mar	A Celebration of Schools Music, Snape Maltings, Suffolk
30 Apr- 21 May	Beccles Festival, Beccles, Suffolk
6 -26 Nov	Cambridge Elgar Festival, Cambridge College Chapels

EAST ANGLIA CUSTOMS

| 7-9 Jan | Whittlesey Straw Bear Festival, Whittlesey, Cambs |
| 2 May | Stilton Cheese Rolling, Stilton, Cambs |

HORSE RACING

Racing at Newmarket	Tel (0638) 663482
Racing at Fakenham	Tel (0328) 862388
Racing at Great Yarmouth	Tel (0493) 842527
Racing at Huntingdon	Tel (0480) 453373

LOCAL THEATRES

You might like to find out what is on at your nearest theatre. Here is a list of theatres and their telephone numbers:

BEDFORDSHIRE

Luton, St. Georges Theatre (0582) 21628

CAMBRIDGESHIRE

Cambridge, Arts Theatre (0223) 352000
Peterborough, Key Theatre (0733)52437
Wisbech, Angles Theatre (0945) 474447

ESSEX

Basildon, Towngate Theatre (0268) 532632
Chelmsford, Civic Theatre (0245) 495028
Colchester
☺ Mercury Theatre (0206) 573948
Lakeside Theatre (0206) 873261
Arts Centre (0206) 577301
☺ **Grays**, Thameside Theatre (0375) 383961
Harlow, The Playhouse (0279) 431945
Southend-on-Sea, Cliffs Pavillion (0702) 351135
Westcliff-on-Sea, Palace Theatre Centre (0702) 342564

NORFOLK

King's Lynn, Arts Centre (0553) 773578
Norwich
☺ Theatre Royal (0603) 630000
Arts Centre (0603) 660352
Maddermarket Theatre (0603) 626560
Puppet Theatre Administration   (0603) 615564
Box Office (0603) 629921

SUFFOLK

☺ **Bury St Edmunds**, Theatre Royal (0284) 755469; Box Office 769505
Eye, Somershey Theatre (0379) 870519
Felixstowe, Spa Pavilion Theatre (0394) 283303
Ipswich
☺ Wolsey Theatre (0473) 253725
Regent Theatre (0473) 281480
☺ Eastern Angles Theatre Co (0473) 218202
Lowestoft, Marina Theatre (0502) 573318
Sudbury, Quay Theatre (0787) 374745
Snape Concert Hall (0728) 452935
Box Office (0728) 453543
Woodbridge, Riverside Theatre (0394) 382174

85

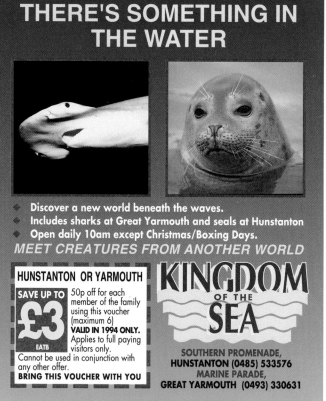

Please mention East Anglia Guide when replying to advertisements

FAMILY FUN

ESSEX

Clacton-on-Sea

Clacton Pier, 1 North Sea: 18 rides, arcades, shops, refreshments, side shows. Roller rink, disco, aquarium and sealion show. *Rides open Mid Feb-30 Nov, Sat,Sun; 1 Jun-30 Sep, daily; Living Ocean and Sealion show, all year, daily, closed 25 Dec; Roller skating, all year, Sat,Sun and school holidays. 50p/free/50p. Unlimited rides £5.50. Tel: (0255) 421115.*

Southend-on-Sea

Never Never Land, Western Esplanade: A unique children's adventure park where fantasy becomes living, animated reality with many fairytale features and special effects. *Apr-Nov, Sat,Sun, 1100-2200, all local school holidays. £1.50/£1.00/£1.00. Tel: (0702) 460618.* &

Peter Pans Playground, Sunken Gardens West, Western Esplanade: Rides and attractions include roller coaster, big wheel fantasy dome, Sky Lab, giant Pirate Ship, the Looping Barracuda. *Jan,Feb,Mar,Oct,Nov,Dec, Sat,Sun only, daily during school hols and Bank Holidays, 1100-1800; 1 Apr-5 Oct, 1000-2200; closed 25 Dec. Ride prices on application. Tel: (0702) 468023.* &

⊛ **Southend-on-Sea Pier**, Western Esplanade: Train ride along the pier approx 1.3 miles. Pier Museum at North Station, amusements, shop, restaurant, pub. Guided tours at Lifeboat House. *1 Jan-27 Mar, Mon-Fri, 0800-1600, Sat, Sun, 0800-1800; 28 Mar-29 May, daily, 0800-2200; 30 May-11 Sep, Mon-Fri, 0800-1800, Sat, Sun, 0800-2000; 12 Sep-31 Dec, Mon-Fri, 0800-1600, Sat, Sun, 0800-1800; Closed 25 Dec. Price on application. Tel: (0702) 355622.* &

Walton-on-the-Naze

Walton on the Naze Pier, Pier Approach: Pier with Arcade having bingo, restaurant, ten pin bowling centre, fishing, adult and junior rides. *Rides 20,27 Mar; 1-10 Apr, daily; 15 Apr-22 May, Sat and Sun; 28 May-30 Sep, daily, from 1000. Tel: (0255) 672288.* &

NORFOLK

Great Yarmouth

Louis Tussauds House of Wax, 18 Regent Road: Waxworks exhibition, torture chambers, chamber of horrors. Hall of funny mirrors. Family amusement arcade. *Apr-Oct, daily, 1030-1830. £2.00/£1.50/£1.50. Tel: (0493) 844851.*

Merrivale Model Village, Marine Parade: Over 200 models in a acre of landscaped ground. Illuminated at night *1-10 Apr, daily; 11 Apr-29 May, daily 1000-1800; 30 May-30 Sep, daily 0930-2200; 1 Oct-30 Nov, 1200-1700. £2.30/£1.30/£2.00. Tel: (0493) 842097.* &

⊛ **Pleasure Beach**, South Beach Parade: Over 70 rides and attractions. Rides are paid for by tokens purchased from pay boxes and machines inside the park or by wristband. *27 Mar-7 Apr & 30 Apr-2 May, daily; Apr-May, Sun, also Fri & Sat evenings in May; 28 May-18 Sep, daily. Opening times are subject to season and weather conditions, Tel to check (0493) 844585.* &

Ripleys Believe It Or Not, The Windmill, 9 Marine Parade: Weird and wonderful assortment of oddities all absolutely genuine. Interactive displays, illusions, videos and special effects. *1 Jan-31 Mar, Sat, Sun, 1000-1700; 1 Apr-31 Oct, daily, 1000-1700 or dusk; 1 Nov-31 Dec, Sat, Sun, 1000-1600; (Full weeks during school holidays) Closed 25 Dec. £2.99/£1.99/£2.20. Tel: (0493) 332217.* &

⊛ **Treasure World**, 11-12 Marine Parade: Diving, treasure and the history of diving, moving audio visual exhibits, restaurant, shop. *All year, daily, 1030-2100. £3.20/£1.20/£2.20. Tel: (0493) 330444.* &

World of Wax, 68 Marine Parade: Waxworks include, fairyland, horrors, crown jewels, pop stars and royalty. *Apr-Nov, daily, 0900-2200; Dec-Mar, weekends, 1100-1700 £1.50/£1.00/£1.00. Tel: (0493) 842203.*

Hunstanton

Jungle Wonderland, Pier Entertainment Centre, First Floor, The Green: Adventure playground catering for children 2-12 years. Soft play area for toddlers, play with the jungle theme. 80 seater diner catering for parties. Height limit of approx 5ft. *1 Apr-30 Sep, 1000-1800, daily. Bank hols and childrens summer holidays, 1000-2030; Oct-Mar, Bank Hols, School Hols and every Fri, Sat, Sun, 1000-1700; Closed 25,26 Dec. 50p/£2.50/30p. Tel: (0485) 535505.*

Reedham

⊛ **Pettitt's Animal Adventure Park**, Camphill: Children entertainment, live shows, tame animals, adventure play complex with ball pond, climbing nets, bouncing castles and mazes. Amusement rides, miniature steam trains, picnic area, events field, crazy golf, organ music at specified times. *3 Apr-31 Oct, Sun-Fri, 1000-1730. £4.95/£3.95/£3.50. Tel: (0493) 700094.* &

SUFFOLK

Felixstowe

⊛ **Charles Manning's Amusement Park**, Sea Road: Traditional amusement park and childrens park "Tenderfoot Territory". Nightclub and lazer shooting. *1 Apr-30 Sep, Sat,Sun and school holidays; Sun and Bank Holidays, 1100-2100; Weekdays, 1300-2100; Times vary with weather. Unlimited rides £4.00. Tel: (0394) 671622.*

Lowestoft

⊛ **East Point Pavilion**, Royal Plain: Edwardian style pavilion providing a blend of play, education, history, also a Tourist Information Centre. Gift shop and restaurant. Toddler play pad (up to 4 years); Play platform (3-10 years); Lowestoft story animated museum. *1 Jan-30 Apr and 1 Oct-end Dec, Mon, 1100-1700, Tue-Sun, 1000-1700; 29 May-30 Sep, Mon, 1000-1800, Tue-Sun, 0900-1800; Closed 25,26 Dec. Toddler play pad £1.50; Play platform £1.95 (last admission to both, 1 hour before closing); Lowestoft Story £1.75/£1.25/£1.25 (last admission 1/2 hour before closing). Tel: (0502) 523000.* &

⊛ **Pleasurewood Hills American Theme Park**, Corton Road: American-style magic every day in summer; you pay only once and then everything's free. Everything you climb and ride on, all the hairy scary rides and all the shows, as many times as you like, and there are over 50 to choose from. *1 Apr-mid May, Sat, Sun and Bank Holidays; Mid May-mid Sep, daily, 1000-1700; Mid Sep-early Oct, Sat and Sun, 1000-1700. £8.95/senior citizens £5.20. Tel: (0502) 508200.* &

Great Yarmouth Pleasure Beach

Prices are in the order Adults/Children/Senior Citizens. Where prices are not available at the time of going to press, the 1993 (93) price is given. If no price is given, admission is free. See Touring Maps on pages 119-124 for locations of places to visit.

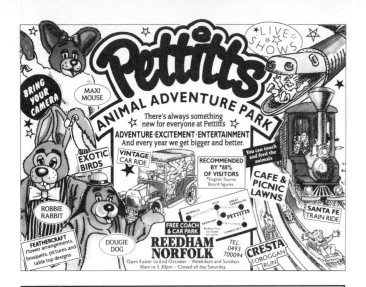

Please mention East Anglia Guide when replying to advertisements

East Anglia offers a full and varied range of opportunities for those who wish to take part in sport and physical recreation. The listing that follows provides some of the basic information to enable visitors to the region to find a suitable facility. Additional advice can be obtained from the Sports Council (Eastern Region). Details can be supplied on indoor sports centres, golf courses, health and fitness centres, sport for people with disabilities and sports organisations. Individual local authorities can also provide more specific details for a particular area.

An annual publication titled **Directory of Sport in the Eastern Region** is produced to support this service. It is available from the Sports Council (Eastern Region) at Crescent House, 19 The Crescent, Bedford, MK40 2QP, Tel: (0234) 345222. A cover charge of £5.00 is made to assist with production and postage costs.

ARTIFICIAL SKI SLOPES

Bassingbourn
Bassingbourn Ski Club, Bassingbourn Barracks, Tel: (0462) 434107

Brentwood
The Ski Centre at Brentwood Park, Warley Gap, Tel: (0277) 211994

Harlow
Harlow Ski School, Harlow Sports Centre, Tel: (0279) 21792

Ipswich
Suffolk Ski Centre & Golf Driving Range, Bourne Terrace, Wherstead, Tel: (0473) 602347.

Norwich
Norfolk Ski Club Ltd, Whitlingham Lane, Trowse, Tel: (0603) 662781 for details and practice times.

GOLF COURSES

Stoke By Nayland Golf Club, Keepers Lane, Leavenheath: Two 18 hole courses laid out over natural meadowland. Restrictions on visitors at weekends and Bank Holidays.

A comprehensive list of Golf Courses in East Anglia is available from the East Anglia Tourist Board, see address on inside front cover. Price 50p.

ICE SKATING

Chelmsford
Riverside Ice and Leisure Centre, Victoria Road, Tel: (0245) 269417: Ice rink, 3 pools, 6 court sports hall, gymnasium, squash courts, snooker hall and health suite.

LEISURE POOLS

BEDFORDSHIRE
Oasis Leisure Pool, Cardington Road, Bedford, Tel: (0234) 272100: Waterslides, fountains, bubble burst, outside river ride, quiet pool, spa baths. Conditioning gym, sauna and sunbeds.

ESSEX
Blackwater Leisure Centre, Maldon, Tel (0621) 851898: Leisure pool with flumes, baby/toddlers pool, health and fitness area, solarium, cafeteria.

Colchester Leisure World, Cowdray Avenue, Tel: (0206) 766500: Extensive leisure complex offering a wide range of facilities including leisure pool , bubble lounge, children's fountain, 25m competition pool and teaching pool. Also badminton courts, sauna, jacuzzi, bar and restaurant and concert hall.

NORFOLK
Great Yarmouth's Marina Leisure and Fitness Centre, Marine Parade, Gt Yarmouth, Tel: (0493) 851521: Tropical leisure pool with wave machine and Aquaglide, sports hall, multigym. Table tennis, snooker, pool, squash courts, sauna/solarium, restaurants, bars, childrens play area, entertainment, indoor bowls, roller skating, conference facilities.

Hunstanton Oasis (Promenade), Tel: (0485) 534227: Exciting family leisure centre on seafront. Indoor and outdoor leisure pools, aquaslide, toddler pools, whirlpool spa, soft play area with toddler slides, swings and see-saw, indoor bowls, squash courts, cafeteria, bar, sun lounge.

Norwich Sport Village & Broadland Aquapark, Drayton High Road, Hellesdon, Tel: (0603) 788912: Indoor and outdoor tennis, squash, multi sports hall, health & fitness centre including gymnasium, sauna/steam rooms, plunge & spa pool, bars, restaurants and hotel. The Aquapark is a 6 lane, 25m competition pool and has 2 giant water flumes.

The Splash Leisure Pool, Weybourne Road, Sheringham, Tel: (0263) 825675: Giant waterslide and splash pool, wave pool, childrens paddling pool and walrus slide. Health and fitness club. Ice-cream parlour, poolside bar and fastfood. Shop.

SUFFOLK
Bury St Edmunds Leisure Centre, Beetons Way, Tel: (0284) 753496/7: 33m pool, 20m learner pool, leisure pool with flumes. Sports hall, 2 ancillary halls, 3 squash courts, climbing wall, weight and fitness training, sporturf all weather pitches, saunaworld. Cafe and bar.

Felixstowe Leisure Centre, Undercliff Road West, Tel: (0394) 670411. Features include leisure swimming pool, learner pool, sauna, sunbeds, bowls hall, fully licensed lounges and bars, multi-purpose entertainment and conference hall, amusement area, cafe and refreshment facilities, tourist information centre.

Crown Pools, Crown Street, Ipswich. Tel: (0473) 219231. Award winning 3 pool complex, 8-lane 25m competition pool, beach entry freeform leisure pool with wave making machine, waterfall fountains, inflatable slide and teaching pool, surrounded by an oasis of tropical plants. Full theatrical lighting system. Bar, restaurant and cafeteria.

Kingfisher Leisure Pool, Friars Meadow, Sudbury, Tel: (0787) 375656. Leisure pool including 25m pool, 55m flume ride, wave machine, water cannon, health suite and gymnasium.

ROLLER SKATING

Bury St Edmunds
Rollerbury, Station Hill, Tel: (0284) 701216: Roller-skating, skating lessons, cafe and bar.

Rollerskating at Colchester's Rollerworld

Colchester
Rollerworld, Eastgates, Tel: (0206) 868868: Great Britain's largest roller-skating rink, 25m x 50m maple floor. Roller hire, roller cafe, roller bar. Sound and lightshow, Quasar at Rollerworld -serious fun with a laser gun.

Ipswich
Roller King Skating Centre, Gloster Road, Martlesham Heath, Tel: (0473) 611333: Maple floor, skate hire, skating lessons, snack bar, licensed bar.

Southend-on-Sea
Roller City, Aviation Way, Tel: (0702) 546344: Roller rink, skate hire, shop, snacks available.

SPORT FOR ALL

SWIMMING POOLS

The swimming pools list gives information about **extra facilities** that can be found at each pool site; the following abbreviations are used:
🏃 Athletic track 🧗 Climbing wall ♿ Provision for those with a disability 🤿 Diving pool
⛳ Golf course ⛨ Health and fitness suite
L Learner pool ≈ Outdoor pool ✳ Outdoor sports pitch ⌂ Sports hall ९ Squash courts

BEDFORDSHIRE

Bedford
Robinson Pool, Bedford Park,
Tel: (0234) 354901. ⛨ *L* ♿

Dunstable
Dunstable Park Recreation Centre,
Court Drive, Tel: (0582) 608107. ⌂ ⛨ ✳
Houghton Regis Sports Centre,
Parkside Drive, Tel: (0582) 866141. ⌂ ♿

Flitwick
Flitwick Pool, Steppingley Road. ⌂

Leighton Buzzard
Tiddenfoot Leisure Centre,
Mentmore Road, Tel: (0525) 37565. ⛨ ♿

Luton
Lea Manor Leisure Centre,
Northwell Drive, Tel: (0582) 599888. ⌂ ♿
Lewsey Park Pool, Pastures Way,
Tel: (0582) 604244. ⛨ ♿
Putteridge Recreation Centre,
Stopsley, Tel: (0582) 31664. ⌂ ♿
Wardown Swimming & Leisure Centre,
Bath Road, Tel: (0582) 20621. *L* ⌂ ♿

Kempston
Kempston Pool, Hillgrounds Road,
Tel: (0234) 843777. ⛨ ♿

CAMBRIDGESHIRE

Bottisham
Bottisham Village College,
Lode Road, Tel: (0223) 812148.

Cambridge
Kings Hedges Pool, Kings Hedges Road,
Tel: (0223) 353248.

Parkside Pool,
Parkside, Tel: (0223) 350008. ⛨ *L* ♿

Ely
Paradise Pool,
Newnham Street, Tel: (0353) 665481. ♿

Eynesbury
St Neots Indoor Pool,
Barford Road, Tel: (0480) 74748. *L*

Huntingdon
Huntingdon Recreation Centre,
St Peters Road, Tel: (0480) 454130. ९ ♿

March
George Campbell Pool,
City Road, Tel: (0354) 53511. ♿

Melbourn
M C Splash, Tel: (0763) 261508. ⛨ ⌂

Peterborough
Jack Hunt Swimming Pool,
Ledbury Road, Tel: (0733) 264644. 🧗 🤿 ♿
Orton Longueville Pool, Orton Longueville School, Tel: (0733) 231971. ⌂
Regional Swimming Pool,
Lancashire Gate, Tel: (0733) 51474. ⛨ *L* ♿

Ramsey
Ramsey Sports Centre,
Abbey Road, Tel: (0487) 710275. ♿

St Ives
St Ivo Recreation Centre, Westwood Road,
Tel: (0480) 64601. 🏃 🧗 ⛨ ⌂ ♿

Swavesey
Swavesey Village College,
Swavesey, Tel: (0954) 30366/30373. ९

Whittlesey
Manor Leisure Centre,
Station Road, Tel: (0733) 202298. ♿

Wisbech
Hudson Pool,
Harecroft Road, Tel: (0945) 584230.

ESSEX

Basildon
Gloucester Park Swimming Pool,
Town Centre, Tel: (0268) 523588. ⛨ ♿

Billericay
Billericay Swimming Pool, Lake Meadow Recreation Ground, Tel: (0277) 657111.

Splash Leisure Pool, Sheringham

Braintree
Riverside Pool,
St John Avenue, Tel: (0376) 23240. ⛨ ९

Brentwood
Brentwood Centre,
Doddinghurst Road, Tel: (0277) 229621. ९ ♿

Canvey Island
Waterside Farm Sports Centre,
Somnes Avenue, Tel: (0268) 696201. ⛨ ⌂ ९

Chelmsford
Riverside Pool,
Victoria Road, Tel: (0245) 269417. ⛨ ९ ♿

Clacton on Sea
Clacton Leisure Centre, Vista Recreation Ground, Tel: (0255) 429647. ⛨ ♿

Corringham
Corringham Swim & Squash Centre,
Springhouse Road, Tel: (0375) 678070. ९ ♿

Dovercourt
Dovercourt Swimming Pool,
Wick Lane, Tel: (0255) 508266. ♿

Dunmow
Dunmow Sports Centre, Helena Romanes School, Tel: (0371) 873782. ⛨ ✳ ९ ♿

Grays
Blackshots Swim & Leisure Centre,
Blackshots Lane, Tel: (0375) 372695. 🏃 ⛨ ✳

Halstead
Halstead Swimming Pool,
Parsonage Street, Tel: (0787) 473706. ⛨

Harlow
Harlow Swimming Pool,
First Avenue, Tel: (0279) 446430. ⛨ ♿
Stewards School Pool,
Stapletye, Tel: (0279) 444503. ⛨ ♿

Hawkwell
Clements Hall Leisure Centre, Clements Hall Way, Tel: (0702) 207777. 🧗 ⛨ ⌂ ९ ♿

Leigh on Sea
Belfairs Swimming Pool,
Fairview Gardens, Tel: (0702) 712155.

Loughton
Loughton Pool,
Traps Hill, Tel: (081) 508 1477. ⛨ ♿

Ongar
Ongar Sports Centre,
Fyfield Road, Tel: (0277) 363969. ⛨ ✳ ♿

Crown Pools, Ipswich

Pitsea
Pitsea Swimming Pool,
Rectory Drive, Tel: (0268) 556734. ⛹

Saffron Walden
Lord Butler Leisure Centre,
Peasland Road, Tel: (0799) 26600. ⛹ ⛹ ⛹

Shenfield
Shenfield Sports Hall,
Oliver Road, Tel: (0277) 226220. *L*

Shoeburyness
Shoeburyness Swimming Pool,
Delaware Road, Tel: (0702) 293558.

South Ockendon
Belhus Park Leisure Complex, Belhus Park,
Tel: (0708) 852248/856297. ⛹ ⛹ ⛹ ⛹

Southend on Sea
Southend Swimming Pool,
Warrior Square, Tel: (0702) 464445. ⛹ ⛹ ⛹

Thundersley
Runnymede Sports Hall, Runnymede Chase,
Tel: (03745) 58717 (Evenings).

Waltham Abbey
Waltham Abbey Pool,
Roundhills Estate, Tel: (0992) 716733. ⛹ ⛹

Wickford
Wickford Swimming Pool,
Market Avenue, Tel: (0268) 765460. ⛹

Witham
Bramston Sports Centre,
Bridge Street, Tel: (0376) 519200. ⛹ ⛹ ⛹

NORFOLK

Bradwell
Phoenix Pool,
Mallard Way, Tel: (0493) 64575. ⛹

Diss
Diss Swimming Pool,
Victoria Road, Tel: (0379) 652754. ⛹ ⛹

Dereham
Breckland Pool,
Quebec Road, Tel: (0362) 693419. ⛹ ⛹

Downham Market
Downham Market Swimming Pool,
War Memorial Playing Fields,
Tel: (0366) 383822. ⛹ ⛹ ⛹

King's Lynn
St James Swimming Pool,
Blackfriars Street, Tel: (0553) 764888.

Norwich
St Augustines Swimming Centre,
St Augustines Gate, Tel: (0603) 620164. ⛹ ⛹ ⛹

Sprowston
Sprowston Swimming Pool, Sprowston High
School, Cannerby Lane, Tel: (0603) 31133.

Thetford
Breckland Sports Centre,
Croxton Road, Tel: (0842) 753110. ⛹ ⛹ ⛹

SUFFOLK

Bungay
Waveney Valley Pool,
St Johns Hill. ⛹

Hadleigh
Hadleigh Swimming Pool,
Stonehouse Road, Tel: (0473) 823470. ⛹

Haverhill
Haverhill Sports Centre, Ehringshausen Way,
Tel: (0440) 702548. ⛹ ⛹ ⛹ ⛹

Ipswich
Fore Street Baths,
Fore Street, Tel: (0473) 253089.

Leiston
Leiston Sports Centre,
Red House Lane, Tel: (0728) 830364. ⛹

Lowestoft
Waveney Sports & Leisure Centre,
Water Lane, Tel: (0502) 69116. ⛹ ⛹ ⛹

Mildenhall
Mildenhall & District Swimming Pool,
Recreation Way, Tel: (0638) 712515. ⛹

Newmarket
Newmarket Swimming Pool,
High Street, Tel: (0638) 661736.

Stowmarket
Mid Suffolk Leisure Centre,
Gainsborough Road, Tel: (0449) 674980. ⛹

Stradbroke
Stradbroke Pool,
Wilby Road, Tel: (0379) 384376. ⛹

Woodbridge
Deben Swimming Pool,
Station Road, Tel: (0394) 380370. ⛹

WATERSPORTS

CAMBRIDGESHIRE

Grafham Water, Huntingdon, Tel: (0480)
810521. Windsurfing, canoeing, dinghy sailing,
cycle trail.

Mepal Outdoor Centre, Ely, Tel: (0354)
692251. Sailing courses, climbing, archery,
residential accommodation, fast-food restaurant.

Tallington Lakes Watersports Centre, Tallington Lakes Leisure Park, Tallington, nr Stamford, Lincs. Main Office Tel: (0778) 346342.
Waterski and jetski Tel: (0778) 347000. Dry ski
slope Tel: (0778) 344990. Windsurf, canoe and
dinghy hire Tel: (0788) 380002.

ESSEX

Bradwell Field Studies and Sailing Centre,
Bradwell Waterside, nr Southminster, Tel:
(0621) 776256. Offshore cruising, dinghy sailing, canoeing, windsurfing. RYA Centre.

**Channels Windsurfing, Mountain Bike and
Canoe Centre**, Belstead Farm Lane, Little Waltham, Chelmsford, Tel: (0245) 441000.

Channels Watersports Centre, Lakeside,
Thurrock, Tel: (0708) 865745. Dingy sailing,
windsurfing, mountain biking, canoeing and
diving.

Chalkwell Windsurfing Club, Chalkwell
Beach, Leigh-on-Sea, Tel: (0702) 79896. Car
parking, toilets. Tuition can be arranged. Regular
racing.

⊛ **Gosfield Lake & Leisure Park**, Church
Road, Gosfield, Halstead, Tel: (0787) 475043:
Water skiing, pitch 'n' putt, fishing, restaurant.

Harlow Outdoor Pursuits Centre, Burntmill
Lane, Harlow, Tel: (0279) 432031. Sailing,
windsurfing, power boats, narrow boats, canoeing, rock climbing. Outside catering facilities.

Southend Marine Activities Centre, Eastern
Esplanade, Southend, Tel: (0702) 612770. Tuition in sailing, canoeing, windsurfing and power
boat driving during evenings, weekends and
school holidays.

Canoeing, an exhilarating sport

NORFOLK

Jubilee Watersports Centre, King's Lynn, Tel:
(0553) 785605.

Roanoke Day Centre, Neatishead, Norwich,
Tel: (0692) 630572. For people with disabilities.

Surf 55, 55 St James's Street, King's Lynn, Tel:
(0553) 764356. Waterbase: Leziate Park, Brow
of the Hill, Leziate, King's Lynn. Windsurf,
mountain bike and kite centre.

SUFFOLK

Windsurfing Seasports, The Beach, Sea Road,
Felixstowe, Tel: (0394) 284504. Car park, club,
changing facilities, toilets, comprehensive rescue facilities. Shop, hire, tuition.

Alton Water Sports Centre, Alton Water, Stutton, Ipswich, Tel: (0473) 328408: Windsurfing,
sailing and canoeing. Tuition and equipment
hire. Cafeteria, chandlery, changing facilities,
toilets. R.Y.A recognised.

Suffolk Water Park, Bramford, Ipswich, Tel:
(0473) 830191 : Windsurfing, canoe hire, jet
skiing, water skiing, tuition, sales, changing
rooms, snack bar, licensed bar.

CRAFTS SPECIALITIES AND GALLERIES

BEDFORDSHIRE

Bromham Mill Gallery
a restored 17th century watermill, now run as a working museum. In addition to the supporting interpretative exhibitions on milling, agriculture and waterways history, the mill houses an art gallery and craft work outlet. The Gallery's rolling programme and exhibition offers high quality professional work from artists within Bedfordshire and the region. During 1994, visitors can see solo, group and themed exhibitions. During October, work under the title 'Fabric' will bring together contrasting work styles and media; printmaking, drawing, painting and mixed media work. Both modern and traditional handmade craft work is also exhibited, much of which is unusual and all of which is of high quality. Most of the art and craft work is for sale. Bromham Mill, picnic area and nature reserve, set amongst river meadow, adjoining the River Great Ouse and 26 arch, 13th century Bromham Bridge, offers a delightful setting for a relaxed family outing. Fresh coffee and speciality teas served during opening hours: Apr-Oct, Wed-Fri, 1030-1630, Sat, Sun and Bank Holidays, 1130-1800. Adults 60p, concessions 30p (1993 prices). Party groups and guided tours welcome, special rates available. Bromham Mill Gallery, West End of Bromham Bridge, Bromham, Bedfordshire. Telephone (0234) 824330 or 228671.

CAMBRIDGESHIRE

Steeplegate
Unusual gifts of good taste in craft gallery beside the cathedral. Tea room. We sell treen, woodwork, leatherware, ceramics, jewellery and toys. Open all year, daily except Sunday, 0900-1730. 16-18 High Street, Ely, Cambs. Tel Ely (0353) 664731.

The Crafty Needle
Set in a converted barn in two acres of idyllic gardens, and with an adventure playground to keep the children happy, this specialist needlework centre is well worth a visit. The Crafty Needle stocks a wide range of fabrics, kits, publications and accessories for embroidery, cross-stitch tapestry and quilting, including a full range of DMC threads, Appletons crewel and tapestry wools. An Aladdin's Cave of finds for the discerning needleperson. Evening group visits available from May to Sept. Open Tue-Saturday 1000-1700, Wed and Sun 1330-1700, closed all day Mon. Free parking. The Crafty Needle, 129 Meldreth Road, Whaddon, Royston. (1 ½ miles off A1198 or A10 between Royston and Cambridge). Telephone (0223) 208103

Sacrewell Farm & Country Centre
is interesting and educational - superb for parties and school visits - but above all it is **friendly** and **fun**. Meet our farmyard animals or enjoy the many "hands on" bygones, quizzes and games. Play on trampolines, roundabouts, swings or get lost in the maze. Travel any of the numerous farm, nature and general interest trails, bury yourself in the history of the place and relish the immense power and ingenuity of our ancient watermill reopened in 1993 after extensive renovation. We are open every day, 0900-2100. "Ye olde hen house", with numerous exhibits and children's toys, provides refreshments and a souvenir/gift shop and is open daily 1100-1730. Admission to the Centre £2.00/£1.00/£1.50 with party rates and conducted tours available. Ample parking; caravans and campers welcome; provision for picnics, inside and out. Situated off the A47, 8 miles west of Peterborough. Telephone David Powell on (0780) 782222.

ESSEX

Trinity Antiques Centre
7 Trinity Street, Colchester, Essex. Tel: (0206) 577775. The Centre is housed in a 15th century building adjoining Tymperleys Clock Museum. 8 dealers with a variety of silver, jewellery, china, furniture, oriental items, postcards, copper, brass, linen etc. Open Mon-Sat, 0930-1700.

Dedham Art & Craft Centre
This thriving centre is set in the heart of Constable Country. The GROUND FLOOR houses the working pottery, and a huge array of British and other crafts. The Centrre provides local artists and craftspeople with an excellent showcase and gallery for their work. There is a fascinating display of silkpainting. The restaurant/coffee shop serves an excellent range of wholefood/vegetarian fayre all day (lunches 1200-1400). On the FIRST FLOOR is a wide range of items from designer knitwear and jewellery to ladies clothes, brass and copperware. Resident artists can often be seen at work. TOY MUSEUM - see entry in Museums section. The Skylight Gallery on the SECOND FLOOR is an excellent venue for a further display as well as studio/workshops for our modelmaker, dried flower arranger and seamstresses. Open Mon-Sun, 1000-1700 all year (but closed Mon during Jan-Mar). Admission 40p/20p (family £1). High Street, Dedham, Nr Colchester, Essex. 1 mile off main A12 between Colchester and Ipswich. Tel: (0206) 322666. Restaurant (0206) 322677.

NORFOLK

The Mustard Shop
Norwich is the home of Colmans, who have been milling mustard for over 160 years. Some varieties sold at this shop-cum-museum of mustard making are not generally available elsewhere. Reproductions of famous Colman posters, tea-towels, aprons, etc. 3 Bridewell Alley, Norwich. Tel. (0603) 627889

Alby Crafts

The Gallery contains the skills of many British craftsmen, shown to perfection in this beautifully restored set of Norfolk farm buildings. Also Studio-workshops, Furniture Showroom, Lace Museum, Bottle Museum and Gift Shop. The Tea Room serves a varied menu of home made food. Extensive and interesting Gardens. Free car park. Coaches by appointment. Open 15 Jan-11 Mar, Sat & Sun 1000-1700; 12 Mar-18 Dec, Tue-Sun, 1000-1700. On A140 between Cromer and Aylsham. Tel (0263) 761590

The Textile Centre
GREAT WALSINGHAM

Hand Printed Textiles, Cards, Books and Gifts.

The Textile Centre

Now established in traditional Norfolk barns, the Textile Centre offers the opportunity to see the fascinating designs of Sheila Rowse being put to print. Sold country-wide for many years, her textile designs present a unique sense of personality rarely seen before. The screen printing and making up processes can be viewed during weekdays. Textiles and a variety of unusual gifts are on sale in the Craft Shop where coffee, tea and home-made scones, etc., are served. Free car parking, facilities for the disabled. Open mid Mar-mid Dec, Mon-Fri, 0930-1730. Weekends & Bank Hols, 1000-1700. Educational and group visits welcomed by appointment. B1388 Hindringham Road , Great Walsingham, Norfolk. Tel (0328) 820009.

Taverham Craft Centre

Taverham Craft Centre is a purpose-built centre for the finest in traditional crafts, hand made on the premises by local crafts people in a glorious countryside setting in the heart of the Wensum Valley to the west of Norwich. The workshops have been built to the highest standards in traditional style, and are grouped around a charming paved quadrangle. Inside you'll find many different crafts, from embroidery and lacemaking to sugar craft, painting and framing. Watch the crafts people at work, talk to them about their skills, and come away with a pretty and practical keepsake. Plus garden centre, coffee bar, pet food and corn stores. Facilities for the disabled: coach parties welcome. Car parking for 1000 cars. Open daily, 1000-1700. Taverham Craft Centre, Fir Covert Road, Taverham, Norwich (situated 7 miles from Norwich on the A1067 Norwich /Fakenham road). Tel: (0603) 860522. Please phone before calling for specific crafts and/or purchases.

THE PARTICULAR POTTERY

The Particular Pottery

A Particular Baptist Chapel (1807) has been sympathetically restored resulting in a working pottery and craft showroom. At the Particular Pottery one can watch the resident potters at work and view finished pieces for sale in the upstairs Gallery. Gillian Anderson produces a stoneware range of functional oven to tableware. Peter concentrates on hand-built pots and makes sculptures of animal and human figures. David Walters prefers throwing porcelain. He creates bowls of all sizes, and large platters, urns and containers, covered with distinctive brush decoration. Kenninghall is on the B1113, not far from Banham Zoo, and the pottery is open seven days a week, 0900-1700. Visitors are very welcome. Tel: (0953) 888476.

Sutton Windmill Pottery

Sutton Windmill Pottery

Sutton is a small Broadland village 17 miles north-east of Norwich via the A1151, and 16 miles north of Great Yarmouth just off the A149. Malcolm Flatman makes and designs a large range of microwave and dishwasher safe stoneware pottery and tableware items in a selection of glazes. Many lamps and decorative pieces are "one-offs", and Malcolm will produce items to customers' own designs. Visitors are welcome in the workshop to see work in progress and to purchase from a selection of finished pottery. Please telephone at weekends, and before a long journey. A price list is available on request, and telephone and postal enquiries are welcome. Pottery can be posted to customers if required. Sutton Windmill Pottery, Church Road, Sutton, Norwich, Norfolk. Telephone Stalham (0692) 580595.

The Picturecraft Art Gallery
North Norfolk's Art Centre

Discover one of the largest, privately owned art galleries in the country when visiting the historic Georgian town of Holt. Gold Award Winners of the coveted NatWest Business Award Scheme 1991. Difficult to find, so look for the brown & white "Art Gallery'' Tourist Information signs in the town centre. No admission charges and large free car park. Extensive artists' material shop and specialist picture framing service. Video presentations on painting techniques. Demonstrations and one-man-shows. Easy access to all departments makes wheel-chair visitors especially welcome. Members of the Fine Art Trade Guild and Guild of Master Craftsmen. Open Mon-Sat 0900-1700. (Thu 0900-1300). Telephone Holt (0263) 711040 Gallery; 713259 Frame Desk; 712256 Art Shop. 23 Lees Courtyard, Off Bull Street, Holt. NR25 6HP

Black Horse Bookshop

Latest books on a wide range of subjects, including almost everything in print about East Anglia. Other departments include maps, art books, architecture and reference books. Books posted to all parts of the world. Open 6 days a week. Official agent for HMSO. 8 & 10 Wensum St, Norwich. Tel (0603) 626871 and 613828

NORFOLK CHILDREN'S BOOK CENTRE
SPECIALIST CHILDREN'S BOOKSHOP

Norfolk Children's Book Centre

Surrounded by fields, the Centre displays what we are told is the best collection of children's and teachers' books in East Anglia. Here you will find a warm welcome, expert advice and an abundance of the best, the latest and the classics in children's fiction and non-fiction. Open during school holidays Mon-Sat 1000-1600, term time Wed 1000-1200 and Sat 1000-1600. Teachers welcome any time, please phone. Find us between Aylsham and Cromer just off the A140. Look out for the signposted left turn 600 yards north of Alby Crafts. Telephone (0263) 761402.

See Glassmaking at **Caithness Crystal** *King's Lynn*

Caithness Crystal

You are welcome to view the glassmaking at no charge and watch them shaping and blowing glass in the manner it has been made for centuries. You will be able to view the operation at close quarters and see the skill of the glassmaker creating items from molten glass. Well stocked factory shop, open throughout the year 7 days a week, June-mid Sep and 6 days a week for the rest of the year. Glassmaking throughout the year Mon-Fri and including Sat from Easter-Dec plus Sun from 29 May-10 Sep. Well worth a visit, a bargain all year. Caithness Crystal, Oldmedow Road, Hardwick Industrial Estate, King's Lynn. Tel (0553) 765111.

Norfolk Children's Book Centre

Please mention East Anglia Guide when replying to advertisements

Willow Farm Flowers

Willow Farm Flowers are situated at Neatishead, near Wroxham, in the heart of the Norfolk Broads. A small farm specialising in growing and supplying quality dried flowers direct to the public. The Shop and Flower Arranging workshop are open throughout the year with advice and help readily available. A huge selection of flowers by the bunch; baskets of all sizes, sundries and books. Dozens of Dried Flower Arrangements, large and small are always in stock or made to special order. Details of winter day classes available on request. Evening group demonstrations by appointment. A selection of flowers can be seen growing during the summer, Well signposted off the A1151 Wroxham to Stalham road. Open 7 days a week throughout the year (except closed Dec 24-31) Mon-Sat 1000-1600; Sun 1100-1600. Tel: Wroxham (0603) 783588.

Great Bircham Windmill

Norfolk's finest corn mill, set in unspoilt countryside on a site used for wind-milling since the 1700s. Climb the five floors to the top and view the milling machinery which is in working order. Tea Rooms, Bakery and Gift Shop. Open daily from 1 Apr-end Sep except Sat, 1000-1800. Tel (048523) 393.

Appleyard Craft Court

The old 1816 stockfeed and harness barn and surrounding farm buildings have been sympathetically renovated to provide a courtyard of crafts and shops to delight any visitor. Experience the aroma of freshly baked bread and pastries from our bakery or enjoy morning coffee in the adjacent coffee shop. Pantiles Bistro and new bar 'The Horse & Harness' offers mouth watering menus and a select choice of local ales. Watch cider being made the Norfolk way and sample straight from the barrel or simply browse amongst the crafts and curios in the old Craft Barn. Why not finish your day with a trip to Banham Zoo - just opposite the courtyard. Coaches always welcome. Open 1000-1700 daily. Situated between Diss and Attleborough on the B1113. Tel: (0953) 887771.

The Candlemaker and Model Centre

The Candlemaker and Model Centre at Stokesby, situated 9 miles from Great Yarmouth on the banks of the River Bure, boasts England's largest variety of handcrafted candles, with many that are unique. The Centre also has a good selection of modelling kits. The candle shop and workshop is open daily (except Sat) from Easter to the end of Oct from 0900-1730 and during Nov and Dec from Thu to Sat 1000-1600 with free admission. Free parking and river moorings in village. Telephone Great Yarmouth (0493) 750242.

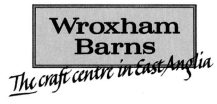

Wroxham Barns Ltd

This collection of beautifully restored 18th century barns, set in 10 acres of Norfolk parkland, provides the setting for one of the finest rural craft centres in East Anglia. Situated 1½ miles north of Wroxham you will find 14 craft workshops where resident craftsmen may be seen manufacturing a wide range of individual craftware. The Gallery Craft Shop offers an exciting selection of unusual gifts, crafts and clothing, whilst the Old Barn Tea Room can provide delicious home made cakes, traditional cream teas and light lunches. As well as Williamson's traditional funfair, the parkland is home to Junior Farm - a farmyard full of friendly animals where children can help bottle feed the baby goats and piglets. Open daily 1000-1800 (winter opening 1000-1700). Tel. Wroxham (0603) 783762.

The Handworkers Market

Situated at the entrance to the main car park is this needlework and embroidery specialist shop. Well known for its marvellous stock of materials both here and abroad. We stock the full range of DMC threads. St Epin crewel wool in over 70 colours. Appleton's wool, both tapestry and crewel in over 390 colours. A vast selection of trammed and painted canvasses. Single and double thread canvas in French, German and English. Evenweave linens and cottons as well as many other fabrics. Over 80 different gold and silver threads. Real kid. Books on the many different aspects of needlework and design. We will gladly post whatever you want. Open all the year round 0930-1700. Closed lunch time 1300-1400 and all day Thu. The Handworkers' Market, 18 Chapel Yard, Holt. Telephone Holt (0263) 711251.

A **BLACK SHEEP** SHOP

Black Sheep

Invite you to visit their Farm Store at Ingworth or Town Shop in Penfold Street, Aylsham both en route to Blickling. The Farm Store is open daily ex Mon, including Sun and Bank Hols and closed mid Jan-Easter. The Town Shop is open daily Mon-Sat. In either you can be sure of a warm welcome. Knitting at Aylsham is often in progress and you will see the transformation of this superb wool into a collection of high quality country clothes, together with an exciting range of gifts. At Ingworth, from the Farm Store windows you just may catch a glimpse of a few members of the World renowned pedigree flock of Black Welsh Mountain Sheep! We've something for every member of the family – sweaters that are chunky, classic, patterned or plain; jackets, coats, skirts and hats; gloves, scarves, belts, mugs – even knitting wools and tweeds to make up to your own design. No tour of East Anglia is complete without visiting us, so don't conform – become a Black Sheep – come and pay us a visit! If you find it impossible to visit us then SEND FOR FREE COLOUR CATALOGUE to Black Sheep Ltd., Ingworth, Norwich, Norfolk NR11 6PJ, England. Aylsham (0263) 733142/732006.

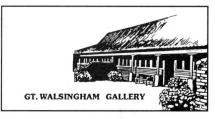

GT. WALSINGHAM GALLERY

Great Walsingham Gallery

The Gallery is set in a beautiful courtyard of converted barns in the picturesque village of Great Walsingham. Exhibitions are held by contemporary and traditional artists together with displays of patchwork quilts and cushions, etc, handmade furniture, baskets and pottery. On sale are framed and unframed fine art prints, photograph frames, mirrors and greeting cards. A picture framing service is offered as well as weekend painting and craft courses. Member of the Fine Art Trade Guild. Open Easter to end of Oct, Mon-Fri, 0900-1730, Weekends, 1000-1700; other times of the year, Mon-Fri, 0930-1700, Sat 1000-1230. Follow signs for the Textile Centre. Parking. Telephone (0328) 820900.

Suffolk Craft Society Exhibition (see page 96)

CRAFTS, SPECIALITIES AND GALLERIES

Park Farm Snettisham
Farmyard Craft Centre

Our resident craftsmen welcome visitors to their splendid workshops set in the beautifully restored Norfolk Carrstone farm buildings. The Centre now includes an art gallery offering original and limited editions from local artists. This traditional building also houses the Orchard Tea Room and Gift Shop. Ample free car parking and free admission to the Centre ensures a worthwhile visit to admire the craftsmens skills and watch art being created. Ideal for purchasing that unique gift manufactured by our craftsmen. Open from Mar-end Dec, daily from 1030. The Farmyard Craft Centre is one of the facilities available at Park Farm, the popular visitor attraction for all ages, which offers deer safaris, an open farm, pets corner, the gigantic adventure playground and lots more. Park Farm, Snettisham, near King's Lynn, Norfolk PE31 7NQ. Tel: (0485) 542425.

The Curiosity Street Experience

New for 1994 we illustrate Britain's fascinating shopping past with thousands of exhibits covering a variety of products; brought to life through personal audio tours. Housed in the Victorian Reepham Station other displays tell of its railway history. Off-road cycle hire for miles of safe family fun, based on the old railway line, is another attraction, as well as giant outdoor games. Light refreshments and unusual gifts too. The Curiosity Street Experience, Reepham Station, Station Road, Reepham, Norfolk NR10 4LJ (midway Norwich and Holt). Telephone (0603) 871187. Open Apr-Oct, daily, 1000-1600.

SUFFOLK

NURSEY & SON LTD

Nursey & Son Ltd

Established 1790. Specialist in Sheepskin and Leather Clothing. Sheepskin Hats, Gloves, Mittens, Moccasins, Rugskins etc. The Factory shop has a good selection especially for Gifts, also a wide variety of sub-standard Products and Oddments. Mon - Fri 9-1, 2-5. Closed 24 July. Reopen 8 August. Access, Visa. 12 Upper Olland St, Bungay. Tel: (0986) 892821

Suffolk Craft Society

The Suffolk Craft Society represents the best professional craftsmen in Suffolk. Details of the 160 members - Basketmakers, Bookbinders, Calligraphers, Furniture-makers, Glass engravers, Jewellers, Musical instrument makers, Potters, Print makers, Sculptors, Textile artists, Wood carvers & turners - can be found in **Living Crafts in Suffolk**, £3.50 from selected East Anglian bookshops. The Annual Exhibition at the Peter Pears Gallery, Aldeburgh, from 23 Jul until 29 Aug, attracts over 10,000 visitors. You will find good craftsmanship, modestly priced and beautifully displayed. Or you could telephone an individual maker to arrange a studio visit and place an order. For further details (or the book at £4.25 inc postage): Sue Wilson, 2 Rose Terrace, Marlesford, Woodbridge, Suffolk IP13 0AR.

BERNARD ROOKE POTTERY

Bernard Rooke Pottery

A pottery gallery selling all the pottery and paintings produced by Bernard Rooke and his sons Aaron and Felix in adjoining studios in an old flour mill. Bernard studied at Ipswich School of Art and Goldsmith's College, London. The pottery was established in London in 1960 and moved to the Mill in 1967. The Gallery was opened in 1971 and is now sited in the old cart shed next to the old steam mill and base to the old post mill. A large range of table lamps, standard lamps, paintings, animal sculptures and vases are on display and for sale all year round. The pottery is situated 6 miles N of Ipswich, opposite Swilland water tower, just off the B1078 midway between Wickham Market and Needham Market. Tel (0473) 785460.

Ascot House Crafts
Earl Stonham – Norwich Road A140

1000 square feet of attractive and fragrant display welcomes visitors who browse our selection of Pottery, Objets D'Art, Turkish Copperware, Craft Jewellery, Colour Box Miniatures, Collectables, Pictures, Corn Dollies, Dried Flowers, Toys, Cards and Giftwrap. Pine furniture is also featured. Sensible prices and well worth a visit. Situated on the main A140 Ipswich to Norwich road at the crossing with the A1120 Stowmarket/Yoxford road. Good parking and only 15 minutes from Ipswich. Jan-Jul open daily except Mon & Tue. Jul-Jan open daily except Mon. Hours 1000-1730. Open Bank Holiday Mon. Tel: Stowmarket (0449) 711495.

Watson's Potteries

Earliest record of Wattisfield potters is 1646. The Watson family have perpetuated the craft for more than 170 years. Original Suffolk Collection of printed terra-cotta ware includes kitchen and gift items, unique terra-cotta wine coolers, herb, spice and storage jars, lasagne dishes, bread bakers, etc. See original kiln, tour factory by appointment, visit shop selling quality seconds. Wattisfield (A143 between Bury and Diss). Tel Stanton (0359) 51239.

Bruisyard Vineyard & Herbs Centre

10-acre vineyard and winery producing the estate-bottled Bruisyard St Peter wine, situated west of Saxmundham. Wines, vines, herbs, souvenirs, etc for sale. Open 2 Jan-24 Dec, daily, 1030-1700. Conducted tours. Parties of 20 or more by appointment. Large herb and water gardens, shop, restaurant, children's play area and picnic area. Free wine tasting for vineyard and winery visitors. Bruisyard Wines, Church Road, Bruisyard, Saxmundham, Suffolk IP17 2EF. Tel: Badingham (072875) 281.

The National Horseracing Museum

Horseracing is part of British history. Explore this fascinating story at the National Horseracing Museum. A beautiful collection of racing art, personalities, objects and history, to interest both racing enthusiasts and casual visitor alike. Fine gift shop, gardens, licensed cafeteria. Open: Tue 29 Mar-Sun 4 Dec, Tue-Sat 1000-1700, Sun 1400-1700, closed Mon except Bank Hols. Jul and Aug Mon-Sat 1000-1700, Sun 1200-1700. Adults £3.30, over 60 £2.00, Child £1.00. 10% Reduction for adults and over 60's in group of 20 or more. Equine tours available, charges on request (booking essential). The National Horseracing Museum, 99 High Street, Newmarket, CB8 8JL. Tel: (0638) 667333.

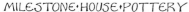

Aldringham Craft Market

Established in 1958. Wide selection of British craft products. Studio, domestic and garden pottery, wood, leather, glass, jewellery and metalwork. Original paintings, drawings, etchings and prints. Sculpture. Toys, ladies clothes, toiletries, books, maps, etc. Frequent exhibitions. Light refreshments. Children's play area. Easy car parking. Open Mon-Sat 1000-1730, Sun 1000-1200, 1400-1730. Evening party visits by arrangement. Aldringham, Nr Leiston, Suffolk. Tel: Leiston (0728) 830397.

Milestone House Pottery

Turn off the A12 into Yoxford High Street to find this pottery with its attractive Trafalgar balcony. We make our stoneware domestic pottery on the premises and import a selected few from Africa. Also available are greeting cards, kites, jam made in the village and many other things to make a visit worthwhile and interesting. Open Easter-Christmas, 1000-1700. Closed Wed 1300 and Sun. Winter opening Thu-Sat, 1000-1700. Milestone House Pottery, High Street, Yoxford, near Saxmundham, Suffolk, IP17 3EP. Tel: (072877) 465

For all who love Flowers

Swan Craft Gallery

Welcome to the restored stable of a former 17th century Inn. Enjoy browsing amid a carefully selected collection of quality Creative Crafts and an unique mix of new and traditional hand decorated accessories and gifts. The whole range is displayed in such an imaginative style that it will make your visit a sheer delight. From our own Workshops, flower designer and author Mary Lawrence, produces original Real Flower jewellery which is sold worldwide. We are situated on the main A1120 at Ashfield between Stowmarket and Yoxford. Open from Apr to Christmas on Tue to Sat and Bank Holidays 0930-1700. On Sun from 1400-1700. Tel: (0728) 685703.

Corncraft

At Monks Eleigh, in the heart of the Suffolk countryside between Hadleigh and Lavenham, Corn Craft specialise in growing and supplying corn dollies and dried flowers for the gift trade. A wide range of their own products, along with an extensive selection of other British crafts is available from their craft shop, beautifully set amongst the farm buildings. Coffee, cream teas, home made cakes and other light refreshments are served in the converted granary adjoining the shop. Ample space and easy parking. Evening demonstrations of corn dolly making are given by arrangement. Contact Mrs Win Gage. Open every day throughout the year from 1000-1700. Bridge Farm, Monks Eleigh, Suffolk. Tel: (0449) 740456.

Snape Maltings

This remarkable collection of old maltings buildings is set on the banks of the River Alde on the Suffolk Heritage Coast. Shops and galleries include House and Garden (furniture, rugs, quilts, kitchenware and fine foods plus pots and plants in the garden); Snape Craft Shop; Gallery; Countrywear; Maltings Music; Children's Shop and a special Christmas Shop (open Sep to Dec). Fresh home-cooked food in the Granary Tea Shop, River Bar and the Plough and Sail pub. Open all year, daily 1000-1800 (1000-1700 in winter). Snape Maltings, near Saxmundham, Suffolk IP17 1SR. Telephone (0728) 688303/5

CRAFTS SPECIALITIES AND GALLERIES

The Parish Lantern
I am sure you will agree that there is something for everyone at the Parish Lantern including delicious light refreshments and a warm and friendly welcome. Before the advent of street lamps the only light in the village was provided by the moon which was called The Parish Lantern. Walberswick is one of the few villages still using the moon in this way. Open daily, 1000-1730. Fri, Sat & Sun only during Jan, Feb and Mar. Tel: Southwold (0502) 723173.

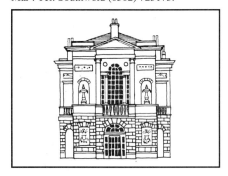

Bury St Edmunds Art Gallery
Robert Adam's only public building in the East of England. The magnificent cruciform upper floor is used for a programme of changing exhibitions across the visual arts with a special emphasis on contemporary craftwork. Craft shop with a selection of prints, ceramics, wood, glass, textiles and jewellery, books, cards and children's gifts. Open all year, Tue-Sat, 1030-1630; closed 25 Dec-2 Jan and 1 Apr. Disabled access. Entrance 50p concessions 30p. Tel: (0284) 762081.

Sutton Windmill Pottery
Reduction Stoneware 8-piece Wine Set

AFTERNOON TEAS

What can be more tempting than a traditional English cream tea? You can be sure of a delicious selection of home made goodies at any of the following tea rooms, so forget about your waist line, and treat yourself!
To help you find the tearooms nearest to you we have marked the locations with a teacup symbol on the maps on pages 119-124. Establishments which are members of the Tourist Board have a ☺ after the text.

CAMBRIDGESHIRE

ELY
Steeplegate
16/18 High Street.
Tel: (0353) 664731
Proprietor: Mr J S Ambrose
Seats: 40
Open: Daily except Sun
Home-made cakes, scones and fresh cream teas served in historic building backing onto cathedral. Medieval vault on view. Craft goods also sold. Small groups welcome.☺

ST IVES
The Cafe Upstairs
Crown Place (situated beside Woolworths)
Tel: (0480) 494214
Proprietor: Mrs S Summerside
Seats: 34
Open: Mon-Sat from 1000.
Morning coffee, wide range of homemade light hot and cold meals, sandwiches, homemade cakes and scones served all day. Ice-creams a speciality. Large no smoking area. Young children welcome! Parties, especially for cream teas, welcome by prior appointment. ☺

ESSEX

BURNHAM-ON-CROUCH
Copper Kettle Coffee Shop
101 Station Road
Tel: (0621) 782203
Proprietor: Howard G Watling
Seats: 55 indoors, 25 in garden
Open: All year, daily.
Homemade cakes, scones, cream teas, breakfasts, light lunches, salads, jacket potatoes, homemade soup, soft ice creams and sundaes. Friendly service, smoking and non smoking areas. Children and elderly welcome, disabled facilities. Reservations accepted. Easy parking. Coaches by appointment.

DEDHAM
The Essex Rose Tea House
Royal Square.
Tel: (0206) 323101
Proprietors: Mr and Mrs Bower and Mandy
Seats: 80
Open: Daily
This pretty pink-washed 15c teahouse in the heart of Constable country serves morning coffee, salad lunches and sandwiches and of course traditional cream teas and special gateaux. Also a large selection of craft goods, paintings, home-made chocs and fudge.

THAXTED
The Cake Table Tea Room
4/5 Fishmarket Street, Thaxted
Tel: (0371) 831206
Proprietor: Mrs K M Albon
Seats: 30 inside plus extra 10 on patio
Open: Mon-Fri 1100-1700, Sat and Sun 1100-1730
The Cake Table Tearoom lies in the heart of this very pretty town, between its splendid old church and the recently restored John Webb's windmill. Winner of the Tea Council's Top Tea Place of the Year Award 1991, the tearoom has an old world charm rarely found today and is famous for its freshly baked cakes and scones.☺

HERTFORDSHIRE

BISHOPS STORTFORD
Tickle Manor Tea Room
3 High Street
Tel: (0279) 466646
Proprietor: Mrs Gloria Gomez
Seats: 62
Open: All year, daily except Sun, 0900-1730
Open for morning coffee, light lunch and afternoon tea. Genuinely home-made cakes and scones to Tickle Manor's unique and delicious recipes, served in beautiful 18th century Dickensian fronted shop in the heart of Bishops Stortford. Families, parties and bookings welcome.

HARE STREET VILLAGE
The Old Swan Tea Shop
Nr Buntingford (on B1368)
Proprietors: Lynda & Bill Sullivan
Tel: (0763) 289265
Seats: 40 inside. 50 in garden.
Open: Apr-Oct, daily exc. Wed, 1000-1900, Nov-Mar, Thu-Sun, 1000-1800
A picturesque 15th century Hall House within two acres of gardens and orchard, situated in beautiful East Hertfordshire. Specialising in traditional home baking. Licensed and open for morning coffee, lunches, afternoon teas, early evening meals. Also Sunday roasts, but please book. Large non-smoking area. Parties welcome by arrangement.☺

Tickle Manor Tea Rooms, Lavenham

NORFOLK

BANHAM
Banham Bakery and Coffee shop
The Appleyard, (Opposite Banham Zoo)
Tel: (0953) 887771 Ext. 255
Seats: 28+ Courtyard seating (weather permitting)
Open: All year (except 25 & 26 Dec)
Set in beautifully restored and converted timber and flint buildings Banham Bakery and Coffee shop is the ideal venue for that relaxed morning coffee and afternoon tea. The smell of baking fills the air, tempting you to purchase from the superb selection of cakes, pastries, pies, gateaux and breads. Parties and groups welcome by prior arrangement. ☺

ERPINGHAM
Alby Crafts Tea Rooms
Cromer Road (on A140).
Tel: (0263) 768719
Proprietor: Mrs C Ingram
Seats: 60
Open: 15 Jan-11 Mar, Sat & Sun, 1000-1700; 12 Mar-18 Dec, Tue- Sun, 1000-1700.
Situated in the centre of a working Craft Centre serving freshly ground coffee, home made cakes and scones, light lunches and snacks. Coach parties and groups welcome by appointment.☺

GREAT BIRCHAM
Great Bircham Windmill
Nr King's Lynn.
Tel: (048523) 393
Proprietors: Mr and Mrs Wagg
Seats: 45
Open: 27 Mar-30 Sep, daily (ex. Sat), 1000-1800. Tea rooms adjacent to the windmill. Cream teas, home-made cakes, free car park.☺

GREAT YARMOUTH
HoneyBuns
Clippesby Holidays
Proprietor: Jean Miller
Tel: (0493) 369217
Situated in beautiful parkland, a warm friendly welcome awaits you at HoneyBuns. Freshly made pots of tea, including a range of speciality blends, honey-sweetened cakes baked on the premises and freshly made butter scones served with Norfolk honey. ☺

HEACHAM
Norfolk Lavender Ltd
Caley Mill, Heacham.
Tel: Heacham (0485) 71965/70384
Seats: 38
Open: Daily, 1000-1700. Closed for Christmas holiday.
Average price: £1.65
Cakes and scones home-made, cream teas a speciality. Tea room in old millers cottage in the middle of lavender/herb gardens.☺

HORSHAM ST FAITHS
Elm Farm Chalet Hotel (Off A140 Cromer Road)
Nr Norwich.
Tel: (0603) 898366
Proprietor: W. R. Parker
Open: All year, Mon-Sat, 1000-1700
Situated in centre of picturesque village. Home-made cakes, scones, cream teas, fruit and cream served in garden or lounge. Light lunches. Parties welcome by prior appointment.☺

KING'S LYNN
Caithness Crystal
Oldmedow Road, Hardwick Industrial Estate
Tel: (0553) 765111
Seats:70
Open: All year, Mon-Fri, 0930-1630, Sat, 0930-1530, Sun 29 May-10 Sep, 1100-1600.
Pleasant tea room serving a large selection of tasty home made fruit pies and cakes, tea and coffee. Light lunches and cream teas.☺

NORWICH
The Sue Ryder Coffee Room
St Michael-at-Plea Church, Redwell St
Tel: (0603) 666930
Seats: 55
Open: 0930-1630, Mon-Sat
Light refreshments: cakes and pastries home-made. Coach parties welcome by appointment please write to the Manageress at the above address for details.

Norwich Cathedral Visitors Centre and Buffet
62 The Close, Norwich NR1 1EH
Tel: (0603) 766756
Seats: 68
Open: Mon-Sat, 1030-1630
Refreshments served in an ancient room above the Cloisters, one of the earliest parts of the former monastery. Locally-baked cakes and scones; delicious light lunches, sandwiches etc. Tea, coffee, soft drinks. Open air terrace in summer months.

OVERSTRAND
The Pleasaunce
Overstrand, near Cromer
Tel: (026378) 212
Open: Beginning of Jun-end Sep, Mon, Wed, Thu, 1400-1600.
Admission £2.50 (includes cream tea).
Ground floor and gardens. House designed by Sir Edward Lutyens; gardens originally laid out by Gertrude Jekyll, although much modified.

SHERINGHAM WOODS
Pretty Corner Restaurant and Buttery with Tea and Coffee Gardens
Nr Pretty Corner Main Car Park, A148
Tel: Sheringham (0263) 822358
Open: Easter-Oct, daily from 1000.
Buttery and Restaurant in creatively laid out Gardens with split-level and sheltered terraces. Home-made Dutch, Indonesian and English specialities, lunches and evening meals.☺

SNETTISHAM
Orchard Tea Room
Park Farm, Snettisham, Nr King's Lynn
Tel: (0485) 542425
Seats: 45 Plus Orchard picnic seating (during fine weather)
Open: Mar-end Dec, daily from 1030.
Our beautifully restored Norfolk Carrstone Barn is situated adjacent to The Orchard at the popular Park Farm visitor attraction. This traditional building also boasts craft workshops and an art gallery. Home made cakes, scones and light meals are available. Personal service to individuals and pre-booked coach parties. ☺

THURSFORD
The Thursford Collection
Thursford, Fakenham,
Tel: (0328) 878477
Proprietor: Mr J. Cushing
Seats: 70 inside, 120 outside.
Admission: £4.20/£1.80/£3.80

Afternoon cream teas on the lawn served from our Garden Conservatory. Teas and light refreshments also served in our "Barn". ☺

WALSINGHAM
Sue Ryder Coffee Room and Retreat House
The Martyrs House, High St.
Tel: (0328) 820622
Seats: 35
Open: All year, 0900-1730.
Light refreshments: cakes and pastries home-made. Coach parties welcome by appointment. Bed & Breakfast accommodation available with evening meal if required.

SUFFOLK

ALDRINGHAM
Aldringham Craft Market, Aldringham, nr Aldeburgh.
Tel: Leiston (0728) 830397
Contact: Margaret Huddle
Seats: Inside: 6, Outside: 30
Open: Spring-late Autumn, Mon-Sat 1000-1730, Sun, 1000-1200, 1400-1730.
Home-made cakes, scones, fresh coffee, etc, offered in our Coffee Shop. Adjacent lawn, climbing frame, etc, provides ideal venue for family break when visiting our extensive arts, crafts and gifts Gallery. Easy car parking.☺

AFTERNOON TEAS

BRUISYARD
Vineyard and Herb Centre Restaurant
West of Saxmundham.
Tel: (072875) 281
Seats: Inside: 25, Outside: 24
Open: 2 Jan-24 Dec, daily 1030-1630

Morning coffees, light lunches, afternoon teas. Home-made cakes and scones, herbal and speciality teas. Winery tours and tastings, herb and water gardens. Vineyard shop with wines, vines, herbs, crafts and gifts.☺

BUTLEY
Butley Pottery and Tea Room
Mill Lane, Butley, Woodbridge
Tel: (0394) 450785
Seats: 30 plus outside
Open: Apr-Sep, daily; Oct-Mar, Wed-Sun;, 1030-1700

A selection of tasty lunches with salad; home made cakes and scones; tea and coffee. Served in the relaxed atmosphere of the renovated thatched barn in peaceful rural surroundings. Live music most Sunday lunch times. Turn off the B1084 in Butley down Mill Lane. Evening parties can be catered for by appointment.

CAVENDISH
The Sue Ryder Coffee Room and Museum
High St,
Tel: (0787) 280252
Seats: 110
Admission to museum: 80p/40p
Open: Daily, 1000-1730, closed 25 Dec.

Lunches and light refreshments: cakes and pastries home-made. Gift shop.

CREETING ST MARY
Alder Carr Farm Shop & Tea Room
Off A45 to Needham Market (between Stowmarket and Ipswich) follow signs.
Tel: (0449) 720820
Proprietors: Nick & Joan Hardingham
Open: May-Christmas (seasonal) phone for details.

On the River Gipping, near picturesque Needham Market producing usual and unusual fruit and vegetables, ready picked and PYO. Adjacent in converted farm buildings are the Tea Room offering home-made cakes and light lunches and the unique old Piggery Pottery.

FELIXSTOWE
Ferry Cafe
Felixstowe Ferry
Tel: (0394) 276305
Proprietor: Laura Balsom
Seats: 48
Open: All year, 7 days a week

Teas with home made scones, cakes and pies, served in unique setting alongside mouth of River Deben with extensive fishing and boating activities. Also golf course nearby. Early breakfasts, superb fish and chips, and light meals all day. Parties catered for with free parking.

HELMINGHAM
Helmingham Hall
between Ipswich and Debenham on B1077
Tel: (0473) 890363
Owner: Lord Tollemache
Open: 1 May-11 Sep, Sun only 1400-1800
Admission: £2.50/£1.50/£2.30

Home made cakes and scones served in the old Coach House or outside in the courtyard, make a welcome end to a visit to the gardens at Helmingham Hall.

IPSWICH
The Sue Ryder Coffee Room
Sue Ryder Home, The Chantry, Hadleigh Road
Tel: (0473) 287999
Seats: 75
Open: Tue-Sun, 1000-1600

Light refreshments, cakes and pastries home-made. Coach parties welcome by appointment. Please write to: Mr Paul Payne.

KERSEY
The Bell Inn
The Street, Kersey, Nr Hadleigh, IP7 6DY
Tel/Fax: (0473) 823229
Open: Oct-Mar; weekends 1430-1700 weekdays by pre-booking only. Apr-Sep open every day.
Traditional Suffolk cream and afternoon teas served in this 14th century property. Fresh cream is used only. Assam, Earl Grey, Darjeeling and traditional "3 star" tea. Parking for 50 vehicles. Groups over 10 please book in advance. Seats 80.☺

LAVENHAM
Tickle Manor Tea Room
17 High St.
Tel: (0787) 248438
Proprietors: Mrs M Hartshorn
Seats: 35

Open for morning coffee, light lunch and afternoon tea, until 1730. Home made cakes and scones with fresh cream from a local Jersey herd, served in a beautiful 16th century timber framed tea room in the centre of this famous medieval village. Speciality cakes include Sticky Toffee Pudding, Suffolk Honey Cake and Hot Chocolate Fudge Cake. Families, parties & bookings welcome. Licensed. As featured on Anglia TV's "Food Guide".

The Vestry Tea Rooms
The Centre, High Street, Lavenham.
Tel: (0787) 247548
Proprietor: Mr K Morgan
Seats: 40
Open: All year, daily 1030-1730

This cosy tea room is set in a converted Victorian chapel which is now a shopping centre. Morning coffee, snacks, afternoon teas, home made cakes. Hot meals are available all day. Sunday roast, including sweet and coffee, £5.50. Easy parking and wheelchair access. Coach parties and groups welcome, by appointment if possible.

LONG MELFORD
Kentwell Hall
Lunches & Teas available to the public when visiting the Hall
Tel: Sudbury (0787) 310207
Owners: Mr and Mrs J P M Phillips
Seats: Old Kitchen 45, Undercroft 120

Home-made lunches plus cakes, scones and biscuits. Pre-booked coach parties welcome. *For admission prices and opening details please refer to Historic Houses entry.*☺

MONKS ELEIGH
Corn-Craft
Bridge Farm, Monks Eleigh, Nr Lavenham
Tel: (0449) 740456

Seats: 40 inside, 30 outside
Open: All year, daily, 1000-1700
Corn-Craft serves morning coffee, cream teas, delicious home-made cakes and other light refreshments in a converted granary, beautifully set amongst farm buildings adjoining the craft shop. Ample parking. Coach parties welcome by appointment. *For details of the craft shop refer to entry in Crafts section.*☺

ORFORD
The Old Warehouse
Quay Street.
Tel: Orford (0394) 450210
Owners: Jean Bostock & Charles Jackson
Open: All year, Tue-Sun, includung evenings.

Teas, coffees, home baked cakes and scones, full and varied lunch menu including local fish dishes, vegetarian meals and traditional Sunday roast. Seating outside with views of river and quay. Full restaurant licence. Permanent art gallery and gift shop. ☺

STONHAM PARVA
Whistling Mouse Crafts & Tea Room
Norwich Road , Stonham Parva, Stowmarket
Tel: (0449) 711000
Proprietor: Cora Pullen
Open: All year, Wed-Sun & Bank Hols 1000-1730
Seats: 24 + 10 on patio
On the A140 at Little Stonham (near Magpie Inn) the Tea Room serves home made cakes and scones, coffee, assorted teas and locally made dairy ice cream. It adjoins the well stocked craft shop with ample parking next to house.

THORPENESS
Gallery Coffee Shop
Barn Hall.
Tel: Aldeburgh (0728) 453105
Proprietors: Mr and Mrs J Strowger
Seats: 60 inside, 100 outside
Open: All year, 0930 to dusk.
A licensed restaurant situated next to beach with pleasant garden overlooking boating lake. Specialising in cream teas, gateaux and ice cream desserts, with extensive craft and gift shop. Coach parties welcome by appointment.

WALBERSWICK
Mary's
The Street.
Tel: (0502) 723243
Proprietors: Rob & Felicity Jelliff
Seats: 45
Open: Apr-Oct, daily (ex for Mon, other than Bank Holidays. Open Mon in Aug); Nov-Mar, Fri, Sat and Sun.

Morning coffee, lunch, afternoon and high teas, dinner Friday and Saturday. Home-made cakes and cream teas a speciality, served in the garden in fine weather. Parties welcome by appointment. and lunch/dinner reservations advisable.

The Parish Lantern
on the Village Green
Tel: (0502) 723173
Proprietors: Mary Allen and Sarah Bellina
Open: Jan- Mar, Fri, Sat and Sun only. Apr-Dec, Daily

Visit our tea room and garden where you can enjoy morning coffee, light refreshments, cream teas and home baked cakes. Also original crafts, gifts and pictures. We serve all day. You will be very welcome.☺

LOCAL PRODUCE

RESTAURANTS

Editor, Steven Saunders, owner of The Pink Geranium at Melbourn, Royston.
Co-Editor, Nicola Bothway, also of The Pink Geranium.

Welcome to my home, East Anglia, and in particular welcome to the restaurants section of this guide, some of which I have known personally for many years, others I am getting to know personally and enjoying every moment of it.

Having been 'born and bred' in East Anglia and spent most of my life here, I feel completely confident and very comfortable writing about some of our restaurants and hotels for the East Anglia Tourist Board. For food and wine is not only my life but my love, and I enjoy writing about it as much as eating or cooking it.

East Anglia has a most beautiful countryside, a horticulturists dream of fertile fields and arable farmlands stretching to the sea from the Thames estuary in Essex up to the Wash.

Our waters thrive with fish and shellfish and many fishing villages have developed their own speciality. Cromer in Norfolk is famous for its crabs and the ports of Great Yarmouth and Lowestoft are historically known for their red herrings. An abundance of shellfish is found all around the East Anglian coast and fresh water fish like eels, pike and zander are found in our counties rivers.

More than a third of the country's entire vegetable crop comes from East Anglia and a quarter of all the soft fruits of England and Wales are grown here.

In Cambridgeshire (where I live), we have many orchards and an abundance of farms selling homegrown strawberries, gooseberries, raspberries and currants.

Game is also plentiful in East Anglia and our countryside with its fields high with wheat, its marshes, fens and broads makes it the ideal habitat for most game birds.

An area so rich in grain is obviously going to produce some first class beer made from fermented barley and hops and there are several well known independent breweries in our region. East Anglia has also become one of the most important grape growing regions in the country because of our climate - supposed sunny summers! with relatively low rainfall ! and warm autumns, help ripen the grapes followed by cold winters allowing the vines to rest.

Our vineyards are scattered throughout the region. Many welcome visitors and sell wine on the premises. (see page for vineyards).

To summarise, East Anglia is a region to feel enthusiastic about and rightly so. It is at least 'a guide' full of interesting places to visit and a multiplicity of hotels and restaurants in the most varyuing of markets. With the help of my 'inspector' Nicola and staff at the East Anglia Tourist Board, we have together selected a list of hostelries across our region in various styles. We would welcome your comments, good or bad on any listed, and please feel free to say that 'we' recommended you when booking a table. I hope that you have a really happy and memorable time in East Anglia and that you enjoy our regions food, wine and hospitality. Bon Appetit!

Prices are intended as a guide only and may change over the course of the year We recommend that you check details when you book. Prices do not usually include drinks with your meal. Please mention East Anglia Guide when replying to advertisements.

CAMBRIDGESHIRE

KEYSTON (off A604 between Huntingdon & Thrapston)	**MADINGLEY (4m NW Cambridge)**	**ELY**

The Pheasant Inn
Tel: (08014) 241

A delightful thatched village pub, its 17th century interior decorated with farming by-gones on high white walls beneath the old beams. Chef Patron Roger Jones produces a sophisticated menu which is acclaimed in every major national guide. In both the restaurant and the bar you can enjoy imaginative and interesting dishes, competitively priced and finely presented, with real ales and wine by the glass. Should the sun shine, enjoy eating outside overlooking the village green. *Open: daily. Average prices: lunch or dinner a la carte £18.00, bar food from £3.95*

Three Horseshoes
Tel: (0954) 210221

Just outside Cambridge, this enchanting thatched village inn with exposed oak beams, is well worth a visit. The very pretty restaurant and conservatory is the setting for the high-class, creative cooking of Chef Patron Richard Stokes. There is a welcoming bar (which offers over ten wines by the glass) and imaginative bar snacks are available every lunchtime and evening. The large garden is beautifully maintained. *Open: daily. Average prices: lunch & dinner à la carte £22.00, bar food from £3.95.*

Steeplegate Tea Rooms
16/18 High Street
Tel: (0353) 664731

Steeplegate Tea Rooms nestle next to Ely's magnificent cathedral. Upstairs, pictures line the walls of the white painted tea rooms, which are divided into areas for smokers and non-smokers. The simple menu includes delicious freshly baked quiches and flans, cakes, pics, scones and shortbread, as well as a selection of different teas. Downstairs is a craft shop and the vaulted undercroft is used for art and craft exhibitions. *Open: Mon, Wed, Thur, Fri & Sat 1000-1700. Average prices: lunch £2.50-£3.75*

CAMBRIDGE

Panos
Hills Road
Tel: (0223) 212958

This popular central Cambridge restaurant cooks stylish French/Greek style dishes and even offers a traditional 'Mezze' as a first course amongst a special 3 course set dinner. The service here is extremely welcoming and the food is delicious. There is a good variety on the menu including classic Greek dishes like Fillet Suvlaki to more French style dishes like Crevette Provençales with rice and Greek Salad. The lunch menu is imaginative and varied and is very competitively priced at £11.95 for 3 courses and there is always a daily 'special' available. Desserts are all home-made and are quite delicious, they include Crêpe Suzette and Baklava. Turkish coffee is offered in addition to regular house coffee. A wide selection of wines are available at reasonable cost. *Open: Mon-Fri, 1300-2330, Sat dinner, Sun, closed. Average price: £17.95 for 3 courses excluding wine.*

HUNTINGDON

The Old Bridge Hotel
Tel: (0480) 52681

The ultimate "country hotel in a town". The lounges extend into a really splendid conservatory with attractive and comfortable cane chairs and tables amidst lush green plants in great tubs. Here one can enjoy exceptional bar-food, with a lavish buffet including a huge range of interesting salads, Baron of rare roast beef, whole Scotch salmon and spectactular sweet trolley. Also a top-class, panelled restaurant with a wine list which won Egon Ronay's "Cellar of the Year" for 1989. *Open: daily. Average prices: 3 course meal £28.00. Hot bar food from £3.95.*

STAMFORD

The George of Stamford
Tel: (0780) 55171

Here is a restaurant in the very best English tradition of the coaching inn. The fine oak panelled dining room is a place for serious eating. There are ribs of beef, racks of lambs and just the odd Italian dish reflecting the taste of Ivo Vannocci, Director of this small hotel group. There is an outstanding wine list. Less formal food is served in the airy Garden Lounge and in the summer the flower-decked courtyard is a most delightful place to meet and eat. Stamford provides a beautiful backdrop for this historic hotel. *Open: daily. Average prices: lunch & dinner, 3 course £28, bar snacks from £4.45.*

WANSFORD-IN-ENGLAND (Just off the A1)

The Haycock Hotel
Tel: (0780) 782223

The Haycock is a splendid 17th century coaching inn. The atmosphere is warm and informal. Especially popular is the cold buffet, which includes whole salmon, traditional beef, moist turkeys, hams, home made pies and all manner of salads. The restaurant itself is well known for its traditional English food: roast beef, steak and kidney pies or puddings, game in season and excellent, fresh, Fenland vegetables. Do not miss the splendid riverside gardens, a winner of the Tourist Board's annual garden competition. *Open: daily. Average prices: à la carte £25,00, buffet £4.95-£9.95, bar food from £4.25.*

FENSTANTON

King William IV
High Street
Tel: (0480) 462467

A charming 17th century Inn in a pretty village off the A604 near St Ives. There is a pleasant relaxing atmosphere in this low beamed pub run by the very hospitable landlord, Jeremy Schonfeldt and his staff. All food is fresh, well varied and reasonably priced. The menu is comprised of things like Seafood Pancake, Steak and Kidney Pudding (in a suet case), or Lamb and Apricot pie with Ginger. There are always 2 or 3 vegetarian dishes available and a wide selection of wines and beers. Every Wednesday evening they have a Blues or Jazz band playing and they frequently have speciality evenings. During the summer you can relax outside and there is ample parking around the attractive village. Seats 50 in the restaurant, half of which is non-smoking.

CAMBRIDGE

Vivat Bar & Brasserie
The Cellars, 1 King's Parade
Tel: (0223) 359506

Situated opposite Kings College, Vivat is a very popular venue. The restaurant seats 70 and has a relaxed atmosphere. A good wide selection of food is on offer including Garlic mushrooms, home-made soups and Scottish smoked salmon slices, to main courses like Goats Cheese Salad, Fillet Steak Salad, Pasta dishes, Grilled steaks and an interesting selection of old English dishes like Beef and Ale pie and Bangers and Mash. Puddings

too are varied and home-made including Banoffee Pie and Chocolate fudge cake. A good selection of wines and drinks are available at fair prices and include new world wines from Australia and South Africa. The staff here are friendly, efficient and smart and offer you good food and service at very reasonable prices. Ideal place to pop into and have lunch (or dinner) whilst shopping in Cambridge or visiting the Colleges. *Open: 7 days a week, bar 1100-2300, restaurant 1200-2300. Average price: £15 per head including a bottle of wine*

CAMBRIDGE

Park Terrace
Tel: (0223) 67480

Tucked away behind the University Arms Hotel and bordering the cricket square of Parker's Piece is Hobbs Pavilion. A selection of savoury and sweet pancakes are filled with fascinating combinations from Bumper Vegetarian (Cheese, Spinach, Basil, Tomatoes), to Hobbs Special Steak with mashed potatoes. A full range of first courses is available from the blackboard, we had Gazpacho which was one of the most flavoursome I had ever tasted even to Spanish standards. To follow I had the Super Pizza Pancake filled with Cheese, Tomatoes, Basil and Garlic Mushrooms which was also delicious (£4.15). Also on the blckboard is a selection of wines served by the bottle or glass, and there is a good selection of soft drinks available including 'Citron Presse' (lemon juice, water and sugar on the side). I also found the list of 'Digestifs' interesting and enterprising which included Marc de Bourgogne, Marc de Gigondas and some single estate Cognac all at £4 per large measure. This is a good place to take kids of all ages. Seats 60. *Open: 1200-1415 lunch, 1900-2145 dinner. Closed Sun, Mon, Bank Holidays, mid Aug-mid Sep. Average price: £14.50 dinner with coffee, per head.*

MELBOURN

The Pink Geranium
Tel: (0763) 260215

A real gem of a restaurant. Steven Saunders understands that eating out is as much about relaxation and enjoyment as it is about eating. He somehow manages to make all his guests feel that they are personally welcome. Cooking is of an unusually high standard. We enjoyed a delightfully light mousseline of fish and shellfish, courgette flowers with soft cheese in a light pastry tart, and then splendid crispy duck, a famous dish of the house. Puddings are light and sensational. A la carte prices are reasonable for such high standards of cooking. Sunday lunch inclusive menu is particularly good value. On a sunny day or a warm evening one can enjoy a drink in the delightful garden, surrounded, of course, by pink geraniums. *Open: Tue-Fri, lunch & dinner, Sat dinner, Sun lunch. Average prices: evening a la carte approx £35.00, set menu £29.95, Sunday lunch £17.95, weekday lunch £17.95*

ST IVES

The Manor Kitchen

The Manor Kitchens
Manor Mews, Bridge Street
Tel: (0480) 464921

Overlooking the River Ouse, The Manor Kitchens is a small building with a superb view of barges, boats and swans. Owned by James and Ann Underwood. James runs the well stocked cheese and delicatessen counter, which also sells a huge variety of loose leaf teas and freshly ground coffees whilst Ann looks after the restaurant business. There are 70 cheeses available from the delicatessen and hand cured Dunmow Ham. The small 32 cover restaurant is filled with old pine tables and chairs and offers a snack type menu of ploughmans (from the cheese counter) a vegetarian special, salads and sandwiches. Home baked cakes and scones and hand made jam are also available. A good selection of quality teas and herbal teas are on offer and all food and beverages are free from artificial flavourings and additives. No alcoholic wines and drinks are available but there are plenty of soft drinks to to choose from. This is the perfect place for a good old English afternoon tea or for a quality, tasty lunchtime snack. The Brixworth Paté Ploughman was delicious at £3.30 and do try the excellent Coffee cake to follow. *Open: Mon-Wed and Sat & Fri, 0900-1700; Sun, 1100-1700. Average price: Varies from 95p (for filled rolls) to £3.75 for afternoon tea. Soft drinks are very reasonably priced and good real cream ice creams available from £1.10.*

ESSEX

HARWICH
Pier at Harwich
The Quay
Tel: (0255) 241212

Nothing could be more titillating gastronomically, than the idea of eating freshly caught fish in a harbourside restaurant. The restaurant upstairs has the feel of a bridge of a jolly ship with a pianist as captain where the food ranges from the simple and familiar appeal of such things as a delicious fish pie to the distinctly luxurious suggested by crab, turbot or halibut in sophisticated sauces, as well as stunningly good lobster Thermidor. The Ha'penny Pier on the ground floor is geared to family eating and offers cheap and cheerful grub like spanking fresh fish and chips. A veritable piscatorial playground. *Average prices: restaurant £15-£20, Ha'penny pier £5-£8.*

ARDLEIGH, nr COLCHESTER

The Wooden Fender
Harwich Road
Tel: (0206) 230466

The Wooden Fender is easily recognised by its brightly coloured fairy lights, on the Colchester to Harwich road. It is renowned for its history as the meeting place of Matthew Hopkins, the "Witchfinder General" and his henchmen who decided the fate of 29 local witches over a pint or two of local ale. The ale is still excellent, with Adnams and Greene King as well as guest beers to be sampled. Eat either à la carte in the restaurant, or in the bar where bar snacks are good value and the choice is extensive – there are 4 different versions of lasagne alone! *Open: lunch & bar meals daily, restaurant nightly except Tues evening. Average prices: bar meals £2.60-£4. Access, Visa & Amex accepted.*

ROXWELL, Nr CHELMSFORD

Farmhouse Feast
The Street
Tel: (0245) 248583

The name of this restaurant conjures up an image of kitchen tables laden with nourishing and delicious country products, and indeed the feeling of plenty comes across as soon as you enter and are confronted by a table groaning under the weight of assorted hors d'oeuvres. Make your choice, but I advice restraint: save space for the rest of the meal! A tureen of home-made soup is to follow and then a choice of four main courses including vegetarian dishes. For dessert there is no problem with indecision for you help yourself from the buffet and can sample a little of two or even three extravaganzas. Coffee and petits fours complete the feast. *Open for lunch Tue-Fri, average price £12, dinner. Tue-Sat. 5 courses £23, 3 courses (exc. Sat) £13.50.*

STONES GREEN (Nr Wix, Harwich)

The Green Swan

The Green Swan
Tel: (0255) 870243

If you like to drink real ale and enjoy classical French country cooking, then The Green Swan at Stones Green, near Wix is for you. This is an informal, French Cafe masquerading as a country pub, owned by Colette and Chris Dudley. Colette, from the Vendée region of France, cooks everything herself from recipes handed down through generations, from mother to daughter. There is an extensive à la carte menu, or a choice of two 5 course set meals. Choosing what to eat is a difficult decision, alleviated somewhat by Chris explaining each dish in detail while offering you a taste of the house wine for approval. There is also a good wine list. My Champignons a la Bourguignonne were delicious and the Tarte aux Fruits was just Tart enough to bring the meal to a refreshing close. *The Green Swan is open each evening from Tue- Sun. Average price: £28 per person excluding wine.*

BURNHAM-ON-CROUCH

Clouds
20A High Street
Tel: (0621) 782965

Legend has it that Clouds was named after Sir Edward Heath's yacht 'Morning Cloud' from a time when he was competing in the Burnham Week Regatta and the yacht could be seen from the window. Lyn and Robin Bassil have been established here since 1986 and their friendly warm welcome makes you feel immediately at home. Situated in Burnham High Street, this one time sail-makers loft retains the original oak beams and red brick. There is an excellent Table D'Hote menu at under £10 or you can choose from a wide selction of dishes from the à la carte menu. Our starters were beautifully presented and were generous portions - half a melon filled to overflowing with exotic fruits, a delicious 'Cocktail Crustacea' - local crabs and peeled prawn cocktail - and 1/2 dozen succulant local oysters. A la carte main courses range from Dover Sole to Steak dishes like Steak Diane and a wide variety of vegetarian dishes. Each main course is served with an enormous helping of vegetables. Clouds has a relaxed atmosphere, you don't feel as though the staff are hovering in the hope that you'll hurry up and go. So much so that you feel like rounding off the meal with plenty of coffee and a large brandy! *Open: Wed-Sun for dinner and for Sun lunch. It is advisable to book for Sun dinner. A la carte menu is about £25 per head, including a bottle of house wine. Table D'Hote menu is from about £10.*

HERTFORDSHIRE

HATFIELD

The Old Palace
Hatfield Park
Tel: (0707) 262030

If you are in the mood for something completely different, The Old Palce is the place for you! Every Tuesday, Thursday, Friday and Saturday evening a magnificent banquet is held in The Great Hall of Hatfield Park and comprises a five course meal of royal proportions including red or white wine or mead. You will be served by buxom serving wenches in constant attendance and your glass is frequently replenished. On Tuesdays and Fridays, in addition to the fun and games of the Elizabethan era, you can enjoy the jests and songs of an earlier era, that of Henry VIII who joins you in his full splendour. The Great Hall is laid with long banqueting tables joining all folks together and merriment from a troupe of costumed minstrels and players singing songs and performing ceremonies will keep you more than entertained. Warming soup is poured from huge earthenware jugs and a traditional English Fare is served. The staff are amazingly helpful and friendly and an endless supply of food and wine is served. Inclusive prices from £24.50. See Historic Houses entry for Hatfield House.

ALDBURY (Nr Tring)

Stocks Country House Hotel
Stocks Road
Tel: (0442) 85341

Stocks is an elegant 18th Century Georgian mansion set in its own grounds just outside the picturesque village of Aldbury. The atmosphere is homely and relaxing and the staff really cater for the needs of the customer here. The 'Tapestry Restaurant' is an elegant, high ceilinged room with attractive tapestries and a large mirror giving a grand spacious feeling. Relax in the elegant lounge and choose from the varied selection on the menu including Homecured Gravadlax, Quenelles of Pink Sea Trout (which melts in your mouth!), and main courses like Sliced Breast of Maigret Duck with Calvados and Steak au Poivre. A good selection of puddings are offered followed by coffee and a comprehensive selection of petits fours which, during the summer months, can be served to you by the hotel pool overlooking the popular 18 hole championship golf course. Stocks makes an ideal setting for board meetings and senior level conferences. *Table D'Hote available lunch and evening (including Sunday lunch). Bar snacks available all day. Average price: A la carte £20-£25 for 3 courses. Table D'Hote £18.50 for 3 courses plus coffee.*

NORFOLK

CAWSTON (10m N of Norwich)

Grey Gables Country House Hotel
and Restaurant
Tel: (0603) 871259

A beautiful former rectory set in wooded grounds. In the winter there is an inviting log fire which, together with the elegant candlelit dining room, make Grey Gables the ideal setting for a relaxing, romantic meal. The cooking is traditionally prepared and cooked by Chef/Proprietor, Rosalind Snaith using fresh, local produce. There is a fine wine cellar with many French & German classics, as well as ports and wines from Italy, Spain, Australia, New Zealand, California, Washington, Chile, England and The Lebanon. The sweets are gorgeous and each customer is served with three sweets to sample-an excellent idea! *Open: daily. Average prices: lunch bookings by arrangement, dinner £17 per person. Light supper also available Sun-Thu, £10.00 per person.*

KING'S LYNN

The Garden Restaurant, Knights Hill Hotel
Knights Hill Village, South Wootton
Tel: (0553) 675566

Dinner at the Garden Restaurant is a civilised and leisurely affair in stylish, elegant surroundings overlooking the walled garden. On arrival you will be invited to relax in the lobby bar while you choose your meal. The fare is light and caters for all tastes. Lobster and sole mousse make a delicious starter. There is a variety of mouth watering main courses including breast of duck with strawberry and Cointreau sauce and pasta, peppers and cashew nuts. *Open: daily for dinner. Average price: £15-£20.*

NORWICH

The Trafalgar Restaurant
Hotel Nelson, Prince of Wales Road
Tel: (0603) 760260

We recommend the Trafalgar Room for your meal. At lunchtime they present a spectacular hors d'oeuvre/buffet, or you can choose from two splendid roast joints, together with puddings or cheese and coffee. In the evening the Trafalgar Room has a comfortable atmosphere with views across the River Wensum, and it serves good local produce. Good light meals and snacks at the Quarter-Deck Buttery. *Open: daily (ex Sat lunch). Average prices: lunch £9.75, table d'hote £12.50, à la carte dinner £10-£15.*

KING'S LYNN

The Farmers Arms
Knights Hill Village, South Wootton
Tel: (0553) 675566

When next in King's Lynn call at this popular inn. Originally a barn, the rustic atmosphere has been skilfully retained. Beams, exposed brickwork and farm implements abound. The menu is unpretentious and very reasonable in price. It features favourites like chargrilled ground burgers and jacket potatoes. A speciality of the house is Norfolk kebab-pitta bread filled with slices of roast turkey on a bed of salad topped with mayonnaise. A smooth pint of draught Bass is a perfect accompaniment. *Open: daily, both Farmers Arms Inn and Restaurant. Average price: Farmers Arms Restaurant lunch or dinner £11, Farmers Arms Inn, bar snacks £4.*

GREAT YARMOUTH

Imperial Hotel, North Drive
Tel: (0493) 851113

The Rambouillet Restaurant at the Imperial Hotel has an outstanding reputation for the quality of its cuisine. In addition to the chef's table d'hote and the à la carte menus, there is usually a gastronomique menu with French regional dishes or local specialities, all prepared by the restaurant's award-winning chefs. Only the finest and freshest ingredients are used, the wine list is excellent and the service is always professional and attentive. *Open: daily, closed for Saturday lunch. Average prices: lunch (table d'hote) £10.50, dinner (table d'hote) £16.50.*

WELLS-NEXT-THE-SEA

Crown Hotel & Restaurant, The Buttlands
Tel: (0328) 710209

Set in North Norfolk's finest coastal scenery this old coaching inn attracts people from around the world. "The sort of small hotel tired travellers dream about" as The Times said of this famous hotel in this picturesque old port. A busy popular bar with lots of local character makes this an ideal meeting place. Bar meals and snacks are always available. The food offered is freshly prepared and is of a high standard. The Restaurant under the direction of Mr Foyers and his four chefs offers both English and French cuisine and is open for both lunch and dinner. *Open: daily. Average prices: Bar snacks from £1.75, luncheon from 11.50, dinner from £17.00.*

GRIMSTON (nr King's Lynn)

THE ORANGERY RESTAURANT

Congham Hall Country House Hotel
Tel: (0485) 600250

For excellent food, go to Congham Hall. Chef Murray Chapman interprets "modern English cooking" intelligently and with a fine balance of taste and decoration. The restaurant and "orangery" is delightfully decorated in the Georgian manner. On hot summer days we particularly recommend Congham's outdoor lunches-ask about the luncheon club; but eating in the dining room or on the lawn one has the feeling of being part of an English Country Home, which is what Trevor and Christine Forecast set out to achieve when they established Congham as a country house hotel and now appropriately a member of the "Pride of Britain" group and Johansens Hotel of the Year 1993. *Open: daily. Average prices: lunch table d'hote £15, Sunday lunch £15, dinner from £21.50.*

LONG STRATTON

Snickerdoodles Restaurant
The Street
Tel: (0508) 31845

For those who like classic bistro cooking, this place is a must. Guests walk in off the pavement into a delightful little sitting room, crammed with Victoriana and the dining room too is filled with a charming collection of stripped pine, pictures and artefacts. The Gibbs (Ray cooks, Penny hosts) offer a 5-course set menu, starting with classics such as mussels, pan-fried mushrooms or melon with port. The 12 or so main courses-wild duck, fillet steak, salmon, lamb and halibut-come with sumptuous sauces. Puddings are home-made and portions, especially fresh vegetables, are very generous. *Average price per person for 5 courses, with wine, £25.*

NORWICH

Pizza One Pancakes Too!
24 Tombland
Tel: (0603) 621583

Norwich's own Pizzas, Pastas and French Crèpes. A favourite haunt, where food still has that homemade taste. It's usually crowded with families, businessmen, students and tourists alike. Situated along the Cathedral wall in Tombland, the historic heart of the city, it is the perfect place to stop for lunch, afternoon pancakes or dinner. *Open daily 1200 -2300, Sun 1200-2200 (closed 25 Dec and 1 Jan). Average price £5.85 – children's portions available.*

BUNWELL

Bunwell Manor
Tel: (0953) 788304

At the end of a quiet country lane, Bunwell Manor overlooks wooded lawns, reed-fringed ponds and a terrace. The beamed restaurant with its polished wood sideboard, has a cosy upper level perfect for romantic dinners. There is a bar menu, a good value table d'hote, and an à la carte restaurant menu. Specialities include fillet steak with peppercorns, stilton, whisky and cream or steak and pheasant pie; and chocoholics will adore the chocolate mousse topped with white and dark chocolate flakes! *Open: 7 days, lunch 1200-1400; dinner 1900-2130. Average prices: Table d'hote £12.75, à la carte £14-£18.*

BANHAM

Pantiles Bistro
with "The Horse and Harness" Bar at
The Appleyard (opposite Banham Zoo)
Tel: (0953) 887709

Pantiles Bistro, already recommended in the Best Hotels and Restaurant guide continues to evolve and now boasts a fine fully licensed bar serving fine local ales and ciders. "The Horse and Harness" designed to reflect the rural setting of the establishment now offers excellent "pub grub" alongside our now well known Bistro menu. Dishes as different as Steak, Kidney and Ale pie and Pan Fried Chicken Breast with Walnut Stuffing basted in Pear Cider gravy vie for your attention. *Open 7 days a week. Bistro menu Fri and Sat evenings only. Pub Grub every day. Full function/outside catering facilities available upon request. "Pub Grub" main meal plus a pint from £5. Bistro 3 course, no wine £13.*

NORWICH

FREE HOUSE
MUSIC | CAFE | BAR
24 Tombland
Tel: (0603) 626099

Take time out to enjoy the truly continental feeling of the new Boswells. Situated along the cathedral wall in Tombland in the historic heart of the city, it is in an ideal spot to stop for lunch or afternoon tea next time you are shopping or sightseeing. The Brasserie style menu is varied and delicious, ranging from spectacular sandwiches to three course meals. The unique decor and atmosphere are further enhanced by its "all day every day" opening hours and live Jazz, old movies and traditional Sunday lunch. You can now enjoy all this in the open air on the fully licenced forecourt terrace. *Open: Sun 1100-1800; Mon-Sat 1200-0200. Average price under £6 (specials for children are available).*

HETHERSETT (Nr Norwich)

Park Farm Hotel & Restaurant
Tel: (0603) 810264 Fax: (0603) 812104

Park Farm Hotel has earned a well deserved reputation for good food, a warm welcome and excellent service in this family-run hotel and restaurant. Set in beautiful surroundings, Park Farm provides both French and English cooking prepared with the best local produce. A good selection of menus, both à la carte and table d'hote, whilst the chef's speciality menus have more skilfully prepared dishes. Bar meals are also available. *Open: daily. Average prices: lunch £10 (table d'hote), dinner £14 (table d'hote), £18-£20 (à la carte).*

DISS

Weavers Wine Bar & Eating House
Market Hill
Tel: (0379) 642411

Wilma and William Bavin and their staff work hard to make this 'Bistro style' restaurant and wine bar the roaring success that it is. The bustling but well looked after establishment offers a simple decor of wooden tables and chairs downstairs, whilst upstairs there are more intimate alcoves and cosy corners with high backed chairs. The food is very much 'country style home cooking' with plenty of meat, fish and vegetarian options and interesting salads and desserts. The service here is welcomning, friendly and attentive, hence it has a good following from local regulars who simply enjoy the good food and lively atmosphere that Weavers has to offer. *Open: Mon-Sat dinner, Mon-Fri, lunch. Prices: á la carte approx £17 for 3 courses, lunch approx £7. (Visa & Access)*

PRETTY CORNER, nr SHERINGHAM on A148

PRETTY CORNER
CONTINENTAL CAFÉ
& RESTAURANT

Tea Garden-Buttery

Tel: (0263) 822358

At Pretty Corner, a variety of food is available to suit different tastes and appetites. The restaurant has continental style decor and excels in continental and Indonesian food. The Dutch-Indonesian Rice Table nights with 14-20 different dishes, are a speciality of the house. Alternatively, in the summer you can eat at the Tea Garden Buttery next door, which serves drinks and light snacks indoors or in the split level terraced gardens with pond, where dogs are welcome. Disabled facilities. *Restaurant open Thu, Fri and Sat, 1930, buttery open 1000-1730. Booking recommended for Rice Table nights. Tea Garden Buttery open Easter-mid Oct, daily 1000-1730.*

WEST RUNTON (Nr SHERINGHAM)

The Pepperpot
Tel: (0263) 837578

Tucked away down a narrow lane leading to the beach, it is only the illuminated sign that distinguises this restaurant from the other private houses. A warm welcome is offered by hostess Barbara (who with husband Ron has run the Pepperpot since March 1992) that complements the immediate feeling of hospitality, comfort and intimacy that suggests itself upon arrival. The A la Carte menu offering three courses, is understated and modest, for the emphasis is on quality through dishes such as delicious breast fillets of duck in peach sauce and incredibly lean steak in a brandy and cream sauce, without forgetting quantity. Desserts are lavish and the wine list is small but thoughtful. *Price per head without wine: 2 courses £13.95, 3 courses from £13-£23.*

NORWICH

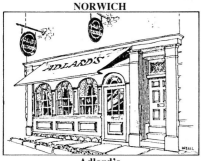

Adlard's
79, Upper St Giles Street
Tel: (0603) 633522

In an emerald green jewel of a restaurant a few hundred yards above the market place, chef-proprietor David Adlard and his lovely American wife Mary are responsible for some of the most serious food in East Anglia, served in a genial and unstuffy manner. Awarded 'County Restaurant of the Year' in 'The Good Food Guide 1994', David's perfectly judged and meticulously prepared dishes utilise much seasonal and local produce including wild mushrooms from a local stud-owner. Sauces which accompany noisettes of English lamb, breast of Gressingham duck or fillets of brill are always based on excellent stocks, carefully reduced. Pastry for a delicious apple tart surrounded by caramel sabayon is buttery and feather-light, and ice cream silky and smooth. *Open: Tue-Sat, lunch 1230-1345, dinner 1930-2230. Average price per head, without wine, lunch £18, dinner £30.*

NORWICH

The Black Horse
Earlham Road
Tel: (0603) 624682

A walk through the garden takes you into the carvery restaurant. The menu is traditional, Roast Beef, Roast Pork, Gammon, and you can help yourself to a selection of fresh vegetables or a wide selection of imaginitive salads. Do try the freshly made Black Horse Cheesecake which was delicious. The Black Horse also has a good vegetarian selection including 'Crispy coated Brie with Cranberry dip and nut cutlets with provençal sauce'. Real ale is served over the bar alongside a good selection of wines by the glass. It is a good smart pub well run by owners Anthea and Roger Cawdron and their helpful, friendly staff. *Carvery open: daily, 1200-1400 & 1900-2200. Average price per head: £9.95 for 3 courses excluding wine.*

WELLS-NEXT-THE-SEA

Freeman Street
Tel: (0328) 710478

Situated near the beautiful Brancaster beach, this busy pub offers bar snacks all day. Children are well catered for from the children's menu (under 12 year olds only) priced at only £1.95. A good variety of food in the pub is on offer from home-made Steak and Kidney Pie to Cod and Chips. A separate restaurant area offers more variety including T-Bone steaks and plenty of fresh fish. There is an interesting selection of lagers from the blackboard in the bar ranging from Singapore to Canadian brands. *Open: Mon-Sat all day; Sun 1200-1700, 1900-2230 (bar); 1200-1430, 1900-2130 (restaurant). Average price: Bar snacks £3.50 approx (hot dish/salad), £1.50 approx (sandwiches). Restaurant £7.50-£16.00 3 course evening meal (excluding wine).*

NORWICH

Walnut Tree Shades
Old Post Office Court
Tel: (0603) 620166

Situated just off the busy pedestrian shopping area of Norwich. A multi-storey car park is only approximately 10 minutes walk away. The restaurant has comfortable bench/sofa seats and walls are packed with American style posters and prints. A large juke box sits prominently by the bar and rock and blues music plays in the background. It has a young electric atmosphere and attracts families with children because of the special menu for kids which has puzzles and games for their amusement. The adult menu has a variety of American style starters like Buffalo Wings and Chilli Potato Skins to a more conservative Prawn Cocktail and Paté and Toast. Main courses are also varied from New York style Hot Dogs to Peppered Steak and Teriyaki Chicken. There is also a good selection of good quality burgers. A stunning cocktail list ranges from Margarita's to Sangria and there is always a special reduced cocktail on offer each night. The wine list is more limited but offers some interesting Californian wines and a sparkling German wine. The staff are very welcoming and helpful and all in all it is a well run successful operation. *Open: Mon-Sat, 1145-1415 and 1830-late. Average price: £12 (excluding wine) for 3 courses.*

NORWICH

Jarrold's Store Restaurant
London Street
Tel: (0603) 660661

There are three restaurants in this large department store. 'Below Decks' in the basement sells sandwiches, coffee, teas, cakes and scones. It is self service - seating approximately 50 and open from 0915-1715. The middle restaurant is called 'Benjamins', has waitress service and offers dishes like homemade soup (£1.95), hot specials from the blackboard (£3.10) and some imaginative vegetarian dishes. They also have slimmers dishes comprising salads with cottage cheese, prawns, etc., and actually list the calories per dish. No alcoholic drinks are available but a wide range of Benjamin's soft drinks, inlcuding hot chocolate and iced coffee are available. A minimum charge of £1.25 is levied between 1145 and 1415 - and food is served up to 1700. The staff are very pleasant and attentive and walk about with hot coffee offering second cups. The third restauarant on the top floor seats 200 people and is open between 0900 and 1715. It offers a wide choice of salads, hot meals, open sandwiches (Chinese and other adventurous ideas). Wine and low alcohol lager plus a selection of soft drinks are available. This bustling attentive restaurant has good views of the city if you get a table by the window.

WOLTERTON (Nr Erpingham)

The Saracens Head
Tel: (0263) 768909

Only 20 minutes from Norwich, The Saracen's Head is a civilised free house without the intrusion of piped music and fruit machines. It was built in the early 19th Century by Lord Walpole as a coaching Inn for his estate. There are log fires, terra-cotta walls, leather bound settles, wicker fireside chairs and fresh flowers on the mantlepieces. It is a well kept, well run house, more a restaurant than a pub. The staff are both welcoming and helpful and the food is fresh and delicious. The Paté Maison was full of flavour and not too rich and the steaks were cooked to perfection. Other dishes include braised local rabbit, grilled fillets of Smoked Mackerel, Venison, Duck and Steaks. Puddings are fairly traditional, e.g., Bread and Butter Pudding, Sticky Toffee Pudding. The wine list is an impressive selection of 17 interesting wines. It made a pleasant change to see a choice of New Zealand, Australian, Spanish and South African wines as well as many of the more classic French. House wines are also available at £8.25 per bottle. Chef/proprietor Robert Dawson-Smith and his staff run The Saracens Head extremely well and they deserve their popularity. *Open: 7 days a week, 1100-1500, 1800-2300.*

SUFFOLK

ALDEBURGH

Uplands Hotel, Victoria Road
Tel: (0728) 452420

This establishment is a fitting compliment to the charming and tranquil seaside resort of Aldeburgh. The Uplands faces the beautiful 15th century parish church and stands in lovely gardens only a stone's throw from the shingle beach. The table d'hote menu features fresh local produce and is changed daily. There is an interesting wine list and an extensive range of malt whiskies. The elegant dining room overlooks the gardens and is perfect for a traditional, relaxed evening meal. *Open: daily. Average price: Table d'hote dinner £15.00.*

FELIXSTOWE

Waverley Hotel and Wolsey Restaurant
Wolsey Gardens
Tel: (0394) 282811

At the Waverley Hotel you have the choice of dining in the Wolsey Restaurant or the Gladstone Bar and you will be assured of a delicious choice of meals made with fresh local produce. Dramatic views of the North Sea make this a very special place to eat. Conferences, receptions and parties can be catered for. *Open: daily. Average prices: lunch £11.25, dinner £14.95. Fax (0394) 670185.*

IPSWICH

The Marlborough Hotel, Henley Road
Tel: (0473) 257677

Tucked away in a quiet residential quarter, this solid, red-brick Victorian hotel exudes a strong feeling of comfortable dependability. A beguiling and unexpected inner garden soothes the spirit, as do adventurous dishes such as Oriental Duck Samosa and other exciting combinations from the well-priced set menu. The only unrestrained note is sounded by the flambé dishes, which run the gamut from beef Stroganov to Crépe Suzette, providing diners with moments of fun and high drama. An efficient young staff, led by the owners Robert and Karen Gough, treat parties, businessmen and private diners alike with skill and courtesy. *Average price per head, without wine, £15-£20.*

BURY ST EDMUNDS

The Angel Hotel, Angel Hill
Tel: (0284) 753926

If most of the houses in Bury St Edmunds look as edible as angel cake, the creeper-clad Angel Hotel must be the plum pudding. In an imposing position overlooking the Abbey Gardens, this fine hotel with its Dickensian connections is owned and run with pleasing professionalism by the Gough family. With three dining areas to choose from, the impressive Norman vaulted cellars, cosy Pickwick bar or handsome Regency restaurant, the food ranges from sandwiches made from local bread through homely brasserie dishes such as braised oxtail to an up-market, classic Chateaubriand with Bearnaise sauce. Adnams supplies the beers and the wine list is thoughtful and modestly priced. *Average price per head, without wine, £15-£20*

HOLBROOK

The Compasses
Tel: (0473) 328332

Holbrook is at the head of Alton Water, an ideal spot for windsurfing, walking and bird watching. The bar at the Compasses is comfortable, with a varied menu including old favourites as well as some unusual dishes. A fascinating collection of keyrings decorates the walls. The restaurant is tastefully decorated in a delicate pink. The menu offers an excellent variety of fish, meat and poultry dishes, with a vegetarian choice of spinach & mushroom lasagne and mushroom & nut fettuccini and others. Large car park, garden play area, children welcome. *Open: daily for lunch and dinner. Average prices: Restaurant £12, bar meals £4-£5, Sun lunch £9.75 (booking advised).*

LAVENHAM

The Angel
Market Place
Tel: (0787) 247388

In one of the best-loved and best-known of Suffolk's medieval villages, the Angel is so resolutely settled into its corner site overlooking the market square that one almost feels that its strong timbers have grown straight from the soil. Two dining rooms, one informally strewn with pine tables, the other rich with mahogany tables and bric-a-brac, offer home-made fresh food: garlic mushrooms, pates, home-made soups and pies, casseroles of pork and apple or steaks and lamb chops, as well as delicious treacle tart or Suffolk apple flan, with a menu that changes daily. The atmosphere is easy, the staff delightful. *Average price per head, without wine, £10-£15.*

HAVERHILL

Mill House Restaurant
Mill Road
Tel: (0440) 712123

The enthusiastic owners of this pink-washed town house, Mr and Mrs Thorpe, arrange special dining evenings, from Greek to Cajun (featuring a splendid jambalaya), as well as offering two modestly-priced set menus, of traditional English and provincial French fare. House cocktails, taken in the modern conservatory bar, are vital when trying to choose from amongst snails in garlic butter, chicken breast with prawns, or steak chasseur. The generous portions hardly leave room for the most popular pudding, RSJ, a confection of meringues, cream, raspberries and ice cream. The excellent wine list is an example of how much care goes into this restaurant. *Average price per head for 3 courses £12-£17.*

CRETINGHAM

The Cretingham Bell
The Street
Tel: (0728) 685419

This cheerfully renovated village pub with its flagged floors, ubiquitous beams and open dining areas lies in the middle of a labyrinth of twisting lanes in the Suffolk countryside. The menu ranges widely through old favourites such as a pint of prawns, sausages or char-grilled steaks to zappy newcomers like Tiger Tail Prawns and Tagliatelle Carbonara with more than just a cursory nod to vegetarians with dishes like Fruity Curry and Cheesy Leek and Potato Bake. The menu changes at least twice a year. Real ales including Adnams which can also be drunk in the well kept gardens. Children's play garden at the rear. *Average price for 3 courses £8-£16. Live jazz twice monthly.*

ORFORD

King's Head Inn
Front Street
Tel: (0394) 450271

The King's Head Inn lies at the heart of Orford, a delightful village by the river Ore. Relax at the bar with a drink whilst choosing from a wide selection of local fish dishes, some meat and a vegetarian choice. Meals are served either in the traditional restaurant which is cheerfully decorated in a nautical theme, or in the 'olde worlde' bar. My starter was a delicious sweet half melon, complemented with prawns, followed by halibut with a rich lobster sauce, served with a platter of fresh vegetables. Fresh local seafood and game are a speciality. *Open: daily lunch 1200-1400, dinner 1900-2100 (restaurant closed Sun & Thu evenings, but bar meals always available). Average price: 3 course meal £15. Lunch & bar meals £8.*

KELSALE (Nr Saxmundham)

Hedgehog Hall
Main Road
Tel: (0728) 602420

A charming old thatched house standing in an attractive garden and under the new management of Sara Fox and Peter Hill who were well known for running the excellent Regatta Restaurant in Aldeburgh. Beams and uneven floors and staircases all add to the character of this establishment. The food is excellent and interesting with the menu changing regularly to maximise the use of fresh produce. It is also attractively and competitively priced with dishes such as Smoked Fish Chowder, Potted Shrimps from the Norfolk coast, Roast Barbary Duck with Orange Ginger and Oriental Spices and Poached Skate wing with Capers and Black butter. Puddings too are delicious and include dishes like classic Tiramisu and Lemon tart with thick Jersey cream. Booking is advised well in advance for this popular restaurant. *Open: Tue-Sat, lunch and dinner, Sun, 1200-1430. Average price: £13.50 for 2 courses, £15.75 for 3 courses.*

WOODBRIDGE

Captain's Table
Quay Street
Tel: (0394) 383145

This delightful restaurant is to be found in one of Woodbridge's quaint, narrow streets between the town centre and the yacht haven. The atmosphere is warm and cosy and you will receive the personal and friendly attention of the proprietor's family and helpers. There is a pleasant patio where you can eat during the warmer months, a licensed bar and small car park. As you may have guessed, seafood is the speciality–lobster, oyster, crawfish and fresh salmon when available and there is a comprehensive wine list. *Open: Tues-Sat. Average prices: lunch £6, dinner £16.50, 3 course fixed price menu £11.95*

YOXFORD

JaCey's Charcoal Pit
High Street
Tel: Yoxford (0728) 668298

An up-to-the-minute, friendly, informal village restaurant which serves Maderian Kebabs, generous skewers of marinated Lamb, King Parawns, Tarragon Chicken or the house special, Tender Beef, Salami, Mushrooms and Bacon. All th eKebabs are cunningly presented on iron serving stands fixed to the tables, you are then invited to lubricate the kebab with garlic and herby butters. They also serve many popular dishes such as Chicken Piri Piri, Burgers, Steaks, Roast Lamb, Pasta and a plate hanging rib of beef for the *very* hungry. The blckboard has specials of the day such as wonderful fish dishes and things that use seasonal ingredients. The homemade bread is terrific as is the fabulously rich Banoffi pie and Pavlova, among other puddings. The very modestly priced wine list is small and interesting. This restaurant makes eating fun. *Open: dinner Mon-Sat, lunch Thu-Sat. Main course prices range from £5-£11 with lots to choose from at £5/8. Main courses include salad,rice, chips or potatoes.*

HINTLESHAM

Hintlesham Hall
Tel: (0473) 652334/268

Set in 170 acres of parkland and golf course, Hintlesham Hall with 33 bedrooms and suites, is renowned for its excellent cuisine and luxurious accommodation. Hintlesham Hall is a member of Small Luxury Hotels of the World. There are 5 reception rooms, including the splendid Salon, the intimate book-lined Library, and the mellow pine-panelled Parlour. Throughout the hotel, individuality is displayed in the eclectic selection of modern and traditional works of art, and the fine antiques. The style of cooking is modern British, using local and home-grown produce for the seasonal menus. Above all, the service from the young team is unfailingly pleasant and helpful. *Open: daily, except Sat - lunch time. Average prices: House lunch (A la carte) including coffee and petits fours £21. Table d'hote menu Sun to Thu £22.00. Full à la carte every day. £18.50 table d'hote lunch.*

FRESSINGFIELD, Nr DISS

Fox and Goose Inn
Tel: (0379) 586247

In 1509 the Fox and Goose was built in the Fressingfield churchyard , parishioners up to that time having eaten and drunk in the nave of the church. Still owned by the church the Inn was taken over by Ruth Watson (ex-owner of Hintlesham Hall) in 1990 who combines the informality of a British pub with the genuine dedication to good cooking of a family-owned French restaurant. The eclectic menu, from which you can choose most dishes in either starter or main course sizes, ranges from Peking duck or Japanese tempura to local cod and chips or English lamb with rosemary sauce, finishing with sticky toffee pudding or chocolate St Emillion. The extensive wine list is reasonably marked up and has won awards from all the major guides. *Average price per head, without wine, £20.*

WRENTHAM (Nr Beccles)

Quiggins Restaurant
High Street
Tel: (050275) 397

Only 2 miles from the Suffolk coast in the centre of Wrentham, this 250 year old listed building has retained some of the original beams especially in the dining room area. There is a warm, homely atmosphere. The menu has an extensive selection of freshly prepared fish dishes ranging from Dover Sole to Quiggins' own Seafood Medley, all priced very reasonably at daily market prices. There is also a wide selection of meat dishes available from classic Tournedos Rossini to a Huntsman's Pie made from venison and other game. Proprietors, Jill and Dudley McNally, have a good reputation in the area for traditional English and French cooking and in particular, Sunday lunch is always very popular. *Open: Tue-Sun, lunch 1200-1400, dinner Tue-Sat from 1900. Average price: £17.95 for 3 courses including vegetables, excluding wine.*

ALDEBURGH

THE CAPTAIN'S CABIN

LICENSED RESTAURANT AND TEA ROOMS

Captain's Cabin
170-172 High Street
Tel: (0728) 452520

The Captain's Cabin is a handsome listed building on Aldeburgh High Street. It has a cosy and friendly atmosphere and offers an inexpensive family meal. The menu is kept simple and prepared with local produce; Home made soup, scampi, cod, steak pie, cottage pie, etc., most meals are served with chips or jacket potato and vegetables. A good selection of desserts is always available. It has a cheerful ambience and is ideal for a family luncheon or afternoon tea. There is even a children;s menu and a choice of vegetarian dishes too. The service is prompt and affable, and the servings are always generous. The walls are decorated with seascapes and pictures of ships to remind you that you are in The Captain's Cabin. *Open: daily, 1000-1700. Morning coffee, lunch, afternoon tea. Evening meals daily, Easter-Sep,ffrom 1700-1900 and in winter on Sat and Sun only. Average price: £5-£10.*

BILDESTON

The Bow Window
116 High Street
Tel: (0449) 740748

Situated in one of the nicest village squares in Suffolk, this pretty pink washed restaurant has an abundance of oak beams, a large inglenook with log fires in season and a walled flower garden for the summer. The restaurant offers simple, high quality food all prepared on the premises with emphasis on taste and flavours. The menu is essentially British with additional selections from around the world for the more adventurous. Chef/proprietress Hilary Pixton believes that her employment at Marks and Spencer has taught her how to provide the optimum in quality and value for money. A wide range of modestly priced wines are available to accompany your meal in the relaxed and informal atmosphere. *Open: Wed-Sat evenings. Typical 2 course meal for 2 around £24. Sun lunch - 3 courses plus coffee £10.95. House wines £7.25. Bookings always advisable. Ideal for special occasions - with your own personally chosen menu.*

STOWMARKET

Tot Hill House Restaurant
Bury Road
Tel: (0449) 673375

This charming restored 16th century timber-framed house fronted with local Woolpit bricks is found on the A45 between Stowmarket and Haughley. You will receive a warm welcome and friendly efficient service from John and Jean McBain. The kitchen is under the control of their son Andrew who will offer you freshly prepared dishes made from the best of local produce such as rack of Suffolk lamb and Lowestoft plaice or more exotic delights such as Swordfish steak marinated in lemon and lime, baked with prawns and parsley. Your meal is taken in the pleasant, comfortable restaurant with views across the lawns and gardens. The fixed price 4 course Gourmet Menu is changed regularly. There is also a carefully selected wine list. *Open: Tues-Sat evenings and lunch on Sundays. Gourmet menu currently £16.75 also à la carte menu. Sunday lunch £8.50. Access/Visa.*

NEWMARKET

THE LANTERN RESTAURANT

15 The Rookery
Tel: (0638) 665098

Just off Newmarket High Street is 'The Rookery' which encapsulates a selection of shops and 'The Lantern Restaurant'. Relaxing classical music plays in the background whilst you read from the large selection of à la carte dishes or from a three course set dinner menu. The à la carte menu includes Baked Avacado with Crab and Prawns in a cheese sauce, Escargots with Garlic Butter, Grilled Steaks and Ceasers Duck in a dark plum and Brandy sauce, Salmon Cutlet Seville - poached salmon with a creamy orange and vermouth sauce. Puddings are all made by joint owner Ray King and include Greengages poached in Wine and Lemon (which were fabulous), Créme Brûleé and Summer Pudding. The delicious food is created by th eother joint owner and chef Adrian Savin. A luncheon menu is also available comprising a selection of light dishes like Omelettes, Jacket Potatoes and T. Bone Steaks. The comprehensive wine list offers very reasonably priced wines by the bottle and by the glass. A set Sunday Luncheon is also available for £8.95 for 3 courses. *Open: Tue-Sat & Sun lunch, 1130-1400; Tue-Fri, 1830-2200; Sat, 1800-2230. Average price per head, à la carte: £15.*

CAMBRIDGESHIRE

NORFOLK

Le'Strange Arms Hotel

Golf Course Road
Old Hunstanton
Norfolk

This fine Country House hotel standing in its own grounds, with lawns sweeping down to the beach. A wide range of bedrooms including Family Suites are available, whilst the hotels restaurant and Ancient Mariner Bar are known for their standard of food and quality of service.

Telephone: 0485 534411 Fax: 0485 534724
RAC ★ ★ ★

THE NYTON
7 Barton Road, Ely

APPROVED

Situated in a quiet residential area of the city in 2 acres of attractive grounds adjoining 18 hole golf course, on which green fees granted to guests. Bed and breakfast from £27. Evening meals from £15 per person. All bedrooms with en-suite facilities. Fully licensed.
AA/RAC ★
Tel. Ely (0353) 662459

Tel: Bunwell (0953) 788304
Fully Licensed AA ★★ RAC ★★
Just 12 miles south of Norwich, off the B1113. Our country house hotel dates originally from the 16th century. 2 acres of lovely grounds and 10 bedrooms all en-suite. Carefully prepared à la carte and table d'hôte menus. Ideally peaceful base for touring Norfolk, Suffolk and Cambridgeshire. Full Central heating and welcoming log fire in winter. Children and dogs welcome.
Special Breaks available all year.
Bunwell Manor
Bunwell, Norfolk, NR16 1QU

COMMENDED

Spindrift

AA

PRIVATE HOTEL APPROVED

Adjacent sea front, bowling greens, tennis courts, waterways. Front bedrooms have sea views. All bedrooms have colour TV, tea/coffee, central heating. Some en-suites. Payphone. Open all year from £14 per night

36 Wellesley Road, Gt. Yarmouth, NR30 1EU
Tel: 0493 858674

HERTFORDSHIRE

The Bobsleigh Inn

Privately owned Country Hotel/Restaurant with reputation for good food and service. Elegantly furnished throughout with 39 ensuite bedrooms. From £25.00 per person including full English Breakfast. Golf course nearby. Easy access M1 and M25. Luton and London Airport.

Hempstead Road, Bovingdon, Herts. HP3 0DS
Telephone: 0442-833276 Fax: 0442 832471

AA ★★ (1 rosette) COMMENDED

Elm Farm
Chalet Hotel
ST. FAITHS,
NORWICH NR10 3HH

Tel. Norwich (0603) 898366
Fax. (0603) 897129

Attractive 17th C farmhouse and chalet accommodation in charming village, 4 miles north of Norwich. Ideal for touring Norfolk & Suffolk. En-suite rooms recently refurbished. Dining room and some bedrooms non-smoking, all have colour television, room telephone, hair dryers, facilities for tea & coffee making. Ample Parking.

COMMENDED

NORTH NORFOLK COTTAGES, HOUSES and APARTMENTS.

Attractive self-catering cottages and ideal holiday homes for everyone, located in some of the prettiest parts of picturesque North Norfolk; coastal, near the coast, heart of the county, country, towns and waterway locations all within easy access to all amenities. We guarantee a holiday in comfort.
Quote Ref: EATB when writing or telephoning for our COLOUR BROCHURE.

North Norfolk Holiday Homes, Lee Warner Avenue, Fakenham, Norfolk NR21 8ER.

Autumn, Christmas & Winter DISCOUNT TARIFFS

FOR OUR BROCHURE TELEPHONE: (0328) 855322

There's so much to do!

STOCKS COUNTRY HOUSE HOTEL
Stocks Road, Aldbury, Nr Tring, Herts. HP3 5RX
Tel: 0442-285341 Fax: 0442-285253
Your "Home from Home" in the Country
A warm and friendly welcome awaits you at Stocks, an 18th Century Georgian Mansion, which is set amidst 182 acres of its own picturesque grounds, just outside the lovely village of Aldbury.
We are open daily for breakfast, morning coffee, bar drinks and snacks, lunch, afternoon tea, accommodation and dinner in our Tapestry Restaurant.
Stocks has 18 individually decorated bedrooms including several suites with views across the gardens and parklands.
Leisure facilities include a new 18 hole golf course, tennis courts, sauna, large jacuzzi, gymnasium, heated outdoor swimming pool (May to September), croquet lawn and full size snooker table. Our own riding stables cater for both the novice and experienced rider.
Stocks is the perfect location for those special occasions and we can cater for private dinners, wedding receptions, conferences and hospitality days.
Stocks is only 10 miles from junction 8 off the M1 and junctions 19 or 20 off the M25. The new A41(T) dual carriageway and Tring Station (mainline Euston – London) are both only 2 miles away.

APPLIED

THE OLD COURT HOUSE
ROLLESBY,
Nr GT. YARMOUTH

Peaceful country hotel, set in 4 acres of grounds with an outdoor swimming pool, heated during the summer. 7 comfortable bedrooms including 2 ground floor suites and 2 family suites with colour TV and tea/coffee making facilities. Cosy bar for residents only. Delicious home cooking. Games room. Bicycles for hire. Fishing, tennis, riding, boating and seaside nearby. **Tel: Gt. Yarmouth (0493) 369665**

COMMENDED

Near Great Yarmouth it's the ideal family holiday resort. ● New Pavilions complex
● Indoor pool with watershute

HOPTON Norfolk
Holiday Village

● Wide range of entertainment
● Restaurants and bars
● Luxury caravans offering great value for money

0345 508508 LOCAL CALL RATE

Please send me your free brochure on Hopton Holiday Village.
Name _____
Address _____
_____
_____ Postcode _____
British Holidays, FREEPOST, Normandy Court, 1 Wolsey Road, Hemel Hempstead HP2 4BR

HOEA

Norwich and Norfolk Holiday Homes

English Tourist Board REGISTERED AGENCY

Historic City – Beautiful County.
Well equipped, convenient city properties and delightful country cottages.
Visit coast, Broads and Stately Homes.
All properties personally inspected.
We offer a friendly service and will send a Free Brochure on request.
18 Keswick Road, Cringleford, Norwich
Norfolk, NR4 6UG
Tel: (0603) 503389 Fax: (0603) 55123

Grey Gables
Norwich Road, Cawston, Norwich NR10 4EY
Country House Hotel and Restaurant
Tel 0603 871259
A beautiful former rectory, comfortably furnished with many antiques, in a pleasant rural setting 10 miles from Norwich, coast and the Broads. 7 en suite bedrooms. £19-£40 single, £48-£58 double. Special Breaks 2 nights or more

---

Please mention East Anglia Guide when replying to advertisements

PLACES TO STAY

Congham Hall
COUNTRY HOUSE HOTEL & RESTAURANT

GRIMSTON, KING'S LYNN, NORFOLK
Luxurious Georgian Manor, 40 acres
6 miles King's Lynn   5 miles Sandringham

A superb hotel created from a Georgian Manor House and acclaimed by many leading guides. Offering peaceful relaxation and high quality accommodation and cuisine. Under personal supervision of the owners. RAC Blue Ribbon, AA 3 red star and two Rosettes. Egon Ronay. Johansens Hotel of the Year 1993

HIGHLY COMMENDED

'A Pride of Britain Hotel'
**Dining and Hotel Reservations:
(0485) 600250**

The Historical Thomas Paine Hotel and Restaurant

Tel: Thetford (0842) 755631

Reputed birthplace of Thomas Paine, Thetford's most famous son, and author of "The Rights of Man". Small, privately owned, family run hotel. Warm welcome, fine food and superb service assured. All bedrooms are tastefully furnished with bathrooms en suite, colour TV, and tea/coffee facilities. Getaway weekend breaks available all year.

MALT HOUSE
Palgrave, Diss, Norfolk. IP22 1AE
Tel: (0379) 642107 Fax: (0379) 640315

17c Malt House, overlooking Palgrave village Green and duck pond. All luxury modern amenities, en-suite rooms, colour TV, tea/coffe making facilities. Set in landscaped gardens with Victorian walled kitchen garden. Bressingham Gardens 2 miles. No smoking. Colour brochure available.

HIGHLY COMMENDED

Park View HOTEL

BLACKFRIARS STREET, KING'S LYNN, NORFOLK PE30 1NN. TEL: 0553-775146
This 46 bedroomed hotel is situated in the centre of town overlooking beautiful St. James's Park. All rooms are en-suite with tea/coffee making facilities, colour TV and direct dial telephone. The elegant Drawing Room Restaurant serves Table D'Hote and A La Carte. Shopping centre, cinema and theatre close by. Known for its friendly, family atmosphere.

BARGAIN BREAKS AVAILABLE ALL YEAR

King's Head Hotel

LYNN ROAD, GREAT BIRCHAM, KING'S LYNN, NORFOLK (on B1153)
Country Hotel & Restaurant Situated Close to Sandringham, King's Lynn & the Coast.
WINE AND DINE IN THE LODGE RESTAURANT OF AN OLDE WORLDE COUNTRY HOTEL
FOOD ESPECIALLY PREPARED BY THE PROPRIETOR
English & Italian Cuisine • Fresh Norfolk Seafood & Produce A La Carte Available Lunchtimes & Evenings
TRADITIONAL SUNDAY LUNCH
Weddings & Parties Catered for
BAR MEALS AND FISH SPECIALITIES
ACCOMMODATION WITH EN SUITE FACILITIES
AMPLE PARKING
TELEPHONE (048523) 265

KEYS HOLIDAYS

A selection of over 70 cottages, houses, flats and bungalows in the Sheringham, Cromer, Holt and Blakeney area. All personally inspected by our staff.

Season commences March until October, some properties cater for out of season holidays also.

Come and enjoy the beautiful coast and countryside of Norfolk in one of our self-catering properties.

Colour brochure on request.
Tel: 0263 823010

or by writing to:

Keys Holidays,
18 Station Road, Sheringham, Norfolk NR26 8RE

THE RED LION HOTEL

A hundred years ago the Victorians discovered the best of the Norfolk coast. Today you can rediscover the dramatic beauty of this coastline at the Red Lion Hotel.

The atmosphere reflects the unhurried life of north Norfolk. The centrally heated accommodation and excellent facilities make it a hotel for all seasons – ideal for a holiday, a business stop-over or a leisurely weekend.

The bedrooms are spacious and tastefully furnished. Many have sea views and all are equipped with colour television, piped videos, tea/coffee making facilites, and a luxury en-suite bathroom. There is a sauna, a solarium, a snooker room, a resident's bar and a first-class restaurant. Energetic guests have the use of a gymnasium. The Victorian Function Room is available.

**Red Lion Hotel, Brooke Street, Cromer, NR27 9HD
Telephone: (0263) 514964**

LES ROUTIERS   COMMENDED   2 Star ★ ★   AA

Parkdean
HOLIDAYS
at **SUMMERFIELDS** HOLIDAY PARK
BEACH ROAD, SCRATBY, GT. YARMOUTH. TEL: 0493 731419.

ONE OF THE MOST POPULAR PARKS ON THE FAMOUS SANDY SUNNY BEACHES OF NORFOLK – STAR FEATURES INCLUDE
★ Free indoor heated swimming pool ★ Spa bath and solarium ★ Free entertainment and dancing nightly ★ Top class Summerfields Showbar ★ Busy Bee family club with children's club with lots of fun and entertainment everyday, soft drinks and licensed bar ★ Weekly beauty, talent, darts, and pool competitions ★ Amusements, gift shop ★ Children's play area ★ Soft play area for tiny tots ★ Self-service restaurant and take-away ★ Late night cabarets.

Full weeks from £65 per chalet/caravan
Send for a FREE colour brochure to
Parkdean Holidays Limited, Freepost, Newcastle upon Tyne NE6 1BR.

For Holiday reservations and information please telephone:
QUOTE EAST ANGLIA GUIDE   24 hr DIAL-A-BROCHURE **091 224 0500**

Please mention East Anglia Guide when replying to advertisements

112

THE MAIDS HEAD HOTEL

TOMBLAND, NORWICH NR3 1LB

Tel: Norwich (0603) 761111

Fax: (0603) 613688

This 700 year old former coaching inn is situated opposite
the Norman Cathedral in the old part of the City.
Surrounded by cobbled streets and specialist shops,
the Hotel is steeped in atmosphere and tradition
and is a 'must' for visitors to the City.

Special weekend rates available.

Flagstaff House

Burnham Overy Staithe
Tel: (072 875) 637

Once the home of Captain
Woodgett of the Cutty Sark,
Flagstaff House is situated
on the quay at unspoiled
Overy Staithe. Superb views,
sailing. Very well equipped
self catering cottage.

Brick and flint 16th Century cottages, overlooking
village green. Peace and tranquillity. Short breaks
from October to April inclusive. Log fires, electric
blankets, video, freezer, microwave, in fact everything we could think of to make you feel at home.
Owner supervised.

**Church Farm Cottages,
Brisley, Dereham,
Norfolk NR20 5LL
Tel: 0362-668332**

HOLIDAY HOMES & CYCLE TOURS

*Relaxing cottages, coastal or countryside,
throughout Norfolk, sleeping 2-8,
from £120 a week.
Also bike hire, picnic hampers and boat trip.*

TEL: (0692) 650286 FOR BROCHURE & BOOKINGS

*Cley Mill is an early eighteenth century
building now converted into a small
Guest House. It is situated on the North
side of the village in a position of great
tranquility and beauty. The conversion
of the Mill has resulted in a unique
home combining comfort with
character. The ground floor rooms
include a magnificent circular sitting
room with an open fire.
Guests are assured of a friendly
welcome, good food and comfortable
accommodation.*

CLEY WINDMILL
Cley next the Sea, Holt NR25 7NN
Tel: 0263-740209

Just four miles from the historic Georgian town of Holt

SURE SIGNS

OF WHERE TO STAY

**Throughout Britain,
the tourist boards
now inspect over
30,000 places to stay,
every year, to help
you find the ones that
suit you best.**

THE CROWN

Looking for a hotel,
guesthouse, inn, B&B or
farmhouse? Look for the Crown.

THE CLASSIFICATIONS:
'Listed', and then
ONE to FIVE CROWN,
tell you the range of facilities and
services you can expect. The more
Crowns, the wider the range.

**THE CROWN GRADES:
APPROVED, COMMENDED,
HIGHLY COMMENDED and
DE LUXE,** where they appear,
indicate the quality standard
provided. If no grade is shown,
you can still expect a high
standard of cleanliness.

'Listed': Clean and comfortable
accommodation, but the range of
facilities/services may be limited.

ONE CROWN:
Accommodation with additional
facilities, including washbasins in
all bedrooms, a lounge and use
of a phone.

TWO CROWN:
A wider range of facilities and
services, including morning tea
and calls, bedside lights, colour
TV in lounge or bedrooms, 20%
or more of bedrooms with private
WC, bath or shower.

THREE CROWN:
At least half of the bedrooms with
ensuite WC and bath or shower,
plus easy chair, full length mirror.
Shoe cleaning facilities and
hairdryers available. Hot evening
meals available.

FOUR CROWN:
At least 90% of the bedrooms
with ensuite WC and bath/shower
plus colour TV, radio and phone,
24-hour access and lounge
service until midnight. Last orders
for meals 8.30 pm or later.

FIVE CROWN:
All bedrooms having WC, bath
and shower ensuite, plus a wide
range of facilities and services,
including room service, all-night
lounge service and laundry
service. Restaurant open for
breakfast, lunch and dinner.

THE LODGES

THE MOONS: If you are
looking for somewhere
convenient to stop overnight
on a motorway or major road route,
the 'Lodge' Moons are a sure sign of
where to stay. The number of
Moons (1-3) will show the range of
facilities and the quality grades are
indicated by: **APPROVED,
COMMENDED, HIGHLY
COMMENDED AND DE LUXE.**

THE KEYS

Looking for a self-catering
holiday home? Look for the Key.

THE CLASSIFICATIONS:
ONE to FIVE KEY, tell you
the range of facilities and
equipment you can expect.
The more **KEYS,** the wider
the range.

**THE KEY GRADES:
APPROVED, COMMENDED,
HIGHLY COMMENDED and
DE LUXE,** indicate the quality
standard of what is provided.

ONE KEY:
Clean and comfortable, adequate
heating, lighting and seating, TV,
cooker, fridge and crockery.

TWO KEY:
Colour TV, easy chairs or sofas
for all occupants, fridge with ice-
maker, bedside units or shelves,
plus heating in all rooms.

THREE KEY:
Dressing tables, bedside lights,
linen and towels available,
vacuum cleaner, iron/ironing
board.

FOUR KEY:
All sleeping in beds or bunks,
supplementary lighting in living
areas, more kitchen equipment,
use of an automatic washing
machine and tumble dryer.

FIVE KEY:
Automatically controlled heating,
own washing machine and
tumble dryer, bath & shower,
telephone, dishwasher,
microwave and fridge freezer.

THE QUALITY Q

Looking for a holiday caravan,
chalet or camping park? Look
for the Quality Q symbol.

THE QUALITY Q GRADES:
1-5 ✓s within the **Q,** for
quality symbol tell you
the quality standard of
what is provided. The more ✓s,
the higher the standard.

Every classified place to stay has a
Fire Certificate, where this is required
under the Fire Precautions Act, and all
carry Public Liability Insurance.

Every **Crown** or **Key** classified place to
stay is likely to provide some of the
facilities and services of a higher
classification. More information is given
in a free *SURE SIGN* leaflet, available
at any Tourist Information Centre.

We've checked them out
before you check in!

SUFFOLK

The Crown & Castle ⚜⚜ COMMENDED
Orford, Nr. Woodbridge,
Suffolk IP12 2LJ
Tel: Orford (0394) 450205   Fax: (0394) 450176
The hotel is an attractive timbered building situated opposite the Castle. There are 20 bedrooms, most ensuite, all with telephone, television & coffee/tea making facilities. The table d'hôte menu features fresh local produce & is changed daily. Bar snacks are available in our cosy bar, open to non-residents. A very relaxed, friendly atmosphere.

A good selection of top quality self catering houses, cottages and flats at affordable prices in and around Norwich, Norfolk and Suffolk including properties in the Broadlands.
ALBION ROSE PROPERTIES
94 SOUTHWOLD ROAD, WRENTHAM NR34 7JF
TELEPHONE 0502-75757

The Waverley Hotel

The Waverley Hotel, Wolsey Gardens,
Felixstowe, Suffolk IP11 7DF
**Telephone: Felixstowe (0394) 282811
Fax: (0394) 670185**

All bedrooms have en suite bathrooms, trouser presses, colour television, tea and coffee making facilities, and direct dial telephones. Our Wolsey Restaurant features a high standard of a la carte cuisine featuring fresh local produce.
Please contact us for details of weekend breaks, colour brochure and tariff.

THE HOUSE IN THE CLOUDS
THORPENESS · Near LEISTON · SUFFOLK

**AVAILABLE FOR HOLIDAYS AND SHORT BREAKS
A FANTASY UNMATCHED IN ENGLAND**
Sleeps 10 in 2 double bedded rooms, 3 twin bedded rooms, and for the extra 2 guests an additional double sofa bed. 3 bathrooms, drawing room, kitchen, dining rooms and 'The Room at the Top' with the finest views in Suffolk.
Situated in 1 acre of grounds overlooking Thorpeness Golf Course, Thorpeness Mere and the sea. Close to Snape Maltings, home of Aldeburgh Festival and to Minsmere and other bird and nature reserves.
For further information and bookings please telephone: 071-252 0743   COMMENDED

The Cedars Hotel and Restaurant

A delightful 16th cent. farmhouse which has been extended and modernised to offer character and comfort. Weekend rates from £35 per person.
**Needham Road, Stowmarket.
(0449) 612668**

The SANDLINGS Centre
Modern fully self contained pine lodges in quiet surrounds on the southern heritage coast close to Havergate island. Superb coastal marshes and forest walks.
LODGE ROAD, HOLLESLEY
WOODBRIDGE, SUFFOLK IP12 2RR
Suffolk's Coastal Retreat
Tel. (0394) 411422

THE DOLPHIN HOTEL
**41 Beach Station Road
Felixstowe, Suffolk**
Near to Beach and Passenger Terminal and Town Centre, Bars, meals, functions, TV in all bedrooms.
Proprietor: H. Hoffacker
Tel. (0394) 282261

Ipswich Moat House
COPDOCK,   IPSWICH,   SUFFOLK   IP8 3JD
Tel: (0473) 730444   Fax: (0473) 730801
Queens Moat Houses

INTERNATIONAL HOTELIERS
Delightful modern hotel set in 5 acres of landscaped gardens, rurally located close to the heart of Constable Country, 3 miles south of Ipswich, just off the A12. 75 bedrooms with private bathrooms and colour TV. Leisure Centre. Special weekend and summer rates, family rooms available.

⚜⚜⚜ HIGHLY COMMENDED
Weekend Breaks available
Six Mile Bottom, Newmarket CB8 0UE, England.
Telephone: (063-870) 234 Facsimile: (063-870) 283

Swynford Paddock stands in 60 acres just 6 miles from Newmarket and 8 from Cambridge.
Once the country retreat of Poet Lord Byron, it is now a deluxe country-house hotel with 15 large and individually decorated bedrooms.
All rooms have private bathroom with WC & shower, colour TV, clock radio/alarm, tea and coffee facilities, direct-dial telephone, mini-bar, trouser-press and hair-drier.
A warm welcome, log fires and a sumptuous lounge, friendly attentive staff, and a first class restaurant combine to make Swynford Paddocks the ideal base for exploring East Anglia.

The Wentworth Hotel stands of the edge of the Suffolk coast at the old fishing town of Aldeburgh and has the comfort and style of a country house with open fires and antique furniture. All individually decorated bedrooms have colour television, radio, telephone, hairdryers and optional tea facilities. The restaurant serves a wide range of dishes using fresh produce and the lunch time bar menu can be enjoyed in the sunken terrace garden.
Aldeburgh has quality shops, two excellent golf courses and nearby are long walks, Minsmere bird reserve, Snape Maltings concert hall and of course, miles of beach to sit upon and watch the sea.
Selection of breaks available throughout the year.
WENTWORTH HOTEL, ⚜⚜⚜ HIGHLY COMMENDED
Wentworth Road, Aldeburgh, Suffolk IP15 5BD   Telephone: (0728) 452312

THE GRANGE HOTEL
Barton Road, Thurston,
Nr. Bury St. Edmunds, Suffolk IP31 3PQ
Telephone: Pakenham 31260

The Grange Hotel is a family-owned country house set in two acres of grounds, only four miles from Bury St. Edmunds. There are fifteen bedrooms, most with facilities. There are two golf courses within five miles, also riding, fishing and shooting within easy distance. We are also just two miles from main roads to Cambridge, Norwich and Ipswich and 30 minutes from the coast at Felixstowe. Bargain break week ends available all year round. ⚜⚜⚜ APPROVED

⚜⚜⚜ APPROVED
The Bell Hotel
Clare, Sudbury, West Suffolk,
England CO10 8NN
Telephone Clare (0787) 27 7741
16c. posting house with beams, restaurant and wine bar. Within easy reach of ports, yet only 60 miles to London.

THE ANGEL
Market Place, Lavenham CO10 9QZ
Tel: 0787 247388
This family-run inn overlooks the market place and offers relaxation in a calm and quiet environment. Dating from 1420, it retains a wealth of period features and is ideal for exploring the area which is of great historic interest. The 7 en suite bedrooms all have telephone, colour TV and tea/coffee making facilities. The restaurant menu changes daily and features fresh local ingredients. Amenities include good music, attractive gardens and free parking. Logis of Great Britain. AA.
⚜⚜⚜ HIGHLY COMMENDED
Special Breaks: 3 nights for the price of 2.
Also available half board with menu choice.
November to March.

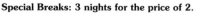

TRAVEL

Bedford	(0234) 269686
Bury St Edmunds	(0473) 693396
Cambridge	(0223) 311999
Chelmsford	(0245) 252111
Clacton-on-Sea	(0206) 564777
Colchester	(0206) 564777
Great Yarmouth	(0603) 632055
Harwich/Dovercourt	(0206) 564777
Hitchin	(0582) 27612
Huntingdon	(0480) 454468
Ipswich	(0473) 693396
King's Lynn	(0553) 772021
Lowestoft	(0603) 632055
Luton	(0582) 27612
Norwich	(0603) 632055
Peterborough	(0733) 68181
Southend-on-Sea	(0702) 611811
Stevenage	(0582) 27612
Watford	(0923) 245001

InterCity Anglia, 15-25 Artillery Lane, London E1 7HA. Tel: (071) 465 9000

Avis
Head Office, Tel: 081 848 8765. Bedford (0908) 281334, Cambridge (0223) 212551, Chelmsford (0245) 496655, Colchester (0206) 41133, Great Yarmouth (0493) 851050, Harlow (0279) 414040, Hemel Hempstead (0442) 230092, Ipswich (0473) 273366, Luton (0582) 454040, Luton Airport (0582) 36537, Norwich (0603) 416719, Peterborough (0733) 349489, Stansted (0279) 663030.

Budget Rent-A-Car
Bury St Edmunds (0284) 701345, Cambridge (0223) 323838, Clacton (0255) 222444, Hitchin (0462) 431151, Ipswich (0473) 216149, Luton (0582) 503101.

Candor Motors Ltd
Braintree (0376) 321202, Colchester (0206) 791171.

Europcar
Head Office, Tel: 081 950 4080. Cambridge (0223) 23364, Great Yarmouth (0493) 857818,

Hemel Hempstead (0923) 260026, Ipswich (0473) 211067, Lowestoft (0502) 516982, Luton (0582) 413438, Norwich (0603) 400280, Welwyn Garden City (0483) 715179.

Hertz Rent-A-Car
Cambridge (0223) 416634, Colchester (0206) 866559, Great Yarmouth (0493) 857086, Ipswich (0473) 218506, Luton (0582) 450333, Mildenhall (0638) 717354, Norwich Airport (0603) 404010, Peterborough (0733) 893083, Peterborough station (0733) 65252, Welwyn Garden City (0707) 331433.

🌑 **Willhire Ltd**
Bury St Edmunds (0284) 762888, Cambridge (0223) 414600, Chelmsford (0245) 265853, Colchester (0206) 867888, Great Yarmouth (0493) 857130, Ipswich (0473) 213344, Mildenhall (0638) 712080, Newmarket (0638) 669209, Norwich (0603) 416411, Norwich Airport (0603) 404010, Peterborough (0733) 340493, Southend (0702) 544441, Thetford (0842) 761578.

P & O European Ferries: Felixstowe Tel: (0394) 604100. Zeebrugge-Felixstowe: 2 daily

🌑 **Scandinavian Seaways** Harwich Tel: (0255) 240240. Harwich-Esbjerg: 3 times a week (Mon, Thu, Sat), every other day in summer. Harwich-Hamburg: Nov & Dec (Tue, Thu, Sat). Rest of year every other day. Harwich-Gothenburg: Nov-Feb (Fri & Sun). Mar, Apr, May (Wed, Fri, Sun). Jun-Sep (Mon, Wed, Fri).

🌑 **Stena Line** Harwich Tel: (0255) 243333. Head office Kent (0233) 647047. Hook of Holland-Harwich: twice daily.

Cambridge Airport Teversham Tel: (022329) 3621/2651/3622

Luton Airport Tel: (0582) 405100

Norwich Airport Tel: (0603) 411923

Southend Airport Tel: (0702) 340201. Destinations to Jersey, Guernsey and Malta.

🌑 **Stansted Airport** Bishop's Stortford Tel: (0279) 680500. Information desk Tel: (0279) 662379/662520.

Air UK Tel: (0603) 424288. Destinations from Norwich: Aberdeen, Amsterdam, Bergen, Edinburgh, Humberside, Jersey, Guernsey, Stavanger, Tees-side. Tel: (0279) 680146 Destinations from Stansted: Aberdeen, Amsterdam, Bergen, Brussels, Dusseldorf, Edinburgh, Florence, Frankfurt, Humberside, Jersey, Guernsey, Nice, Paris, Teesside.

Britannia Airways Tel: (0582) 424155. Destinations from Luton: Scheduled flights to Belfast only.

Premier Holidays, Cambridge Tel: (0223) 66122, Channel Islands.

Suckling Airways Reservations Tel: (022329) 3393. Destinations from Cambridge to Amsterdam and Cambridge to Manchester.

🌑 **National Express Ltd**

London	071 730 0202
Cambridge	(0223) 460711
Peterborough	(0733) 237141

There are many bus service operators throughout the region and each county council has an enquiry number as follows:

Bedfordshire	(0234) 228337
Cambridgeshire	(0223) 317740
Essex	(0245) 492211
Hertfordshire Traveline:	
Hertford	(0992) 556765
Hitchin	(0462) 438138
Watford	(0923) 684784
Norfolk	(0603) 613613
Suffolk	(0473) 265676

Information sheet available from the East Anglia Tourist Board, price 50p. See address on inside front cover.

TOURIST INFORMATION CENTRES

Pay a visit to your nearest Tourist Information Centre and you may be surprised by the range of services they offer both for visitors and for local people. Things to do, places to eat, how to get there, what to do if it's raining, places suitable for young children, or for the elderly and disabled... the Tourist Information Centres are expert in answering these kinds of questions. Information covering the whole country can be found at most offices, to help you plan your next destination, or for locals to help you choose your next British holiday. Tourist Information Centres will book accommodation for you, whether in their own area, or further afield using the " Book A Bed Ahead Scheme". If you are looking for a local souvenir or a gift, you may find that you need look no further as many Tourist Information Centres specialise in locally produced crafts or goods and in a wide range of local interest or British travel books. Make the Tourist Information Centre your first stop in every Town!

* Not open all year

Aldeburgh, Suffolk
* The Cinema, High Street, Tel: (0728) 453637. *28 Mar-30 Oct, Mon-Fri 0900-1715, Sat, Sun and Bank Hols 1000-1715.*

Ampthill, Bedfordshire
12 Dunstable Street, Tel: (0525) 402051. *All year, Mon-Thu 0845-1700, Fri 0845-1600. Closed Bank Hols.*

Beccles, Suffolk
* The Quay, Fen Lane, Tel: (0502) 713196. *1 Apr-31 Oct, daily 0900-1300, 1400-1700.*

Bedford, Bedfordshire
10 St Pauls Square, Tel: (0234) 215226. *All year, Mon-Sat 0930-1700, Sun 1300-1700.*

Braintree, Essex
Town Hall Centre, Market Square, Tel: (0376) 550066. *All year, Sat 1000-1600; Jan-31 Mar, Mon-Fri 1000-1600; 1 Apr-30 Sep, Mon-Fri 1000-1700; 1 Oct-31 Dec, Mon-Fri 1000-1600.*

Brentwood, Essex
Old House, 5 Shenfield Road, Tel: (0277) 200300. *All year, Mon-Sat 0930-1330, 1430-1700.*

Bury St Edmunds, Suffolk
6 Angel Hill, Tel: (0284) 764667. *4 Jan-1 Apr, Mon-Fri 1000-1600, Sat 1000-1300; 2 Apr-30 Sep, Mon-Fri 0915-1745, Sat 1000-1500; 1 Jun-30 Sep, Sun 1000-1500; 1 Oct-31 Dec, Mon-Fri 1000-1600, Sat 1000-1300.*

Cambridge, Cambridgeshire
Wheeler Street, Tel: (0223) 322640. *Jan-Easter and Nov-Dec, Mon-Fri 0900-1730; Easter-Jun and Sep-Oct, Mon-Fri 0900-1800; Jul and Aug, Mon-Fri 0900-1900; Easter-Sep, Sun and Bank Hols 1030-1530; All year, Sat 0900-1700; Wed only open 1930.*

Chelmsford, Essex
County Hall, Market Road, Tel: (0245) 283400. *All year, Mon-Fri 0930-1700, Sat 0930-1600.*

Clacton on Sea, Essex
23 Pier Avenue, Tel: (0255) 423400. *Jan-21 May, Mon-Sat 0900-1700; 23 May-4 Sep, daily 0900-1700; 5 Sep-end Dec, Mon-Sat 0900-1700.*

Colchester, Essex
1 Queen Street, Tel: (0206) 712920. *4 Jan-31 Dec, Mon, Tue, Thu, Fri, 0900-1700, Wed 1000-1700, Sat 1000-1300; 7 May-24 Sep, Sat 1000-1700; 4 Jun-25 Sep, Sun 1000-1700; 1 Oct-31 Dec, Sat 1000-1300.*

Cromer, Norfolk
Bus Station, Prince of Wales Road, Tel: (0263) 512497. *4 Jan-28 Mar, daily 1000-1600; 28 Mar-17 Jul, Mon-Sat 1000-1700, Sun 1000-1600; 18 Jul-4 Sep, Mon-Sat 0930-1900, Sun 0930-1800; 5 Sep-30 Oct, Mon-Sat 1000-1700, Sun 1000-1600; 1 Nov-31 Dec, daily 1000-1600.*

Diss, Norfolk
Meres Mouth, Meres Street, Tel: (0379) 650523. *All year, 4 Jan-31 Mar, 1 Nov-31 Dec, Mon-Thu 1030-1400, Fri-Sat 1000-1600; 1 Apr-31 Oct, Mon-Sat 1000-1600.*

Dunstable, Bedfordshire
The Library, Vernon Place, Tel: (0582) 471012. *All year, Mon-Fri 1000-1700, Sat 0930-1600.*

Ely, Cambridgeshire
Oliver Cromwell's House, 29 St Mary's Street, Tel: (0353) 662062. *4 Jan-30 Mar, Mon-Sat 1000-1715; 1 Apr-30 Oct, daily 1000-1800; 1 Nov-31 Dec, Mon-Sat 1000-1715.*

Fakenham, Norfolk
* Red Lion House, Market Place, Tel: (0328) 851981. *28 Mar-10 Apr, Mon-Sat 1000-1700, Sun 1000-1600; 11 Apr-29 May, daily 1000-1400; 30 May-4 Sep, Mon-Sat 1000-1700, Sun 1000-1600; 5 Sep-30 Oct, daily 1000-1400.*

Felixstowe, Suffolk
Leisure Centre, Undercliff Road West, Tel: (0394) 276770. *Jan-31 Mar, Mon-Fri 0845-1715, Sat 1000-1700, Sun 1000-1300; 1 Apr-30 Sep, Mon-Fri 0900-1730, Sat, Sun, 0930-1700; 1 Oct-end Dec, Mon-Fri 0845-1715, Sat 1000-1700, Sun 1000-1300.*

Great Yarmouth, Norfolk
* Marine Parade, Tel: (0493) 842195. *2 Apr-5 Apr, daily 1000-1700; 2 May-27 May, daily 1000-1700; 28 May-18 Sep, Mon-Sat 0930-1730, Sun 1000-1700; 19 Sep-9 Oct, daily 1000-1700. Information can be obtained between Oct-Apr on Tel: 0493 846345.*

Hadleigh, Suffolk
Toppesfield Hall, Tel: (0473) 822922. *All year, Mon-Fri 0900-1715. Closed Bank Hols.*

Harwich, Essex
Parkeston Quay, Tel: (0255) 506139, Fax: 0255 240570. *Jan-31 Mar and 1 Oct-end Dec, Tue-Fri 1200-1900, Sat 1000-1600; 1 Apr-30 Sep, daily 0645-1900.*

Hertford, Hertfordshire
The Castle, Tel: (0992) 584322. *All year, Mon-Fri 0900-1730; 8 Jan-2 Apr, Sat 1100-1500; 9 Apr-29 Oct, Sat 1000-1600; 5 Nov-31 Dec, Sat 1100-1500, Bank Hols 1000-1600.*

Hemel Hempstead, Hertfordshire
Opening Jun 1994, *All year, Mon-Sat 0900-1700, Information can be obtained all year on (0442) 60161.*

Hoveton, Norfolk
* Station Road, Tel: (0603) 782281. *1 Apr-31 Oct, Mon-Sat 0900-1300, 1400-1700.*

Hunstanton, Norfolk
The Green, Tel: (0485) 532610. *Jan-Mar and Oct-Dec, Sun-Thu 0900-1300, 1400-1715, Fri 0900-1300, 1400-1645; Apr-Sep, daily 0900-1745.*

Huntingdon, Cambridgeshire
The Library, Princes Street, Tel: (0480) 425831. *All year, Mon-Fri 0930-1730, Sat 0900-1700; Closed Bank Holidays.*

Ipswich, Suffolk
Town Hall, Princes Street, Tel: (0473) 258070. *4 Jan-31 Mar, Mon-Thu 0900-1700, Fri 0900-1630, Sat 0930-1230; 1 Apr-31 Aug, Mon-Thu 0900-1700, Fri 0900-1630, Sat 1000-1600; 1 Sep-31 Dec, Mon-Thu 0900-1700, Fri 0900-1630, Sat 0930-1230.*

King's Lynn, Norfolk
The Old Gaol House, Saturday Market Place, Tel: (0553) 763044. *All year, Mon-Thu 0915-1700, Fri 0915-1730, Sat 0915-1700, Sun 1000-1700.*

Lavenham, Suffolk
* Lady Street, Tel: (0787) 248207. *28 Mar-30 Sep, daily 1000-1645.*

Lowestoft, Suffolk
The East Point Pavilion, Royal Plain, Tel: (0502) 523000. *1 Jan-30 Apr, and 1 Oct-end Dec, Mon 1100-1700, Tue-Sun 1000-1700; 29 May-30 Sep, Mon 1000-1800, Tue-Sun 0900-1800.*

Luton, Bedfordshire
65-67 Bute Street, Tel: (0582) 401579. *All year, Mon-Fri 0930-1630, Sat 0930-1600.*

Maldon, Essex
Coach Lane, Tel: (0621) 856503. *All year, Mon-Sat 1000-1600.*

East Anglia's newest centre at Lowestoft

Mundesley, Norfolk
* 2a Station Road, Tel: (0263) 721070. *28 Mar-10 Apr, Mon-Sat 1000-1700, Sun 1000-1600; 11 Apr-29 May, daily 1000-1400; 30 May-4 Sep, Mon-Sat 1000-1700, Sun 1000-1600; 5 Sep-30 Oct, daily 1000-1400.*

Newmarket, Suffolk
63 The Rookery, Tel: (0638) 667200. *All year, Mon-Thu 0900-1700, Fri 0900-1930, Sat 0900-1700.*

Norwich, Norfolk
The Guildhall, Goal Hill, Tel: (0603) 666071. *Jan-29 May and 1 Oct-end Dec, Mon-Sat 0930-1730; 30 May-30 Sep, Mon-Sat 0930-1800.*

Peterborough, Cambridgeshire
45 Bridge Street, Tel: (0733) 317336. *All year, Mon-Fri 0900-1700, Sat and Bank Hol Mon, 1000-1600.*

Saffron Walden, Essex
1 Market Place, Tel: (0799) 510444. *4 Jan-31 Mar, Mon-Sat 1000-1700; 1 Apr-31 Oct, Sat 0930-1730; 1 Nov-31 Dec, Mon-Sat 1000-1700.*

St Albans, Hertfordshire
Town Hall, Market Place, Tel: (0727) 864511. *All year, Mon-Fri 1000-1700, Sat 1000-1600.*

Sheringham, Norfolk
* Station Approach, Tel: (0263) 824329. *28 Mar-17 Jul, Mon-Sat 1000-1700, Sun 1000-1600; 18 Jul-4 Sep, Mon-Sat 0930-1900, Sun 0930-1800; 5 Sep-30 Oct, Mon-Sat 1000-1700, Sun 1000-1600.*

Southend on Sea, Essex
High Street Precinct, Tel: (0702) 355120. *All year, Mon-Sat 0930-1700.*

South Mimms, Hertfordshire
M25 Welcome Break Service Area, Bignalls Corner, Tel: (0707) 643233. *All year, Mon-Sat 0930-1730, Sun 0930-1630.*

Southwold, Suffolk
* Town Hall, Market Place, Tel: (0502) 724729. *1 Apr-end Sep, daily 1100-1700.*

Stowmarket, Suffolk
Wilkes Way, Tel: (0449) 676800. *4 Jan-31 Mar, Mon-Fri 0930-1700; Sat 0930-1330; 1 Apr-31 Oct, Mon-Fri 0930-1730, Sat 0930-1630; 1 Nov-23 Dec, Mon-Fri 0930-1700, Sat 0930-1630.*

Sudbury, Suffolk
* Town Hall, Market Hill Tel: (0787) 881320. *28 Mar-30 Sep, Mon-Sat 1000-1645.*

Thurrock, Essex
Motorway Services, M25 Thurrock, Grays, Tel: (0708) 863733. *1 Jan-30 Jun, daily 0900-1700; 1 Jul-31 Aug, daily 0900-1800; 1 Sep-31 Dec, daily 0900-1700.*

Walsingham, Norfolk
* Shire Hall Museum, Common Place, Tel: (0328) 820510. *31 Mar-30 Sep, Mon 1000-1300, 1400-1700, Tue-Sat 1000-1700, Sun 1400-1700; 1-31 Oct, Sat 1000-1700, Sun 1400-1700.*

Waltham Abbey, Essex
54 Sun Street, Tel: (0992) 652295. *All year, Tue 0930-1700, Wed, Thu, Fri 0930-1630, Sat 0930-1700, Sun 1000-1600.*

Wells-next-the-Sea, Norfolk
* Wells Centre, Staithe Street, Tel: (0328) 710885. *28 Mar-17 Jul, Mon-Sat 1000-1700, Sun 1000-1600; 18 Jul-4 Sep, Mon-Sat 0930-1900, Sun 0930-1800; 5 Sep-30 Oct, Mon-Sat 1000-1700, Sun 1000-1600.*

Welwyn Garden City, Hertfordshire
Campus West, The Campus, Tel: (0707) 390653. *All year, Mon, Tue, Wed, Fri 0900-1715, Thu 0900-1300, Sat 1000-1230.*

Wisbech, Cambridgeshire
District Library, Ely Place, Tel: (0945) 583263. *All year, Tue-Fri 1000-1800, Sat 0900-1700.*

TOURIST INFORMATION POINTS

Limited information available, no bed booking service.
* **Not open all year**

* **Aylsham,** Bure Valley Railway Station, Norwich Road, Tel: (0263) 733858. *Apr-Oct*

Beccles, Public Library, Blyburgate, Tel: (0502) 714073. *All year, Mon-Sat 0930-1700.*

Berkhamsted The Library, Kings Road, Tel: (0442) 877638. *All year, Mon, Fri, 0930-1730, Tue, Thu, 0930-2000, Sat 0930-1600. Closed Wed and Bank Hols.*

Borehamwood, Civic Offices, Elstree Way, Tel: (081) 207 7496. *All year, Mon-Thu 0900-1715, Fri 0900-1700.*

* **Dedham,** Duchy Barn, Tel: (0206) 323447. *Easter-Mid Oct, Mon-Sat 1000-1300, 1400-1700, Sun 1400-1700; Mid Sep-mid Oct, closes Sun.*

Downham Market, Town Hall, Bridge Street, Tel: (0366) 387440. *All year, Mon-Sat, Nov-end Mar closes Mon.*

* **Great Yarmouth,** North West Tower, North Quay, Tel: (0493) 332095. *1 Apr-31 Oct, daily 0900-1700.*

* **Halstead,** Lodge Gate, Townsford Mill, Tel: (0787) 477411. *1 Apr-end Sep, Tue-Fri 1000-1600, Sat 1100-1530.*

Hitchin, The Library, Paynes Park, Tel: (0462) 434738/450133. *All year, Mon, Tue, Thu, Fri 0930-2000, Sat 0930-1600.*

Holt, Sanders Coaches, Market Place, Tel: (0263) 713100. *All year, Mon-Fri 0900-1700, Sat 0900-1300.*

* **Loddon,** Bridge Stores, 41 Bridge Street, Tel: (0508) 20690. *1 Apr-31 Oct, Mon-Fri 0900-1730.*

* **Ranworth,** Norfolk, The Staithe, Tel: (060549) 453. *1 Apr-31 Oct, daily 0900-1300, 1400-1700.*

Rickmansworth, Three Rivers House, Northway, Tel: (0923) 776611 ext 1381. *All year, Mon-Thu 0830-1700, Fri 0830-1645.*

* **Santon Downham,** High Lodge Visitor Centre, Tel: (0842) 815434. *Apr-Sep, daily.*

Southend-on-Sea, Civic Centre, Victoria Avenue, Tel: (0702) 355122. *All year, Mon-Thu 0900-1700, Fri 0900-1645.*

Stevenage, The Library, Southgate, Tel: (0438) 369441. *All year, Mon-Thu 0930-2000, Fri 0930-1700, Sat 0930-1600.*

* **Swaffham,** Market Place, Tel: (0760) 722255. *Apr-Oct, Mon-Sat 1000-1630.*

Thetford, Ancient House Museum, 21 White Hart Street, Tel: (0842) 752599. *All year, Mon-Sat 1000-1700; 29 May-25 Sep, Sun 1400-1700.*

* **Walton on the Naze,** Princess Esplanade, Tel: (0255) 675542. *May-Sep, daily 1000-1700.*

* **Watton,** The Clock Tower, High Street, Tel: (0953) 882058/884224. *May-Sep, Mon, Sun 1000-1230, Wed 1000-1500, Fri 1230-1730, Sat 1000-1730.*

* **Woburn Heritage Centre,** Old St Mary's Church, Tel: (0525) 290631. *1 Apr-Oct, Mon-Fri 1400-1630, Sat, Sun 1130-1630.*

Woodbridge, Public Library, New Street, Tel: (0394) 382896. *All year, Mon, Sat 0930-1700, Tue-Fri 0930-1730. Closed Bank Hols.*

* **Wymondham,** Market Cross, Market Place, Tel: (0953) 604721. *Easter-end Sep, Mon-Sat 1000-1600.*

Ely's Tourist Information in Oliver Cromwell's House

Please mention East Anglia Guide when replying to advertisements

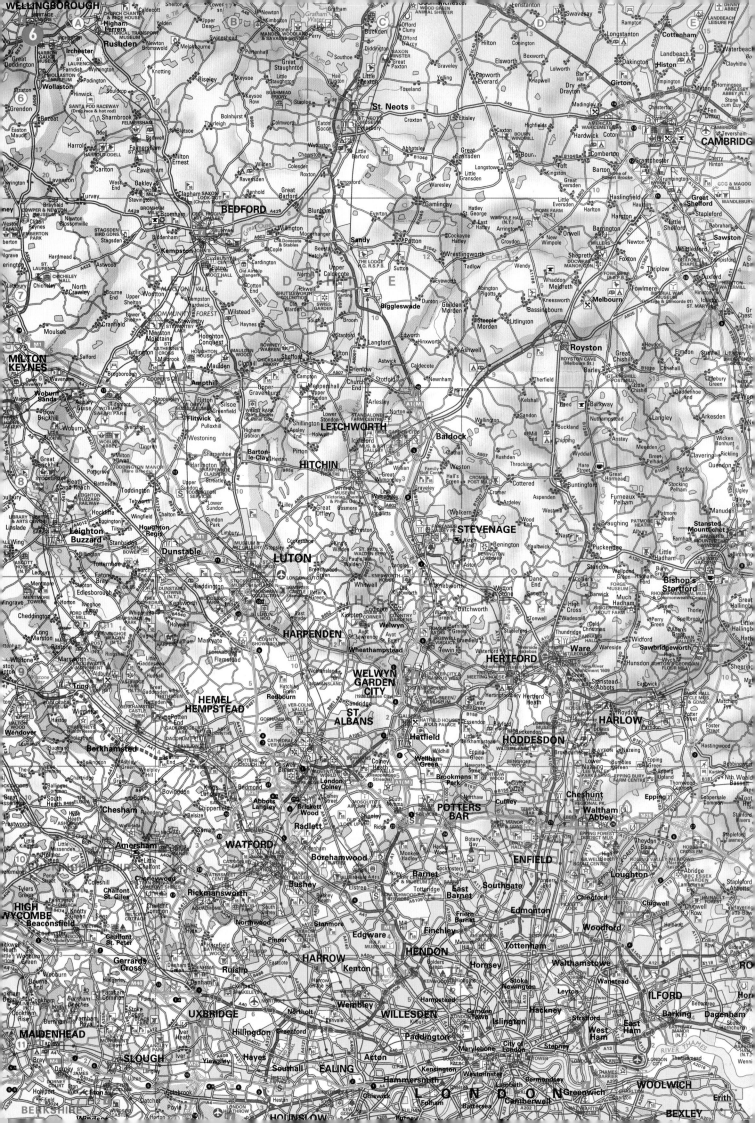

126